Seeing the
Beat Generation

Seeing the Beat Generation
Entering the Literature through Film

Raj Chandarlapaty

McFarland & Company, Inc., Publishers
Jefferson, North Carolina

"Dog" by Lawrence Ferlinghetti, from A CONEY ISLAND OF THE MIND, copyright ©1958 by Lawrence Ferlinghetti. Reprinted by permission of New Directions Publishing Corp.

"Baseball Canto" by Lawrence Ferlinghetti, from THESE ARE MY RIVERS, copyright ©1993 by Lawrence Ferlinghetti. Reprinted by permission of New Directions Publishing Corp.

"Oil" by Gary Snyder. Credit: Copyright © 1957, 1958, 1959, 1960, 1961, 1962, 1963, 1964, 1965, 1965, 1966, 1967, by Gary Snyder, from *The Back Country*. Reprinted by permission of Counterpoint Press.

Selections from an unpublished draft of "Over the Hills and Far Away," by William Burroughs. Copyright © 1961, 2016 by William S. Burroughs Papers at the Berg Collection, New York Public Library, used by permission of The Wylie Agency LLC.

Quotations by William Burroughs copyright © 2016, used by permission of The Wylie Agency LLC.

Excerpt from "Kaddish" by Allen Ginsberg, currently collected in Collected Poems 1947–1997. Copyright © 1961, 2006 Allen Ginsberg LLC, used by permission of The Wylie Agency.

LIBRARY OF CONGRESS CATALOGUING-IN-PUBLICATION DATA

Names: Chandarlapaty, Raj, 1970– author.
Title: Seeing the Beat generation : entering the literature through film / Raj Chandarlapaty.
Description: Jefferson, North Carolina : McFarland & Company, Inc., Publishers, 2019. | Includes bibliographical references and index.
Identifiers: LCCN 2019015264 | ISBN 9781476675756 (paperback : alk. paper) ∞
Subjects: LCSH: Film adaptations—History and criticism. | American fiction—20th century—Film adaptations. | Beat fiction, American— History and criticism.
Classification: LCC PN1997.85 .C425 2019 | DDC 791.43/6587392—dc23
LC record available at https://lccn.loc.gov/2019015264

BRITISH LIBRARY CATALOGUING DATA ARE AVAILABLE

ISBN (print) 978-1-4766-7575-6
ISBN (ebook) 978-1-4766-3670-2

© 2019 Raj Chandarlapaty. All rights reserved

No part of this book may be reproduced or transmitted in any form or by any means, electronic or mechanical, including photocopying or recording, or by any information storage and retrieval system, without permission in writing from the publisher.

On the cover: Front cover: James Franco as Allen Ginsberg in the 2010 film *Howl* (Oscilloscope Pictures/Photofest)

Printed in the United States of America

McFarland & Company, Inc., Publishers
  Box 611, Jefferson, North Carolina 28640
  www.mcfarlandpub.com

Table of Contents

Preface	1
Introduction: New Americanist Visions, Modern Theory and Knowledge, and the Beat "Setting" as Found in Film	11
ONE. Neal Cassady and Jack Kerouac: The Films and the Reinvention of Text	25
TWO. Allen Ginsberg: The Films and Romanticism's True Test	89
THREE. William S. Burroughs: The Films and His Postmodern Techniques of Reinvention	113
FOUR. Amiri Baraka, Lawrence Ferlinghetti, Carolyn Cassady and Gary Snyder: Films on the Relevance of the Lesser-Known Beats	167
Conclusion: Sixty-Five Years Later, and What Did We Learn?	197
Appendix: Audiobooks and Recordings—New Beat Consciousness and Teaching the Beats	201
Chapter Notes	215
Works Cited	221
Index	225

*I see Hermes, well-respected, dying, saying
Do not weep for me, this is not my true country,
I have lived banished from my true country,
I now return to the Celestial Sphere,
Where each of us goes in his turn.*
     —Whitman, "Salut au Monde"

Preface

The idea for this book first appeared when I taught American literature in Afghanistan in January of 2016. It was very unclear how a class of thirty-five Afghans, both men and women, would relate to the social and stylistic content of American literature, or to its historical evolution far from the pale of the literary imagination from Afghanistan or its neighboring countries. I had inherited a frequent pedagogical problem at American University: Western knowledge and philosophies were alien to the conservative, nationalist Islam that held considerable influence, and even farther from Indian/Pakistani societal influences that had nurtured their modern, urban core values through popular arts, cinema, languages, the press, and the constructive edge of the young Asian's rising mode— and art of self-expression. But students were eager to learn. They had been critical, and expected content that would make them think and reflect on the American's specific situation. I thought that this was a novel beginning, and admit that the films helped generate stronger responses in the essay assignments.

But the exchange intrigued me as, to say the least, I had probably misjudged the modern Asian student and his/her capacity to understand, digest, and discuss something far outside their social imagination, insofar as it is connected with one's social understandings of learning and context. American college responses to Beat Generation fiction and poetry were atrocious. In one reading of "Howl" at University of Texas–Pan American, dazed students could not offer a single comment. At Florida Memorial University, a woman scolded Ginsberg and a man wrote angrily about his glorification of drugs and pornography. The American student was, in short, not intellectually lenient and saw the Beats as *poseurs* who built an elaborate fantasy during the mid–20th century, that they were modernist writers. Responses from Afghan students, in tandem, meant projecting their values and inferences from writing, studies, and collaborations. Of course, at AUAF, plagiarism policies were in place: there were many examples of student copying, but many more that included student Web research, Google, news media, government statistics, and Web-derived histories and literature essays allowing them to experiment with concepts and ideas. If there was less novelty—because this constitutes an active education, integrity or not—there was also curiosity, criticism of corruption, grand narrative slashes at replacing America with Islam in the social criticism, and legitimate studies. The Hippie Trail boomed with speculations and tales of adventure, and even students who opted for their "road." I didn't inspire this: it was a gradual, inevitable critical mass speaking an empathetic breath for experimentalism.

Still, the key concept was derived from its American origins: I knew that American students understood that the Beats spoke of vagrant lifestyles, social orders, and histories that conflicted with the realms of more accomplished literature said to write the American experience. Cross-cultural exchanges like these often comprise some of the subject matter for Composition I and II; still, I believe that film nurtures interest and the audience's learning of modernist art's specific personal and internal problems as it forms a social media, and that Afghan students responded to mid–20th century writing anxieties. Without unearthing long novels and their labyrinthine syntax as evidence, let us say that writing responds to perceptions, writings, and ideas graphically evident in today's setting, contrasting itself with narrative forms found in today's English-language cinema. We might then debate whether underground literatures are better taught through film adaptations: in each instance, we are as likely to accept film's necessity in dramatic conceptualizations of history, place, and ideation. Audiences are then more familiar with social and intellectual techniques that are found on screen, a much more interactive reality that turns the deep ethnography of ideas and experiences into more relevant, perceivable collages. The resulting body of historical storytelling and tales advance the interchangeable, absorbable truths condensing prophetic-magic pretense to suit jubilant American adolescence, "the scene" and its confident navigations, and delicious, potent absorptions of the circle's experiences and fantasies. In short, the film's slick, moving sense-expression in voices and visual examples, and the flesh and voice of characters found within Beat rebellion and illumination, provoke adolescent literature's easy conquest of the mainstream at an early stage, enjoining casual, enjoyable rejections of government-Christian authoritarianism. Further, digital films promise new aural and textual immersions for Beat readers:

> [...] the Internet makes it possible for a community of strangers to exchange texts, images, and video sequences, thus enabling a new kind of international communication, one, it is hoped, that is more reciprocal and multi-centered than the old Hollywood-dominated international system [...] the shift to the digital makes for infinite reproducibility without loss of quality [...].[1]

Preface

The teaching of American literature through films is a contested practice, and many methods create writing issues for students that puzzle the ambivalence of the written form, teachings, and translations. Alan Marcus wrote in *Teaching History with Film*, "as fictionalized, dramatic stories, Hollywood movies contain a tremendous load of visual, auditory, and emotional stimulation. In order to attract an audience, and therefore make money, filmmakers take liberty with the stories they tell."[2] Yet a great part of *Teaching History with Film* tends to pedagogy, and to the teacher's specific instructional choices and emphases. Nonetheless, Marcus adds: "When movies dramatize controversial historical events, they often are meant to have meaning for contemporary viewers."[3] Results for the classroom in these cases are twofold: one, historical film enhances learning for minority students who are less proficient in American history; and two, films entice students to understand theories, issues, and conscious expression. Surely, the Beats were and are controversial, and students challenge the gist of author inquiries and prophecies when examining letters, travels, biographies, and commentaries about the outside world. The authors themselves pose as intellectually disenfranchised, lost and fierce hero-mendicants nourishing signs of their self-expression. Still, our focus departs methods summarizing the professor's pragmatic deliberations about authors and literatures: "A key attribute of effective teaching about contemporary controversial issues is presenting and helping students understand multiple viewpoints or alternative frames."[4] The implied questions are deep and painstaking: was it possible to understand the Beat Generation from true modernist literary domains? Would a person from Asia, Africa, or even Europe accept the professor's strict, didactic expression of them to represent its historical isolation, and to carry a failed mechanism that tried to transform American culture? This, of course, would be challenged in pot-friendly Afghanistan: I was quickly rid of the suspicion that conservatism denied students identity through drugs, with several recounting interest in marijuana legalization. More, how do we teach the writers to constitute American "humanism"—particularly when authors, commentators and filmmakers have done their best to crop content and screenplays, giving us American self-reflections? Strengthening Beat ties to humanities studies generates our understanding of the authors' subjective inquiries. We might then assess their separation from modern ideologies carrying greater influence upon minority and non–Western communities. From this partial focus, I found the films insightful, initiating student inquiries situating their own peculiarities through character, knowledge, and aural/visual cues containing richer otherness. Viewers may then ponder and stimulate one's own inquiries erring on the side of their movies, political and lifestyle discussions, and the arc of conservative adult representation in changing times. In short, documentaries and film adaptations plant the central question, "Why?" to state the Beat writer's unique perspectives and comprehensive engagement of humanism from juvenile origins causing us to question, and to re-evaluate, a work's seriousness.

With half of India's population under 25, we would also be amiss to think that conservatives deny Indian cinema and music its journeymen, bands of youth, extra-materialistic values and principles, dope experiences, or rebellious adventures. Abundant examples tell us the college student's wish for a revived education, even as the arc of liberal culture reached them only through pop music forms. If an "All-Soul" was not being born, an interchangeable history, that first challenged industrial-military rule through protest and even the conscious symbolic defiance in sex, vocations, and in the public responsibility. We might then throw off an authorial seriousness dimming the Western picture: a challenge to reform one's estimation of oneself.

The main realization came in the form of the films themselves. I found that most of them include specific conversations bisecting peculiar knowledge or wisdoms that covered the pages of unpublished letters and writings in the library's special collections. I think that, since students understood the writer's biography from the film, a greater learning potential exists in the films, which repeat the moral and rhetorical weights of today's culture and its specific histories catering to populist re-readings of 20th century America. This means stronger retention of basic facts and concrete modernist forms. The accomplishment could be duplicated and superseded in any literature. If films themselves held together positive narrative structure and graphic impact upon the viewer that motivates the idea's viewing and absorption, they could teach specific histories. I began to wonder why the technique was not part of contemporary criticism, and why there were only two books, David Sterritt's *Mad to Be Saved* in 1998 and Michael Prince's short, adaptation-focused study of six Beat films in *Adapting The Beat Poets* in 2016, that were about any kind of cinema that includes movie/TV adaptations of Beat Generation novels.

Beat Generation film criticism began in 1998, when Sterritt published *Mad to Be Saved*, and continued with the 2004 publication of *Screening The Beats*. Certainly Sterritt deserves credit for a history-sensitive treatment of early Beat film, and for his extensive, thoughtful coverage at a suggestive moment in Beat archaeology. The purpose of this work is not to trace those moments of historical-fictional studies or even his liminal *pose*. It is truer that the greater diversity of today's media and sources, contemporary screenplays and visual/oral media and communications, beget very different appraisals of text and symbol in rough translations onto today's poststructuralist narrative. I believe, too, that newer generations can revive the movement's controversial written forms, relaying the weight of inferences about the film's visual and spoken content. They also dismiss controversies drawn from written examples and imagery projecting today's health and vigor. Numerous themes of inquiry arise in a project on Beat Generation films, especially if studies cover a good range of films. One has simply to do with subsets of 20th century American history, or counter-histories that Jack Kerouac rewrote several times starring his childhood and travels. Another forces us to re-appraise the author's moment of authenticity through the film's comparison with early writings that spotlight the imaginative genesis of forms and theory.

In our postmodern world, where ideas and knowledge are understood from man's vision and his subconscious meditations, many facets of authorial thought and narrative skill will be lost or diminished. This is often read to be a grave abstract warning that kept literary works isolated in the college classroom. Do first-run films confirm Beat Generation prophecies and identities, and were the Self's hallucinatory models accurate? Also, could we trace the legend through historical moments, and was the iconography and imagery sufficient to appreciate the Beat's special, coveted range of experiences? A last question applies itself to place. Can we build a useful history of the cities and towns that retell Beat society and travels, so that we understood their influences upon the authors themselves? Might we also understand that the Beats were a carefully evolving literary circle with shared contents and endless conversations about it? Were the geographies culturally rich enough to illustrate Beat transcendences? I believe that the questions are thoughtful: films about American writers could evince the greatest impact if they educate us about the writer's biography, and when unmasking psychedelic imageries and follies. I also believe that Beat films can be used the classroom, to augment literary discussions of American literature, because few textbooks used more than one poem, Allen Ginsberg's "Howl," for American literature courses. Beat literature is seldom taught in the university setting, though English departments did testify to revolutionary and anti-academic developments in the manifold, extra-rational high modernism. The Beats encouraged rebellion and anti-normative change: we may, too, debate whether or not they were part of a complex, negotiating identity rising from class conflict and its central themes: knowledge, selfhood, and communities. Because of literary criticism's discouraging limitations, I felt that film offered us a chance to revisit the form's intensity and brilliance without unshackling authorial isolations found amidst complex rhetorical and narrative inundations in Beat works such as "Howl," *On the Road*, and *Naked Lunch*.

Historical films, as they are a kind of anomaly, cause us to accept the mechanics of contemporary film's consumption, hence its material and conversational development through culture. I think this is why they are useful: after all, any effort is to make learning less academic and to allow us to drop the special authoritarian rhetoric of moral control in our specific, doctrinal education. Conventional morality is a clear limitation skewering academic knowledge in the English field. I understood this when I taught minority students: in practical senses, literature's popular impact proliferates examples to stir more comfortable, inclusive readings, allowing us to visit the human transferences rather than staid, lifeless academic ones denying us modern understandings of mystics and their narcotic tales, memoirs, and dreams found in letters and first drafts of novels and short stories at NYPL's Berg Collection and Harry Ransom Center at The University of Texas. My teaching examples range from specific ideological indoctrinations, such as Allen Ginsberg's "Howl" in the United States, to broadly philosophical re-writing of Beat glories, when Afghan seniors watched *Big Sur* after viewing Hollywood films such as 1999's *Sleepy Hollow*. If films expand horizons and build student writing and ideation, they might spell out literature's re-popularization outside the United States and Europe. Literary worlds are thus living and verdant with greater intellectual possibilities, championing the movement's youthful life, its braggadocio, and its impulsive maze of thought-creations and underground/ *kitsch* ethnographies.

Postmodern stereotypes, as Frederic Jameson wrote them, projected sensory and imaginative limitations, so as to guarantee Western cultural hegemony. The technique also negates or weakens much of culture's dramatic and spiritual content. If we expect the power and sublimity of Beat dreaming to match the innocent moment of cultural discovery, we assume that Beat writers and "beatniks" are understood from our imagination and memories, filled as they are with greater, richer realizations of poststructuralist variety and imageries than in earlier moments of the 20th century. I think that realistic, concrete approaches to literary and media theories are very applicable. After all, the spiritual and romantic adventures of Jack Kerouac, Allen Ginsberg and William S. Burroughs are questionable and strayed far from the mainstream, filled with juvenile comedies that weaken the seriousness of their inquiries. Capturing Beat themes and its coveted *ethos* could not, then, mean living within the Beat moment. Instead, it broadcasted modernity's progressive development to reflect more generalizing, exchangeable formats through other historical films. The candle of countercultural discovery was lit in 1991, when Oliver Stone featured Val Kilmer as Jim Morrison in *The Doors*,[5] a movie that showcases the graphic and visual investments and symbolisms promulgated in 1960s youth culture and transposing the 1990s attentions to body, to cult ritual and national controversy, and to conspiracy theories. Kilmer's copy of the rock idol takes advantage of both physical and sexual instances of the rock star's graphic form, and of multimedia that builds the story's events and mood around poststructuralist streams of images, news clips, and music. In the movie's final minutes, a drunken Morrison watches democracy's eclipse on television, following scenes of Dr. Martin Luther King's assassination, anti–Vietnam War protests, President Richard Nixon's speeches, and riots in U.S. cities, syncopated to John Densmore's drum tracks and Morrison's metered recollections in 1967's "When The Music's Over."[6] Soon, postmodern film techniques adapt their visual template to counterculture, getting us to sense, consume, and valorize the 1950s and 60s, infusing the viewer's dynamic realization of true political-social involvement. A greater range of films on the period followed, projecting global repercussions. I will compare cinematic versions of Beat fiction works with the historical period's other films: I will also make use of Hollywood films that are not historical. These movies use modern screening and content techniques well before history films applied them, changing authenticity's screening.

Does post-technological realism move us forward, or backward, in screenings of history film? It is a meaningful question: even if students prone to pop film and visual imaginations pan historical film as being "racist" or "unintelligible" or even out-of-touch with reality, this is not the abiding sense of either filmmakers or students who are interested in history, even in humanities courses. Ninth-grade Vanita's light, sugary re-reading of a Lord Tennyson poem in 2011's *Dhobi Ghat*[7] eyes the pendulum's diversity, as history is a fact of being and a means of social and personal growth far from its ivory tower in the United States or in Europe. History, most certainly, can be taught and filmed: as a professor, I know that aggressive self-censorship and conformity do not quash dynamic senses. Therefore, improving viewing quality and simulating pop histories challenges artisans in immersion. Literary film's dramas, too, offer us conscious greatness: 1982's *Gandhi*, 1984's *A Passage to India*, and 1984's *Indiana Jones* herald greater involvement, though riddled with diminutive, derogatory stereotypes and pure inaccuracies. Of course, illusions of corporate- or comic-friendly mythologies of place and character offset history's ambivalence and imperfection: could young adults understand it, or better than the writers who are prejudiced? Even if, or when, students reject the past as ignorant and non-referential, they glimpse character's exercise as an artifact of culture, to suggest the Era's transferability as a greater wand of societal diffusion painting greater, and not lesser, possibility in the free world long after literature's decline.

The August 24, 2016, terrorist attack at American University of Afghanistan did incite my greater interest in writing this book. My years there as a professor allowed me to survey diverse Asian lifestyles, attitudes, and points of modern inspiration. I believe that, either inside the classroom or through word-of-mouth associations with street culture, media, and popular music, that the need for good scholarship on the Beats promises a dramatic reconceptualization of them as living forces of America's cultural message. From the 1950s, jazz musicians performed in Japan and in other countries: and certainly, then, Burroughs's cut-ups and short works develop the competitive form of narco-narratives against Asian pop stars praising authority, cyber-transcendence of street decay, and criminal spindling of social evil. Creativity and consciousness aside, street prophecies, visions, and mysticism escape censorship in popular Indian cinema, projecting its heroes and modern political synthesis, gauging self-reflections, histories, and even personal vendettas through myriad scenes of revolution and street synergy. Youth cultures depart realist stereotypes, and censorship's guiding control, after which they may attempt to relate Western liberal fantasies and imaginative rejuvenations from the East. This move anticipates government censorship of sin and anti-government pluralism, pervasively forswearing citizens to redeem family, vocations, and communities. Classroom writing, from this alternate focus, allows for the growth of both knowledge and perspective, protecting both subjective modern navigations of life and sharper criticisms of their elder's shortcomings. I think, too, that, reflexively and comparatively, students who criticize the writer's experiences may exercise that criticism free of propaganda, deciding for themselves what anti–State rebellions are actually "good" for. It is time that we admit to our more mature status, lending ourselves to the world's examinations, and to specific criticisms of Self and Society less consistent with corporate/institutional writings of "the story." Beat film allows them a chance to see and enjoy very different simulations of truth and unadorned dialogue, moving to endorse change and re-entrenchment in today's cultural and popular arts, and breathing life into their own adult representations. Young generations listening to the whole rock period might then derive sustaining themes of mission and counter-knowledge favoring Eastern social-intellectual development.

I thank a number of people who have been helpful in this project. My thanks to students at the American University of Afghanistan for watching and responding to *Big Sur*: this was during the Winter, 2016 course in American Literature, a gregarious and engaging class and a testament to Afghanistan's strong relationship with education. New York Public Library and Harry Ransom Center provided good examples of drug-influenced writing; thanks to Lyndsi Barnes, Joshua McKeon, and Ariel Evans for helping me find such striking examples to feature the writer's untouched and unmediated subjective side, away from canonical theory. An even greater thanks to Dr. Isaac Gewirtz, who discussed the NYPL collections with me about ten years ago, when I first contemplated this project: there is much more, and I hope to continue the tradition of archive research again someday. Thanks also to Savannah Lake at the Wylie Agency and the Allen Ginsberg Trust LLC. Phillip Sipiora and Richard Schwartz are thanked for their continuous encouragement of the writing. Here was and is a studied relationship where, twenty-five years ago at Florida International University, Schwartz first puzzled the difficulties of counting the Beats as modernists during the Cold War period; and where, at University of South Florida, Sipiora reconciled much of their cultural perspectives with more anchoring to the modernist tradition and the works of Ford Maddox Ford, Sherwood Anderson, and others. A thank you to the late Butler Waugh and to Alfred J. Lopez for encouraging me to start work on Kerouac's letters, nearly eighteen years ago. Sincere thanks is also given to Oliver Harris, Regina Weinreich, John Giorno, James Grauerholz, David Sterritt, Maggie McKinley, Kurt Hemmer, and Barry Miles: the expert wand of criticism gained ground from the author's brave, didactic readings. With no personal relationship with the actors and producers, I can only comment in the positive, that the range of films is very rich and we are lucky to have such broad possibilities when re-reading novels, letters, stories and poems. Very special thanks to the authors—Jack Kerouac, Allen Ginsberg, William S. Burroughs, Amiri Baraka, Gary Snyder, Lawrence Ferlinghetti, Neal Cassady, and Carolyn Cassady. I first thought of your works in this light more than twenty years ago, and often wondered what you would accent in our readings as undergraduates, trying to figure out the world's caprices and mysteries.

Introduction

New Americanist Visions, Modern Theory and Knowledge, and the Beat "Setting" as Found in Film

Numerous essays in Donald Pease's volume, *The Future of New Americanist Studies*, speak to the problems resulting from social, economic, racial, and cultural inequality, and motion for a new historicism that drew itself ultimately against mainstream American studies. The Beat Generation fell within this concept's broader meaning as it revisits and rewrites America's imagination. The Beats were among the first American *literateurs* to take psychedelic drugs, writing their drug narrations and visions against formalist and socialist introductions of conscious moral necessity. Prose held together America's very different vocational and communitarian direction that lived and grew far away from meritocracy's rising colossus that defined and promulgated education, capitalism, and scientific realism. They cross and navigate multiracial boundaries while over-suggesting counter-studies about the American Dream, which in its historical moment supposes man's personal and spiritual fulfillment. More, they are de-gendered, casting forth homosexuality, feminism, and hyper-masculinity against meta-narratives that retell the fluidity of America's marital and familial codes. Beat Generation counter-histories rode in the wake of American ethnographic and social developments in the modernist literature analogous to, but contesting, modernist fiction's impact, in works such as Sherwood Anderson's *Winesburg, Ohio* (1921) and John Steinbeck's *East of Eden* (1952). Yet more poignantly, it is harder for us to imagine what this counter-history and its social geographies meant for American social ethics, and not simply because of the conservative, institution-friendly rhetoric of translations. At some point, all of us will note that large parts of American history, and specific development of history's impact on humanity, are left out or gradually amass citizen interest, with stories devoid of their provocative contents as readers instead shoulder the mainstream's ineffable social message.

My sense is that we should teach Beat literature through film, because the authors' lives and times will raise questions, stir up controversies, challenging modernist literature as taught in the classroom. Here lies a classic tension in the critical reception: while the Beats, from the time of Kerouac's 1942 reading of Sebastian Sampas, cherishes the reading and the humanity espoused to learn man's ancient literatures and traditions, critics oft thought it to be a joke, a paean to history that ignored the real, daily motions of a godless universe. This medium operates its traditional bias when teaching 20th-century liberal literatures. Cautionary tales of the American subject's vagrancy and immodesty are also common, to stimulate conservative commentaries and deliberations that limit student responses. American short story textbooks, for instance, feature Alice Walker's "Everyday Use" (1973) about a rebellious Black college girl, Raymond Carver's "Cathedral" (1982), where a blind man learns to paint by smoking marijuana, Joyce Carol Oates's "Where Are You Going, Where Have You Been?" (1966), where a hoodlum kills a girl's parents, and James Baldwin's "Sonny's Blues" (1965), where a mathematics teacher fails to convince his brother to quit his heroin addiction, only to find out that he has been arrested. In the classroom's imaginative setting, teaching stories and their controversial explications document and confirm middle-class morals scourging the left's prose, which had apparently sewn crime and self-destruction. Still, student responses to drug use, too, have changed considerably over time: they are more summoned to the tale and its intricacies, and written and spoken inferences are more joyous or horrid than responses that repeat identifications of drug use with crime and instability. Semiotic changes in writing's structure, and that which speaks to cultural norms that follow mankind's rhetorical simplicity, cause us to re-appraise film's visual and conversational techniques. At least, then, we will understand the author's biographical tone when applied to the writing's form, language, and to unconscious breaches that smote literary theory's guidance.

Postmodern adaptations also promoted historical continuity and the strength of man's resistance to rhetorical norms. These norms presupposed their social rationality. I chose to give as many opportunities as possible to revisit the Beat family's anti-canonical realism when selecting first-run versions of the novel or biographical films that re-introduced a host of literary notables, family members, and outsiders who recalled place and origin thoughtfully against literary forms leading our eyes across the printed page. Few 20th century literary forms merited a collective appraisal from scholars and pundits, and the real dearth of knowledge built the underground's rhetorical and spiritual powers, a guiding wisdom still fresh in an American historical imagination whose origins dated from the 1840s and 50s, with authors that include Nathaniel Hawthorne, Herman Melville, and Edgar Allan Poe. From this literary inception, biographical and narrative films yield populist re-readings of the Beat Generation. Unpublished works and letters, too, incur aggressive documentation of mid–20th century America's plebeian instances of spirit and community, in a counter-writing that could extract Beat literature from its current academic setting and revive its humanism for undergraduates. Films, when they adapt writing and thought, comprise a stepping-stone to vocational, personal, philosophical, and political inquiries that may then change the adult citizen's range of ideas and principles to help them conceive a greater moral universe.

My own awareness of American readings of her history and culture directs much of this exercise and called my attention to what a "counter-history" may mean for American students. We acknowledge the dimensions of cognitive realism: they do not know the details of their country's history, times, culture, arts, or simply the geographies and social conflicts that inform democracy beneath the guarded American social *ethos*. Alongside the dangers implied in this very real and alarming gap, the dearth of knowledge about time, places, fiction works, lineage, cultures, politics, travel, family, ethnicity, and even language forces us to acknowledge the historical film's energy which re-invents history and supposes its brilliance. Audiences will state their need for accuracy and truth: it is likely that much of American history isn't ably taught in the classroom because its impact conflicts with more popular archetypes that confirm core values. The rise of rock in the 1960s, and modernism's decline, speaks to the inequality of social transactions and stories: it is clear that songs, speeches and media examples demand stereotypes' power over us, where Beat histories suggest alternative development of minds, bodies, and communities. Without protecting middle-class similitude, might we understand America for its endless, sweet, though repressed powers, and agency? Could we resurface as students of a much greater tale, and one directing our studies instead of repeating our ruminations on the post-industrial, post-atomic quest for social Being? After all, the proliferation of conspiracy theories about the 60s are matched with weak, passive attentions to dynamic change in our society, ignoring our imaginative histories, swearing off their more penitent depth in silence. In turn, Kerouac's letters tell us of a wealth of future study, geographic diversity, and intellectual directions: when appraising films and documentaries, poetry readings and rare moments of philosophizing, we project a much greater power to the scene's meditations. Ginsberg and Burroughs, too, might be understood more forcefully to be liberal social agents, corrupting or distending our innocent self-limitations as to what history and study mean when we have freed readings, sketches, imageries, and personas of eccentricity's pose. We will understand them as Americans who imagine the fruition and testament to a much wider, hybrid intellectual functioning that scalds our illusions of a special, simple history justifying democratic fighting of the world's corruption, barbarism and totalitarian injustices. We might then understand the man to be an artist freed of his deranging stereotypes, projecting a sharper counterculture that sought answers to the human covenant that often lay dormant in post–World War I American generations. George Orwell's severe warning about Winston Smith's pact of subversion in *1984* (1949) notwithstanding, let us finally understand that greater self-examinations and testaments lay ahead, enlivening writing and poetry to possess both riddles and knowledge distant from our unctious control of plurality and social necessity. Ironically, and with a very refreshing certainty, documentary films lend a more objective unmasking of "gay" or "queer"—they *are men, and men who suppressed the absence of heteronormal desire because they sought to change the world and its ideas.* Should we defer to their closets' political witticisms, and our expunging of them, we may easily accept their philosophical and mystic depth to be parallel with canonical knowledge's growing scientism and mythology. In both, too, a lurking paternalism finds its way to admirers—again, a testament to living forces of modern knowledge and their discussion. There is no longer a riddle to "solve": film allows both men to escape the absurd trajectory of writing's perverse witticisms and overarching, vulgar prophecies of the Earth's doom.

More important, the Beat writer's specific history owns its anxiety and testifies its truths, as knowledge and democratic perspectives grow from historical sources to express what we find true and meaningful. Our ignorance of America's history and characters, too, affects us in ways that aren't imaginative: specific constructions of the republic's *ethos* and messianic virtues truncate or airbrush the author's writing context and his complex, novel re-readings about America and the world during the 1950s. I think that, too, audiences must be weaned away from Protestant, White, middle-class readings nixing a very considerable template of deep, mystifying sensuality and introspections, causing us to use popular culture, music, television, and film to sponsor our own histories and geographies. But I remember my foreground comments to American college students: I told them that their generation held many rebellious intellectual characteristics, and even personas and modes of expression, that repeat generational stereotypes. If we are to foster a learning environment, we must cut through specific mythologies that keep knowledge retention suppressed in the general social milieu. I believe that the Beats' fringe attentions to ethnicity, sexuality, and drug histories preface a second telling of history and the nudging forth of America's experiences and conscious motions. "Counter-histories," set in the hospices of America's Great Depression streets, bars, restaurants and whorehouses, promise a different, yet resonant, national means to express the underclass's romantic resurgences. If we are able to get students to say, "it wasn't really like that" or, "lots of people disagreed with middle-class understandings of America," we perform our first motions toward mature, independent governance of American social histories and ethics.

A guiding limitation has more to do with the privileged moment of literary production. Deconstructing it dispersed much of the mystery that causes us to project genius. When we turn to letters and rare manuscripts, another strict limitation reveals to us that publishing meant restricting content strengthening the time period's polity and newsworthiness. Nonetheless, unpublished drafts, journals, and novellas assemble the writer's didactic growth and subjective maturity versus the endless tide of 20th century ideas and philosophies. We might add that Todd Tietchen's 2016 publication of Kerouac's undiscovered writings in *The Unknown Kerouac* allows us insight to, and fresh appraisals of, Kerouac's literary anxiety, and even of the steps that he took in developing a humanist's written form. "Journal 1951," for instance, relays ambitious literary inspiration that unearths authorial pretense. Kerouac sought sensitivity and place from William Faulkner, Norman Mailer, Thomas Wolfe and Malcolm Lowry. Thus, films document greater symbolic inspirations than in his letters and even the collective literary imaginations that shone in American/British literatures after 1800. More thoughtfully, the written inspiration took on the Bible and Chinese film,[1] in each case advancing his own comical interpretation of human nature. The gritty, subjective force of the written work's learning technique accentuates Kerouac's popular form. These inveigh, in turn, against intellectual and philosophical immersions telling us Kerouac's life experiences had been imperfect and bizarre. At one point, he wrote from memory, "realizing that I was in myself revolutionizing writing by removing literary & that curious 'literary grammatical' inhibition from its moment of inception, removing most of all of course, the obstacles that came from my own rhetorical stupidity."[2] Humorous parables aside, students will ignore literary techniques because films could not preserve the form's integrity. Still, races through Kerouac's jagged imagination suggest that ecstatic prose rose from a brilliant, concrete imagination that reveals spiritual and cultural discoveries. They also will muse the fact that Kerouac's fictional technique operates against gradients of mid–20th century post-industrial fatigue that, when understood logically and institutionally, were realities that either silenced or deranged aesthetic rebellions. There are also many paragraphs in *The Unknown Kerouac*'s prose novels and stories that duplicate the technique, first appearing in *Selected Letters* in 1999. Conversely, we are prone to think that writing operates from Kerouac's perceived intensities and mobility, wielding variable communities and fertile points of imagination bringing together materialist, sensible universes in his quest for redemption. Examples of popular fiction did not depend upon any one breakthrough. Instead, they bequeath to the emerging films a mobile, pleasurable set of the authors' imageries and meditations encouraging colleagues and filmmakers to retell steps of Kerouac's neurotic, if brilliant, rebellion. In this way, friends and critics document Kerouac's anti-modern legitimacy and timeliness, and the resulting sympathies for its romanticism and reticence. Films, of course, may avoid this, denying the meaning of individual inquiries: my finding was that this wasn't the case, and that historiographical attentions build the illusion of a literary genesis friendly with the author's life, times, and perspectives about the world and its history. Film studies of Kerouac, then, could be structured in terms friendly to the author's life, memories, and times. This pushes us past the today's blockbuster films and immersions in visual *kitsch*, which repeat bad or ahistorical readings.

Criticism on Beat Generation history—and those that consider them to be a movement or an impulse to social and political change—introduced Jack Kerouac as the group's greatest author. Hence, the intense and sustained speculation about his writing anxieties, private meditations on America and its social compression, and idylls of reflection and poesy, suggest to us that he might have been even more read and understood in his time. Thus, because of the carefully veiled attention to Kerouac's origins, we have overlooked the film's seriousness. Alternative moments of creation and understanding, too, bravely figure in his ethnography, which define and race around the cultural moment's mystique, immersing the audience with Super 8 films and readings recalling Kerouac's rambling devotions. To this end, films about Kerouac's muse, Neal Cassady, are both generic and uncontrived. One film, 1997's *The Last Time I Committed Suicide*, rewrote a 1946 letter to Kerouac, retelling a day's journey haunted by the sickness of Cassady's girlfriend, Joan. If doing nothing to advance the tactic for literary creation as being shared, *Suicide* conceptualizes the adventuresome moment's virtuosity and artistry, holding together masculine development of character and forms with Beat beginnings. The Beat Generation's social necessity is a key factor left out of much criticism, and so the movement's underground *métier* and its special communications can polarize and redirect the network of friendships. Cassady was belatedly given his due, though without the *bourgeois*-leaning privilege of publication during the writing period of the 1940s and 50s. The other, *Heart Beat*, features Sissy Spacek as Carolyn Cassady and projects a lifelong navigation. Co-starring Irwin (Allen Ginsberg) as Spacek's romantic competitor, *Heart Beat* captured the movement's homosexual anxieties that compete with favored heterosexual form. The film's four main characters travelled scenes and moments of mutual belonging to confirm the inklings and guiding wisdoms of mobile, skilled urban poor adapting to their specific situation. *Heart Beat*'s narrative style supposes intellectual and literary creation as it interfaces with and causes the author's daily life and character, rebuilding the moment's translation. Conversations with critics and notables, and attentions to the larger American historiographical picture, are retold to avoid serious contemplation, in either mainstream or countercultural spheres. Further, the film's avoidance of competing graphic, conversational, and artistic forms suggest the group's purposeful non-recognition, a persistent shadow limiting the characters' voices and impact, despite recurrent minutes of the Beat author's crucial geographic and moral dominance.

Filmed versions of Kerouac's fiction that feature new, Kerouac-inspired storytelling include 1960's *The Subterraneans*, 2004's *Beat Angel*, 2012's *On the Road* and 2013's *Big Sur*. These works usher in filmed navigations of narrative's virtuosity so as to maintain and use graphic controls to illustrate the literary movement's cultural agency. These films ensure the Beat movement's intact relationships and interdependences that encourage the group's notoriety. The only example of Kerouac's imaginative re-creation in our Era, *Beat Angel* renews literary fortitude because of its dynamic clash of Beat and descendant generations, and challenged us to conceive of and relish in the literary acolyte's visions and retellings of Beat tales. When unveiled, these spoken stories and memoirs promise us the ecstatic rebirth of modernist, romanticist, and naturalist world-views. Vincent Balestri's performance, then, operates alongside more pedestrian concerns of daily life and its agency. He thus bridges symbolic and theatrical gaps between the two generations, spelling out discontents and lighting up the eyes and minds of depressed liberal generations through comic, hawked readings of Kerouac's novels, letters and biographies. For scholars and students seeking redemption and life through literature, *Beat Angel* embodies the technique of the artist's rediscovery in a gloomy, darkened postmodern Age that suffocates romanticism and realism through knowledge's distortion and disfigurement, and grandiose *post*-doctrines guard man's material-social similitude.

The Subterraneans gains the most recognition for ably penning the Beat Generation's struggles: starring George Peppard as Leo Percepied, it surveys the group's place and characters with an air for its legitimate presentation. Comic replays are limited to augment the central tension between male and female identity and agency: deep anxieties color the rambling, breakneck ticker of writing's creation and significance, pitting the modernist subject against the realities of social change. Amidst poetry readings, jazz, and dance, the artisans of the Beat Generation nourish and frolic in their community, on the edge of discovery and harrowed by the potent brush of one's realizations through love and family. Regarding the two novel-adapted films, it should be said that Walter Salles and Michael Polish limited Neal Cassady's partial narration, stressing the literary group's interrelationships to further generational questing and to retell of male adult hierarchies and their libations. Techniques for screening isolation and incomprehension from beyond are even more appealing. The Beat moment was frozen in time, with no official-imperial symbols and translations of authority and man's materialistic conformity. The resulting production of scene and context gives more credibility to adolescent workings of time, experience, and vocation than most historical films that try to manifest character-derived messages to instill respect for history's iconographies and themes. Liberties that changed the fabric of history's general dictum rebuild the Beats' imaginative, jubilant thrusting of modern man's social freedoms, and their *déclassé* social front. They encourage us to revisit the development of arts, community, and sexuality away from engaging metaphors that built and crafted Kerouac's nuanced, subjective poetic *métier*. Without theory, and far from Kerouac's purer intensities, audiences collude with *Beat Angel's* social dramas that stage Beat accumulations of fact and poetry by playing the social circle's temperament against its robust, spindled integrity. The architectonic of Kerouac's genius, too, is swayed in cultural re-creation's pure moment. When our viewing is stripped of the movement's participations, we are led through extra-temporal stories that exchange sense-impressions and conversations about mankind's health, revelries, and ruminations with much less historiographical content, and without the written moment that sustains magic realism. In short, the altered signs of authorial greatness reflect a greater social aptitude. One must admit that turning Beat narrative and character content into contemporary form and structures causes us to accept that social change operates from the same adaptive and graphic techniques found in other historical films favoring today's moral attentions for more mobile, dynamic American Selves.

Documentary films like 1988's *Jack Kerouac: King of the Beats* and 1986's *What Happened to Kerouac?* favor technological simulations. Nevertheless, it was also true that the breadth of authorial exposure, the references from literary notables and friends, and the inlays of the scene's moment of written and meditated inceptions invite the makings of a counter-history. Inroads hinted at thoughts and conversations to raise literary genius's spectacle in letters and unpublished stories shackling the author to his written imagination, denying us any historical realism. Super 8 films and interviews capture the movement's critical evolution, from screening techniques that propose valiant, modernist-sweetened counter-graphics which succor its meditations from short stories, to readings of letters and short minutes telling the author's story through his travels and experiences during his formative years. Iconographies are broad and inclusive of critics that had, in the written form, savaged his embryonic content. "Political Fallout of the Beat Generation" heralds Allen Ginsberg, William S. Burroughs, Abbie Hoffman and Timothy Leary in a 90-minute symposium on Beat Generation content and significance: my role will be to piece together the moment's unmediated reflection in the midst of the much broader tide of perspectives that critics kept far from the Beat Generation's reticent gaze. After all, Kerouac's disregard for the hippies was a key theme, and we might suppose that the literary movement's demise owes much to its polarity and antithetical rambling. The Beats had kept out postmodernism's vehicle of semantic and strophic revolutions in works of fiction during the 1960s and 70s, gluing agency's stereotypical deaths onto the main character's legendary *oeuvre* as a hero and social messenger. Renewed attention and development could, then, squeeze out the Beat Generation's real, sociopolitical dissent that critics assault from the 1950s onward. The social circle also anchors the moment's deep realism, and its offhand chance at humanism, which wasn't seriously considered. The members of the Beat Generation ruminate on their beginnings, now at the feet of an uncharted adulation of the icons and their romanticist intensity. "Political Fallout of the Beat Generation" retells the movement's critical shortcomings, too, and the special task for recovering angles of culture's regeneration. My task was to demonstrate simple literary and rhetorical re-invention versus counterculture's failure to change the 1960s political order.

Films that cover the life and authorial significance of Allen Ginsberg inherit special reflections away from the moment of genius. Ideas and visions travel classroom anxiety and the psychiatric ward's horrors, Ginsberg's gay mentoring, and dynamic re-inventions of history and its hallucinatory moments of story. At the outset, it should be admitted that Ginsberg's talents and inventions were not inferior to Kerouac's, and that many of them parallel discoveries that spoke to their imaginative sketching. Their gay relationship instills the romantic reflection to shape Ginsberg's American reflections, and his torch-bearing call out to ethnographies in America, Mexico, and the Orient, before Eastern religious and mystic studies changed his vision of social protest. The dividing line was and is meaningful: Ginsberg appears in a special series of adventures and poststructuralist tales inside his Manhattan apartment, in the streets, and when sensing young love and familial horrors in advance of the tumult and magical escapes filling the jaunt of 60s counterculture with alien truths that concentrate poetry's intent to sing free prophecies that erase literature's special Euro-American prescriptions and prejudices. We will also turn to Ginsberg's biographical origins that make the Beat authors' literary fission between gay and straight—or fringe and normal—in 2010's *Kill Your Darlings*, years before Ginsberg heard any prophetic realizations to redress erasure of man's socioeconomic fulfillment, either as a writer or literary progenitor. Adaptations range from cartoon films to biographic re-creations to those that spell out the teaching moment's imaginative realism. As Linda Hutcheon ably pointed out, these are useful to college-level teaching.

Lastly, *The Life and Times of Allen Ginsberg* conveys both the commentator's talent for sketching and grounding the familial and community poetics of Ginsberg's career as a poet and requires him, at a later point in life, to reveal the angelic details of love, poetic form, and his naturalist rebirth at the dawn of counterculture. The specific tryst with rebellion and the operating powers of Ginsberg's mobilization are tested as to the sincerity and purity of the strophic form. In his last years, Ginsberg re-reads his poetry, pointing to the poems as a tradition consistent with canonical modernist reading.

The films of William S. Burroughs offer us punk and rock adaptations of authorial intent, reflecting psychedelic, underground screening techniques, and the simplicity of place against the postmodern adaptations that spell out the sublime redevelopment of Burroughs's fictional form. Narrative adaptations of literary works, such as 1999's *The Junky's Christmas* and 1993's *Naked Lunch*, include narcotic subcultures and multiple graphic text-image techniques. These forms admit the story's comparison with contemporary film, as it opened adaptation's simplicity and underground imaginative recurrence. Biographical films including 2004's *The Commissioner of Sewers*, 2010's *A Man Within*, and 1986's *Burroughs: The Movie* trace the outcome and lyric form of Burroughs's homosexual relationships and the diffusion of sexed imaginations. These films also told Burroughs's personal reflections when they advance his didactic form, and the considerable afterthought to infest the mind with the details of his anti-modernist pandemic, as mirror images of the misanthropic cycles found in Paul Bowles's novels including 1955's *The Spider's House* and 1949's *The Sheltering Sky*. Without starring a relationship between the two men, broad Moroccan imaginations give narrators many opportunities to tell of the underground tryst with graphic and aural strategies of invention and subversion. We are led through the old man's multiple portraits and fixtures, far from literary inception and even farther from the modernist canon. When watching Burroughs's lectures, we ought to ask of ourselves guiding questions about the writing's graphically simple, dislocating instance. In Burroughs's eyes and from pages in his novels, we understand modernism's catalytic minute of failure, and its foreseeable postmodern eclipse and denouement, a senseless derangement holding neither artistic nor altruistic goals. Burroughs's shocking, disheveled caricature, and more picaresque drafts, develop a broad, thoughtless adaptation to postmodern humors tearing democracy apart. While approximating the movement's psychedelic grandeur, it should be noted that images, narratives and inlays of words and thoughts project broader, more dynamic agency than before. They, too, mix with visual technologies repeating the present moment, capturing our private indifference to modern man's social and intellectual revolutions, as they are distant from the everyday man's daily textual and visual indoctrinations about psychedelic imageries and nonlinearities that ran amuck in the author's penitent depression. At the same time, we examine instances of the literary group's biographies in greater historical detail. Thoughts from Burroughs's friends, protégés and caretakers all interlock with the Beats' presumed absence from middle-class communities, to derive new outcomes as they shelter and surround the author's literary moment with rock's growing subjectivity and the stain of its premature, profane absorption of books eschewing man's private legends. The films examine the writer's social and literary origins. At several points, they also exude compassion for the man the world misunderstood, building and over-building the penultimate concept of a rock "family" that cared for him when mainstream media assaulted his professed underground virtue. Lastly, the scope of Burroughs's films foment his narcotic-fueled ambitions: it is a moment when socialist critique married itself to the ethics and dynamics of modern man's deconstruction, over-suggesting conscious overtures through mind-altering drugs and technologies such as the Flicker. There is abundant true text and, at the same time, examples of criticism's connivance robbing Burroughs of this special authenticity. Thus, critical studies promise discussion and cross-examination to expand Burroughs's increasing canonical weight. Films such as 2004's *The Dreamachine* and 2007's *Destroy All Rational Thought* spearhead our journeys into extra-intellectual or occult learning as they phrase semantic and cultural revolution, tracing necessary biographies linking Burroughs to indie artists such as Brion Gysin. They, too, document the underground's street poetics, their occult re-inventions, and perhaps the refreshed dynamic of new, hitherto totally unexplored, knowledge for which Burroughs claimed credit. They also reopen Burroughs's queries when faced with his academic self-perception. If comparisons with the academically well-received Paul Bowles favor the latter's broad humanism and thorough engagements of the Orient, biographical cues and commentaries suggest Burroughs's more intense, irrational point of learning drawn from treks through Central and South American territories and versus his spoken indifference of, and ignorance to, much-storied Orient arts and experiences. These excursions shadow his erstwhile approval of the rhetoric- and perception-changing technologies such as the Cut-up and the Flicker. I believe that Gysin's mobility in both innovations concur with the elder Burroughs, when cut off from Orient labyrinths of super-creation. Burroughs had been less successful at demonstrating true Orient ethnography, supposing ritual and art techniques in his ideas' written form. This lifetime obsession testifies to the Tangier's shadowy, labyrinthine scene, and the hordes of young beatniks and hippies devoted to unearthing and consuming shards of his revelations.

I saw the merit of film examples about the lesser-known or non-focal Beats—mainly, because I believe that wider historical examinations are possible, and the formal critique of the literary group's fame and excess could be known from race, gender, class, and the contemporary setting. Beginning with Anthony Harvey's 1967 film *Dutchman*, films critique and revisit crucial moments of polarity and promise. As Beat works were published, and racial and sexual *entendres* become more revealing, Harvey's film explores the philosophical and social conflict inherent in the person and setting of Beat knowledge and its pretense to avant-garde lifestyles. Films starring Lawrence Ferlinghetti in 2010's *A Rebirth of Wonder* would also critique the main group's persistent body of myths. From our exegesis of literature, history, and race, there was a much greater beginning, a more realistic display of ideas, ethnic re-writing of liberal intellectual purpose, and a departure from aesthetic simplicity and novelty when replaying modern man's quandaries. 2011's *Love Always, Carolyn* adds critical re-examinations of place and actors: there was a sobering side to its expression of liberal aesthetic and occult talents, and sour re-examinations about literary man's brand of *pathos* and sickness. Jack Shoemaker's 2012 film, *The Practice of the Wild*, contests the aesthetic riddle of Kerouac's joyous and un-thematic journeys: while attesting to the consistency of poetic form, Snyder gives much more socio-politically real, empirical appraisals, summarizing his history from straight translations of Eastern philosophical and religious wisdom.

Film adaptations of literature, and commentaries that exposit literary biography, if they are to be understood, might as easily profuse and distort our academic inclination to teach historical literature. They also build our consumption: it should be said that much of my effort means to document art's partial demise in favor of the timeless rubric of man's graphic freedom from his social responsibilities. Here is a technique found in many historical films that derided authority's control to free the author's origins from censorship's narrowing gaze. It is not beyond our grasp to compare the literary adaptation with mainstream, first-run movies. Audiences are more likely to track the film's effectiveness, constructing its graphic and conversational techniques to star the literary work's recasting. They may then paint special minutes of self-understanding that projects the greater engine of liberal social developments that we understand through the use of screenplays. With this in mind, I have included a number of archival examples: it is just as important to feature what had been lost, and the moment's duality when it was lost. Building the movement's popularity has as much to do with scholarship as it does with their somber *denouement*, as film has in large part replaced writing when assessing counter-history's moments of social and cultural *praxis*.

As a final note, I will say that comparisons between this work and my last, *Re-Creating Paul Bowles, the Other, and the Imagination* ought to at least ensure the completeness of form. Bowles was an Orientalist and governed the Oriental frame tale to beget formalist-poststructuralist intersections that were not authentic and directed the motions of cultural theory towards a greater narrative Self-understanding. Bowles, too, examines the ground of gay ethnography from the pains of graphic and comic abstractions to cement gothic narrative horror in the visual and temporal moment, and ultimately modernism's persistent horror beckoning the Self's internal sickness. It is questionable, then, whether the much deeper gay narrative synthesis approximates any political or cultural logistics of man's modern experience, even if the topic was beguiling and favors undiscovered knowledge. Contrastively, if we attempt a modernist-friendly Beat ethnography, where journeys into the non–Western world are shorter and include a more limited anthropology, we risk a greater postmodern ineptitude due to the absence of archetypes emboldening counter-history's narrative symbols and referents. This will, in the real sense, expand counter-history, and modern discussions retracting authoritarian control. My task, then, was to trace the author's ambitions and indoctrinations, with a greater perceivable form and narrative reflection when considering film.

ONE

Neal Cassady and Jack Kerouac
The Films and the Reinvention of Text

Linda Hutcheon's book *A Theory of Adaptation* is useful for the Beats, as she augments the multifaceted range of changes and innovations that weave a truer humanism, causing us to promote Beat literary origins and man's simple inventions. This symbol-text agency stimulates our appraisal of the group's writings and historical period from largely realist conceptions. Hutcheon writes: "To think of narrative adaptation in terms of a story's fit and its process of mutation and adjustment, through adaptation, to a particular cultural environment is something that I find suggestive. Stories also evolved from adaptation and are not immutable over time."[1] With this in mind, Kerouac's films point to the principles of viewer adaptation and to immersions. One thoughtful thread is that they develop and retell the author's earlier perspectives, whether supposing or paraphrasing the author's works, or in commentaries about the author. They, then, count in the historical drama that comprises Kerouac's modernist forms during the time of his published reception, beginning in 1950 with *The Town and the City*. The Beats read endlessly, and Kerouac wrote and typed hundreds of drafts. The Beat Generation's main nucleus consists of writers who negotiate the specific conditions guarding their lives, personas, and imaginations. For these reasons, I believe that audiences will intensify fictional portraits, extending their semantic, graphic, and philosophical boundaries. Poststructuralist and postmodern semantic revolutions use visual, iconic, and aural techniques to subjugate modernist literary ambition: the distension of characters and heroism record an increasingly difficult, and soon hyperbolic, quest. Biography as a collective body of commentaries and authorial portraits, too, altered the word's power, decentering authorial readings. Films promote the idea that Beat knowledge and perspectives were shared, not individual, advancing the generational idea that Beat literature galvanizes necessary social critique. The idea is not purely admissible: Kerouac's writing, travels, and specific prophecies avoided metaphors that describe or symbolize the literary movement's origins, fully clandestine until his 1965 publication of *Desolation Angels*. New Kerouac criticism draws upon studies of his unpublished writings, hence of the author's idea and its nascence. Since Jacques Derrida told us "the book is dead"[2] in 1984's *Of Grammatology*, many scholars discussed writing's living force from close readings of the author's letters and rough drafts. Changing the scene's formal and historical characteristics attributes historiography to be a recurrent, open social idea and the tool for greater examinations. Changes in scene and content also situate man's social geographies and characterizations. Thus began the author's partial deconstruction, and literary ideas that advance forms of a peculiar, tormented, and special genius whose subjectivity we do not understand.

Without inflating more general questions about Kerouac's childhood, our attentions to Kerouac and to his infancy's special voice, and to that voice's endless societal prescriptions, herald specific details concerning his epistemology, ethnography, and iconography. Should we deduce the young author's comprehensive attentions to the Beat scene and its culture, we at least surmise that the modernist form knew of its grand rewriting in films that includes the writers' vocal expression, perspectives, and private memoirs. These themes recur despite the thesis, from the 1970s onward, that the Beats were original, representing a change in human conscious intentions. Modernism's aesthetic-derived intellections supposed realism's ambitious remaking, and youthful stardom inspires a special whirlwind of personal discovery and internalizations to help mount a counter-history and counter-context that would popularize and vulgarize the 1950s scene.

Before we turn to the films themselves, we should recognize the written work's historiographical power, and hence the movement's deducible power as living instruments that decorate the Beat's special, modernist allusions to man's ecstatic creation of himself as Self. Adolescent forms richly inscribed their psychic and dramatic concentration of facts and reflections when tracing the origins and impact of drugged states, dreams, and personal narrative. Nineteen fifty-two's "The Beginnings of Bop" interweaves Kerouac's visionary attentions to cannabis and jazz. Imagism and interiority depends on Kerouac's crafted vision, where he introduces Harlem's "scene" as the sublime agent of urban divination. Youth's special memoir details the concrete form in a strophic ascent more affective than in the works of Ralph Ellison, James Baldwin, and even Miles Davis:

> The band realized the goof of life that had made them be not only misplaced in a white nation and the goof they felt stringing in their bellies [...] Thelonious was so weird he wandered the twilight streets of Harlem in winter with no hat on his hair, sweating, blowing fog—in his head he heard it all ringing often he heard whole choruses by Lester [...] Thore was a strange English kid hanging around Minton's

who stumbled along the sidewalk hearing Lester in his head too—hours of hundreds of developing choruses in implacable bars—erected in mind's foundation jazz [...].[3]

A basic rhetorical fact lay within Kerouac's iconographic translation of place and memory. Kerouac's own recording of jazz's intensity and novelty unveils the anti-normative vehicle of modern man's communion with non-scriptural transmigrations and transcendences of America's more realistic, class-derived ethics. Kerouac's "tales" read with purer concentration and deeper narcotic fabling than expositions of jazz in his novels: it also purports radical blackness enjoining a distinct social and moral history in White America. Critical iconographies of tenor saxophonist Charlie "Yardbird" Parker reflected sweeter and tighter rhetorical and concrete movements of imagery and thought. They, too, express the Beat group's narcotic experimentalism that intensifies modernist diction and outlook. In fairness to Kerouac, it was this oft-emulated fete that black criticism frequently censors to anoint a more centrist direction:

> Bird, lips hanging dully to hear, is turning slowly in a circle waiting for Diz to swim through the wave of his own grim like factories and atonal at any minute and the logic of the mad, the sock in his belly is sweet, the rock, conga, monga, bang—in white creamed afternoons of blue bird had leaned back dreaming in eternity as Dizzy outlined to him the importance of becoming Mohammedans in order to find a solid basis of race to their ceremony.[4]

Visual and aural angles are exact, and the comic extensions of language are limited, so as to accentuate the poetic angle of rebirth as a transnational extension of consciousness. Conversely, audiences may put Hutcheon's ideas about mutation and narration to the test with our sense of the film's rhetorical and conversational power, and thus the virtual moment's approximation of America's "real" history. In doing so, we may ask questions about social realism's collective body to manifest historical and historiographical truths about the Beats. Films that introduce Jack Kerouac and Neal Cassady intersected with American history's everyday simulation, and re-writings of straightforward attentions to writing and taped conversations among writers that attribute place, intention, and anxiety when reconstructing the literary period. What is most important are screenings of verbal rhetoric and visual style that viewers could understand and appreciate. Staging of Kerouac's shroud-like voice and poetic ramblings and of thoughts and witticisms in his novels and letters mark a glossy, surefooted tone, instilling narrative confidence and discovery's illusory pendulum nesting erratic, uncertain conflicts. Shorn of this guiding concept, we would probably lose the Beat moment in time and assume instead its tepid irrelevance. From conversations at conferences and with students, I found that the most valuable analytical and cultural threads in contemporary literature speak to the form's modern perception and projections. The barest mainstream reading, by contrast, supposes fiction's non-agency, recognizing its dynamism and humanity in light of popular renditions of history and culture. Many postmodern re-writings through film tread this specific danger. Many are the false American histories, and there are even more rhetorical hyperboles and gaps in history textbooks and criticism causing us to reject the historical film as *kitsch* that carries no pragmatic ideas, though it had scandalizes viewers who expect true, careful readings. Even though these are not easy dictums to follow, the accuracy of cultural-social translation in films is even more surprising, despite distortions of presence when adding big-name actors and actresses known for more *kitsch*-directed navigations that repeat postmodern anti-glamor during the 1970s, 80s, and 90s.

We may then type Jack Kerouac to be a much greater catalyst in developing and narrating narcotics epistemology and the altered mind. True, this part of Kerouac's critical reception is muted in favor of the more studied, exotic Burroughs and the communist Ginsberg: it is evident from his letters that visions were happenstance, erratic, and distorted to relay Kerouac's gladiator-like moments of comic exaggeration. Despite this very sanguine fact, Kerouac's written mastery communicates his seriousness about knowing the drugged mind's sincerity and beauty. In this light, films re-introduce the power of drugs as they operate in man's visions, memories, and thoughts, in concrete forms that appear a decade before writers such as Timothy Leary, Allen Ginsberg, Aldous Huxley, Paul Bowles, and William S. Burroughs research them and make it popular, should this second nucleus be said to trace its objective impact. More narrowly, 1952's "Benzedrine Vision" captured the author's extreme delusions and mental transfigurations, posing Kerouac's deepest biographical contentions about himself. In Kerouac's mind, narcotic form displays and tells key modernist imaginative details, reading concrete narrations of the spirit, the mind, and travelers. Because of this, Kerouac deserves much more credit for nixing his formalist anxieties well before *Road's* 1957 publication. In his written confessions, Kerouac traces the limits and the extremities of his mind for crucial answers: he did not propose romantic journeys that instead manifest the destruction of thought and ideations when they had conjured its moral and emotional perspectives. Recalling a night in Mexico City, Kerouac is barely coherent, totally losing his way and his sense of self as he wanders the streets. Kerouac's moment of truth is found ten years before the graphic/geographic thoroughness of Lupita's slum in 1960's *Tristessa*: he puts his God-given romanticism to the conscious test of eclipse:

> I was full of misery—my main misery—my main misery, the fear of not being myself and the fear of not being able to hand out who I am, who myself is and the

fear of god who was somehow mixed in the penalty [...] I began to speak with my mother and to hear her voice counseling berating and as always, consoling me in the cell, the throat choking and when you want none or salvation & eternity then you were made to carry out you cannot cry—because then you've lost you still love love [...].[5]

I think that, if the letter's rhetorical and textual incoherence accomplished the destruction of modernist engagements of mind's thoughts and of the idea's graphic, self-expression in forms of narcotic dream-contexts, and in their raw, tactile, and lingering syntax is strong and resilient. Its pathetic, comic rambling also embraces a sustained romanticism confirming love, maternity, and faith through one's doctrine of perceptual and graphic self-recognition. It, too, nests the Freudian self-conception of his idea's inhibited moment in the mechanics of social-temporal isolation[6]: "love" stands as an undefined sign whose vagueness and emotional depth promise greater excavations of the Soul and the Real through drugs and dreams. Stronger marks could be given to the concrete depth and pure ethnographies in 1960's *Tristessa*. I would simply point out that scholars have ignored the generative content that beckons us to take Kerouac more seriously without comical steps that cause us to profane and denounce his written irrelevance to American thought and its mid–20th century polarity. Might film, even if its screening was narrower, clipping narcotic memories and dreams to herald juvenile escapism rather than learning, sustain literary forms to be guiding, thoughtful social agents? After all, Norman Mailer gave Kerouac the axe: he had, in a note of assurance and complete understanding, said that Kerouac's works were infantile and would not withstand the publisher's critical eye. Thus, we force forward more useful discussions for students trying to get a handle on the modern mind's substantive content. When we deny the erratic work's arguable stress, we are led to believe that the author's individuality nixes his true purpose as the Beat Generation's founder.

The Films of Neal Cassady

The Beats traversed many active or unvisited memories and ideas of modern man's resurgence, so we are apt to ask questions about what literary and social origins meant to express in modernist literary analogues and their specific textual techniques. Why must we deduce literary identity to have been shared and mutual? What specific forms of writing, person, and place will help us embrace further adolescent social development? When these developments are screened, do they form part of a casual narrative inscribing the storyteller's valorous stance as a classless, unadorned hero, and hence the artist who offers us socially necessary dialogue and characterizations? After all, the Beats did not escape criticism's scalding, bruising provocations. Americans were encouraged to drop the literary group's possible meaning, as they felt it had stemmed from false constructions of adolescent moral guilt that were useless to contemporary social-intellectual development. Norman Mailer, in particular, wielded the axe of destruction in a sure calculation. In 1959's *Advertisements for Myself*, he destroys and polarizes the movement's recurrent social angle of mythic productions, stripping the East-imbibed asceticism of its virile potency. In his essay "Hipster and Beatnik," a careful assault disgorges the novel, sublime technique of pure, syntactic and imagistic innovation, revealing the Self's critical weaknesses at the moment of its formalist *nexus*:

> While he comes along with most hipsters on the first tenet of the faith: that one's orgasm is the clue to how well one is living—he has less body to work with in the first place, and so his chances for lifting himself by his sexual bootstraps are commonly nil, especially since each medieval guild in the Beat Generation has invariably formed itself on a more or less common sexual vitality or lack of it. The boys and girls available to the average beatnik are as drained as himself. Natural that the sex of the beatnik circles in, and mysticism becomes the Grail—he ends by using his drug to lash his mind into a higher contemplation of the universe and its secrets, a passive act, onanistic; the trance is coveted more than any desire to trap it later in work or art.[7]

My sense is that the Beat Generation writers have incurred below-the-belt criticisms that target the lack of sexual focus as meaning some cultural-psychic problem. They represent weak social links that initiate their philosophy, romanticism, and reflections. Because of criticism's breadth, we recast the movement's rhetorical and social power through Neal Cassady. From the film's narration of the 1940s that featured scene, time, and the social imagination, we suppose that evidence that heralds Cassady's early narrative mastery without academic instruction tells us that Cassady, not the Columbia-educated Kerouac and Ginsberg, was the group's "natural man" and the true social catalyst. Cassady is made into a messenger of intellectual responsibility and relationship, and a prophetic social adventurer with special, deep and complex tales that spoke of the dilemmas and liaisons found due to his graphic, underground, virile power. Cassady's filmed translation is imperfect, yet states the strongest relationships among lesser-known Beat artists. Poetry is thus reconciled with masculinity, and masculinity with the underground *métier*. *Heart Beat* and *The Last Time I Committed Suicide* struggle with the artistic parable, though very different in its overall structure. When modern man's creativity arose from his adolescent stimulations, it brought the generation's members closer together to cast written iconographies of virtue. Both films visit the obvious socioeconomic contrast. Although Kerouac's authorial identity was carefully guarded, Cassady's was not—a verdict on their ideas and creativity that publishers only recently took up with the publication of *The First Third* and *The Letters of Neal Cassady*. Cassady, too, orchestrates virtuous narrative technique symbolizing modernist truth. Ideas and adventures come from a real, not imagined, personal realism.

Heart Beat

The warm, conversational format of 1980's *Heart Beat* writes didactic, instructional, and practical alternatives to blanket rehashing of a basic Beat Generation history. The film did not make use of complex cinematography, or any narrations of dreams or altered states. In fact, the group's simple narration of its history—focused on American geographies and partying with the Beat Generation stars—extolls the timeless story and should be understood as an introduction to the Beat "family." With Sissy Spacek as Carolyn and Nick Nolte as Neal Cassady, the movie's impetus is to detail and conceptualize the group's social and moral problems, against the tide of libations and artistic pretensions not thickly described to fully unveil their experiences or that sprung from the characters' thoughts. Neal, Jack and Carolyn race through the period's spectacle and place's interiority, and laugh their way through the post–War middle-class American cultural similitude. In doing so, they dredge up some of Neal's peculiar vision and some of the moment's alternation between Nolte as film star and as Beat star. The film's lucid, conversational medium assigns the Beat story's chronology and plots, giving no references to literary history or the writing's specific, deeply aesthetic, ascending *métier*. These are masked, constituting part of the foil speaking to much greater, wilder expositions of the Beat movement's joys and intricacies, sexual gambling and tomfoolery, and jocular, anti–Victorian thrusting of street personas. *Heart Beat* is the first example of the new generation of Beat films. I will stress the ongoing narrative as crucial to marking and opening up familial discussions that pointed to greater historical excavations: in doing so, *Heart Beat* tries to disperse Kerouac's peculiar mysticism.

Sissy Spacek's role as groupie and family head includes the romantic sweetening of *Heart Beat* as a pop-oriented vehicle flavored with 70s stereotypes and easygoing rehashing of the outside world to sustain and accent the literary group's idealism. The group's gusto and revelries, far from the American hearth's collective focus, intends to please viewing audiences and inscribes ribald, speculative juvenile tales as an epochal abstraction and comic necessity. Joyous ambivalence tells the idea of synchronous generations that grows from its vernacular truth. *Heart Beat*, if it is compared to historical films, assumes the contemporary eye's successful unfolding of American history and her special, contrived cultural-generational creation. We then identify and focus upon the historical moment to appear as the dramatic minute, made of man's conversational and social conflicts with knowledge and experience. As extensions of socialist realism's screenplay technique, conversations and screenings of real-life biographical adaptations forecast ideas about the story's production, imbuing the historical portrait with its own reality. The film expresses the tenacity and thoughtfulness of man's ethical comparisons with today's investigation of anti–Victorian freedoms. More likely, expositions of the Beat Generation's internal and external struggles with the authorities, the mainstream world, the publishers, and the renegade movement's unguarded minute of recognition, assuming the form of man's virtuous legend, and not his passing irrelevance. *Heart Beat* uses the simple format of adapting the entire Beat history in its 90-minute replay. With this in mind, it is useful to score the film's patient and thoughtful nudging of the Beat movement into two *ménages a trois*—that of Carolyn-Neal-Jack and Carolyn-Neal-Allen—that embroil a strangely sentient and distinct moral message. It is clear from the group's tapestry of self-conceptions that the press, and popular speculation have led us away from this message, though travelers and artists confirm its wake to open doors to prophecies and self-knowledge.

Scene adaptations are simple enough to understand as bearers of the modern, urban, middle-class visual technique for expression, and ably dislocate the *salon's* interior navigations of artistic pretense and its ascension to the American social imagination. Many of the scenes with Cassady are protracted, nominal journeys repeating the literary group's jocular, penitent isolation. They include the rejection of Kerouac's manuscript, where a short, White man informs him that his work "isn't a novel" and with Ginsberg angrily trashing the institution of publishing,[8] Cassady's drunken stagger through a Beat-friendly café where he lingers over a sign that demands a "$2.50 drink minimum,"[9] his liaison with a prostitute in a hotel, where he throws out sailors.[10] The movie's second half includes scenes from the group's Mexico travels, painted in terms friendly to Carolyn and giving light to none of the shaded pornography of *On the Road*[11]; it is followed with Cassady's arrest by an African-American snitch[12]; and his 1960s stint as the hippies' bus driver in Mexico. As the radio blasts Jimi Hendrix's "Purple Haze" during a phone call to Carolyn, Neal comes to terms with his eclipse as an unrecognized mystic, borne of his own vision.

Ironically, Kerouac's writing career is understood from actor Ron Heard's verbal admonition that writing will ensure a prosperous middle-class life in America.[13] Heard is cast as silent, introspective, piously introverted, and somehow special: this isolation is ensured with Carolyn's visible preference for Neal, who plays a kazoo on the bed as Kerouac begins to type the first pages of *On the Road*.[14] Nonetheless, the technique for expressing the group's familial bonds is brave and misleadingly safe. When Kerouac decides to take the bus to New York, Cassady warns him, "New York's not a good place for a writer."[15] *Heart Beat*, in short, preserves the muse's special, romantic, and joyous postures in his tense suggestion that Kerouac was the object of his hysterical protections; Heard's thoughts are guarded during the foursome's intoxicated, joyous, and lengthy collusion. Carolyn's narrative tone appears amidst vacations in Mexico City with Neal's two children, her spoken admission that she had never loved men like Neal and Jack,[16] as well as Carolyn's basic yet noteworthy and feminist-friendly reticence, *a la* Helene Cixous, to Ginsberg that most men "liked to talk about themselves."[17] Comical, intuitive replays of Cassady's ideas and context find expression in inner-city brownstones, suburban tract homes, bars in urban ghettos, and scenes from the road that retell family experiences and dialogues. But the Beat family was American, with its peculiar and silently, thoughtlessly guided origins and legend. Thus, *Heart Beat* did not complicate the Beat picture, even when it overstates their romantic indifference and insouciant adventures in changing, inhuman-sounding worlds speaking to America's pure incomprehension of the movement's tryst with unkempt vision.

The addition of Nick Nolte as Neal Cassady presumes a special target for new histories that replayed the mid–20th century American experience. Nolte is Heard's friend and wise prophet, and embodies the literary group's tale of libations, parables, and reflections. Nolte counters much of Mailer's thesis—he is prodigal, easy to like, sympathetic, and reflective. What matters more, though, is the situation of American scenery amidst Nolte's everyday navigations of Beat moments, which attach the doctrine of underclass realism to bohemian writings that eschewed political fashioning of its resilient, meandering "spirit." Audiences may then peruse with approval and warmth Nolte's easygoing, silent, or dreamlike contemplations away from Kerouac's typewriter. The implied clash between the Beat movement's aesthete and its founder gives credence to the historical film's mainstream expression. It poses class-sensitive ideations about knowledge stemming from underground circles and from dejected figures that present subjective truths. Thus, the Cassady legend's key steps of self-expression and ideation—or those that predict a truly separate, guiding meditation—attribute the group's reticent pain, and the pains of its expression, to the form of America's geographies and cryptically barren domains of lifestyle, status, and finally recognition. As Cassady relaxes in the Los Gatos home while smoking a joint, looking idly and happily at his children, Kerouac receives the call from an agent offering to publish *On the Road*.[18] Still, *Heart Beat* states substance's meaningful polarity. Was Cassady happy in the passing of his whirlwind, romance-studded adventures and his life impressions? Did writing present a task that his emotions were not prepared for, even as Kerouac wrote his novels? Scenes and minutes of suburban dreaming are part of the publisher's haunting tale. Neal is a street subject, born of the Catholic-spoken happiness and compassion that Kerouac sought. Travels are negotiated easily: minutes of peace and familial and conjugal reflection are a blissful mirage freed of Cassady's wild adventures into the city or beyond. Without reading the primary works or staging any of the "read-ins" documented in *Visions of Cody* by 1951, *Heart Beat* preserves the story's silence against the brilliant casting of manhood that was conversational, intuitive, and easily understood. Fulfillment, of course, is firmly grafted onto corporate-driven America's impassive, tedious poetics. John Harrington accepts Kerouac's commentaries when supporting *Road*'s publication, as a happy Kerouac steals the phone and asks Harrington to talk to Neal.[19] Harrington, his hair greased back and smiling impishly, intones the soupy, *kitsch*-flavored media rhetoric that Ginsberg and Mailer rehearsed at Congressional obscenity trials of "Howl" and *Naked Lunch*: what was destructive to America should be studied and understood.[20] As recounted in the letters, too, there is no hindrance of Neal's easygoing flirting and cheating that brings him to Kerouac's house with Black prostitutes, and later finds him in the city looking for sex.[21] Nolte draws a special talent as a penitent victim of changing times. He is able to laugh, tease, love, and reflect, projecting the persistent mirage that told millions of teenagers to leave their suburban homes. Still, the movie relays their broad instance of generation, suppressing Nolte's ambitions and his private sense. Now aged, haggard, and still seeking Kerouac, he lives in a post–Beat world that recognizes the movement's significance even though defunct when transposing the elder's riddle of philosophy and literature, much of it not divulged to us in the written form. Spacek remorsefully ejects, as the sun sets on the suburban tract homes and Kerouac headed for the road, "I guess you're damned if you do, damned if you don't," recalling the group's *pathos* and Kerouac's endless, transmigrating horizon at the end of his writing career.[22] Spacek's final comment exclaims her deep depression about a literary movement's visible, evocative diminution and derangement: beneath the alcoholic tedium, Spacek's broad brush-stroke assembles both Beat idealism's perceived might and deep, gloomy visions of its total subjection and irrelevance at the movement's sour, whimsical end in the late 1960s. Scholars, writers, readers, and activists alike turned over the Beat Generation's eclipse very early on, and so deserve the summative, meaningful demise as a partial meditation on the literary group's real worth in the changing, and increasingly neurotic, American Dream.

Nolte and Spacek meet a couple obsessed with cleanliness; at one point, Sissy turns upon a drunken, high Nolte and scolds him, saying that he "has no friends."[23] The resulting dinners at the couple's house leave them dismayed and deliriously laughing at the postmodern fetishism's sudden and surreal moment of pure comedy. The house's blaring lights found Nolte and Spacek doffing their literary ardor, instead hanging on the obsessive etiquette that gives way to child-like giggling that dismayed the happy-go-lucky Cassady who had thought himself to be the instance of social change. Many adolescent novels, TV shows, and films screen conflict between social acceptance and renegade partying with high school friends who cling to intuitive thinking and seek to conquer cultural and moral *difference* in the outside world. Even as authority-knowledge dichotomies were part of English literature as early as Henrik Ibsen's *Hedda Gabler* (1891), I think that young artistic pretensions and their comedic happenstance possess a richer, more sensually diverse range of examples and social standards in today's music, TV serials and sitcoms, and commercials. These myriad examples either understate or overstate the authentic minute of youthful understanding, suggesting their reflective grasp that emboldens written perspectives. I think, therefore, that adolescence's penitent illusion and stated *praxis* withstand today's scrutiny: *Heart Beat* nests subversive adolescent inceptions of idea and community in the constitution of the Real, the honest, and the natural vivacity of men and women. Commodity fetishism was also introduced after *Road's* publication, when a drunken Cassady stumbles though a bar created in the wake of his friend's triumph, looking oddly and depressively through tired eyes at the drink prices and the bartender who doesn't know who he is.[24] *Heart Beat* takes advantage of moments of careful social indoctrination. Adolescent contemplations and communities were intact and un-parented. We might also say that Spike Lee's casting of an erratic and independent Mookie in *Do the Right Thing*, or Trey Stiles' promise to his girlfriend, Brenda, not to make her pregnant in 1991's *Boyz n the Hood*, project street rebellion and pleasure as part of the decision-making process that deepen street moral understandings supposing American vocations, family, society, and geographies, that do not answer modern life's seriousness. In *Hood's* final scene, Stiles calls out to Ice Cube, "Yo, Dough, you still got one brother left, man,"[25] a rhetorical full stop restating solid Black adolescent engagements and indoctrinations versus the evils of urban, poor society. Re-entrenching adolescent morals and moral discoveries, I believe, do not happen for Neal, Jack, and Carolyn in *Heart Beat*. Instead, there lay a penitent agony, an assessment of the Beat group's travails to speak of something haunting, yet central to their survival. When shadowed by Cassady and Carolyn, Kerouac's reflective persona is strong and hauntingly so, adding to the living tensions between writers who thought that the Beat's defining power had lapsed in time, bequeathing nothing to future generations.

Re-Writing the Letter and the Narrative of Feeling in *The Last Time I Committed Suicide*

I watched Keanu Reeves when he starred in *Bill and Ted's Excellent Adventure* in 1988. Critics and our generation did not view it to understand history: it projected a total, abominable lapse of historical writing in film and may have spawned more history-spoofs over time with ridiculous plots and oddball visions that fled our serious inquiries. Still, Reeves' succeeding roles in film projected a more heroic character that expresses the instance of American national attitudes and morals. As such, I thought it novel and worthwhile to trace new injections of the spirit that had grown out of a 1950 letter to Kerouac that described Cassady's liaison with Joan, who repeatedly tries to commit suicide. The middling moment in Reeves' career—on the heels of blockbuster success *Speed* and just before his greatest success, 1998's *The Matrix*—re-introduces the adolescent comedy's success when painting romantic and sensual imageries and its instances of place as it re-tells Neal's meditations in the letter, one of Cassady's few publications that first appeared in 1964's *Notes From Underground*. My job is not to assess Reeves's character, as he is a supporting actor; still, his presence in this movie shadowed the historical moment from the towering Hollywood behemoth's gaze, placing crucial control of the letter's content in the format of today's rhetorical imagination. Thus, the operative bias was friendly to life's envisioning as Neal wrote of it, a genuine drama intersecting with today's intellectual diffusion of richly modern ideas and intonations of place. Stephen Kay's screenplay guaranteed the literary group's actions, libations, and dramatic foci that held few passive or reticent moments within the letter's special intimacy. Hence, the strophic moment of *difference* weighs against more conservative emblems of life and their stereotypical dictations of character and plot.

The Last Time I Committed Suicide based itself on a letter to Jack Kerouac on December 17, 1950, and tells one of Cassady's longest tales: it recalls a 1946 memoir of his relationship with a girl named Joan, who resides in intensive care in a hospital. A labyrinthine revisiting of Cassady's pretenses, pleasures, and difficulties at finding success, *Suicide* underscores his writing technique and the written form's imaginative and rhetorical strength. We ought to judge whether or not *Suicide* was truly faithful to the 1946 letter, yet could recognize the composure and complete reflection of writing, and thus the adolescent reflection's density, sweetness and ascriptions to authoritarian moral strength in mid–20th century American urban society. Further, we anticipate the youth's tentative state of being. My sense is that *Suicide* also builds the form of tactility, feeling, and self-gratifications in the filmed tale: these are themes that Kerouac agonized in his quest for fame. In terms of race, *Suicide* bequeaths an essential geographic and sensual whiteness that did not engage the outside world: like *The Town and the City*, motifs and metaphors of prosperity and sexuality are arranged to reflect the American middle class's wealth and continuity, and hence its antagonistic inquisition of the street scene's degenerate followers. Versus Reeves, too, Cassady acts out the triumph of goodness and moral truth against the poolshark's frequent misuse of his business and the weakening state of corrupt young men mistreating those that they know: this, of course, is in stark contrast to repeated dramas and quips in *Visions of Cody* that shadowed Neal's poverty and shiftlessness with the poolshark's visible compassion. I believe it is important to recognize moral conflict as being part of young adult social narratives, telling us what matters most to them about their communities. The letter's richness of reflection adds questions about the accuracy and motions of the characters, scenes, and place's visual renditions, so as to record Cassady's self-vindication against the other Beats, who were better schooled and who accept broad intellectual pretensions in a short period. Cassady writes when discovering Joan at the hospital:

> There was no doubt she was over-joyed to see me, her eyes said so. It was as though the gesture of self-destruction had, in her mind, equalized all the guilt. The courage of committing the act seemed to have justified her to herself. This action on her conviction, no matter how neurotic, had called for all her strength and she was now released.[26]

A very able criticism of the other Beats was vivid and certain: Kerouac's depersonalizing form that is found in his main novels gave no verbal or contemplative inclusion of women or racial minorities in his daring, madcap adventures into the world. Indeed, he maintains rhetorical, conceptual, and organizational control, denying his friends any kind of vocal message telling us that Beat culture and consciousness grew from lesser writers' thoughts and perspectives. Thus, *Suicide* includes striking reflections about womankind's contemplations allowing her to escape or destroy her Victorian confines and guilt with no benefit from her husband's telepathic or transcendental powers. Conversely, Joan's anxieties bore fruit in Cassady's romantic attentions to the mind's individual rigors when facing society. I believe that this, as in many of Cassady's works, repeats the strength of his pulse on humanity and its recurring truths. By contrast, audiences will deduce that Kerouac's suppression of verbal and rhetorical content allows him greater freedom when writing about his reflection's strength and seriousness.

Kerouac's humorous style is confessional and in some instances is tied to literature, religion, and philosophy. Not surprisingly, he addles the White brain in his prose works, synthetically arriving at the conclusion that women and minority characters should be adaptable, and so did not speak of Kerouac's recurrent urban *pathos* that spun out of control. Regarding "Beat," humanity and humanism welded together more direct expressions of mankind's social being, something Kerouac was reluctant to give to characters outside the group's main nucleus. Dominant male traits remained in place. Kerouac develops from the muse's purer simplicity, with the metaphor cresting in examples such as "Joan Rawshanks in the Fog" and the 102-page introduction to *Visions of Cody* that retold Cassady's poverty, hunger, and adolescent discoveries around "the scene."[27] Kerouac and Cassady, too, held similar cultural viewpoints about the world they live in, and letters poured back and forth in the 1940s and early 50s. Terror, isolation, warmth and compassion recurred in Kerouac's description of the Denver poolhalls in *Visions of Cody* and so hung conspicuously on Cassady's feelings of loss and sickness. *Suicide* adopted the poolhall scene's shadowy brilliance: the many young girls that frequent Harry's place re-form the sweetness and errant syntax of Kerouac's visits to Denver whorehouses, happily speaking aloud his juvenilia that builds his meditative power. Depressive urban characteristics, realities, and geographies accentuate the light, pleasure, and redeeming strength of "the words" found in Cassady's long depression and sickness that Kerouac rewrote into Cody Pomeray in *Visions*.

Starring blond-haired, lean and cavalier Thomas Jane as Neal Cassady, *Suicide* projects the honesty, happiness, and real moral and intellectual struggles of the film's main character. Jane expertly performs the demeanor and depressive perceptions of middle-class America. He moves from joy-filled adventures of sex, partying and relationships on the road and in the city, to scenes detailing authority's strong hands and the status's coercive jealousy that kept him unhappy and meandering. The adolescent tale-telling, seen through the eyes of Joan—who tries to commit suicide and grudgingly adopts the spoken and physical attributes of relationship and community—interwove many narrations that recall Cassady's struggle to be a successful writer. Stuck in everyday jobs and dependent on his Beat colleagues and others, Jane steadily navigates the foibles and jealous tangling of his friendships and liaisons with no visible emotional suffering. He moves between subcultures, decides what actions to take, and maintains an honest sensibility that could take on the most intrusive prescriptions from authorities and the underground. He saves himself from

Cherry Mary's dictatorial mother, survives incarceration, and leaves Joan when she attempts suicide the second time.[28] Specific portraits of Cassady's memories are, then, at least accurate when advancing his views and moral sincerity as they could be supposed during the 1940s. By contrast, Reeves is visibly expressive and speaks instances of the contemporary character's much-recognized voice and attitude. The persona, outlook, and moments of inclusion in America's daily life confirm Reeves's noisy provocations, featuring the improvised, shady splendor of his loutish bravado. No attempt is made to change his conversational style, and at best his position in the 1946 memoir is minimal. Jane's beginning in *Suicide* unveils the writer's schizophrenic beginning: Jane is jumpy, on edge, unsure what front to give to his persona, and fails to convince Ben (an Allen Ginsberg lookalike) that he had any new ideas. Several characters, including Ginsberg, repeatedly con him for sex, both ways.[29] The film passes through Denver's homes, bars, and warehouses, allowing us to peer into its depressive picture versus the lucid, yet vague and so deeply meditated, chance at inclusion in a rich society. The most difficult task was clear: *Suicide* explores the conversational depth, querulousness, and criminal shadowing, of voice and presence with the letter not more than a superficial guide. My question has to do with the aural and visual cataloging of the spirit in which the letter itself was intended. In a first reading, the 1946 letter painfully and joyously tells the author's labyrinthine intimacy with the memoir, and of biographical poses of artistry's value. The film projects Cassady's raspy, haggard voice over several passages from the letter. Talks among friends and lesser characters, too, screen a general format favoring romantic attestation to scenes and place, moral and educational dilemmas, and depressive tales about Denver's shiftless, partying youths fed up with their elders. Appropriately, the shadowy, Herculean struggle with his ambitions and private adventures parallel the struggles found in modernist fiction's main characters. We might as well replay Leopold Bloom's night out in the Dublin brothels in 1922's *Ulysses*,[30] or Walter Mitty's delusions of grandeur in 1939's "The Secret Life of Walter Mitty" suggesting the diminished modern man's legitimate axis of rhetorical and physical control.[31] This questing shades itself against the Beat subject's inferiority of purpose: they held no administrative or community power, and their impulses funnel the imagination, friendly collusions, and tight moral judgments saving the poor man's vices and speculation in inner-city dens. Thus, *Suicide* does more than it sets out to do: to dramatize adolescent ramblings, and to say that youths held enough modern meaning to advance the time period's conscious investigations of the Spirit. The portrait of an unaccomplished writer is indeed significant, and openly gay Ben (Adrien Brody) took advantage of his superior intellectual status.

Screened instances of sex and the writer's sexual impulses and responses to changing circumstances are juicy and filled with pleasure's insanity and sweetness, yet call our attention to male and female anxieties that interrupt the Yankee, gusto-high script that promised audiences tales of adventure and pleasure. Scenes depicting sex are graphic yet fell short of pornographic excess: the penis, vagina, and body are excluded and so maintain the censorship and social prescriptions of an "R" rating. Whether in an apartment on a rainy night, or in the country with the others whooping and hollering, or through their partner's ambivalence, *The Last Time I Committed Suicide* underscores America's thirst for undefined, rollicking sexual adventures. Several scenes, including Cassady's nude escape from Cherry Mary's parents into the snow-filled night, are cut: these examples relay the author's navigation of America's romantic thoughts and taboos to avoid authoritarian figures. Further, Cherry Mary advances a chancy technique of the author's *pose*: as Cherry Mary and Cassady leap into a parked stolen car to have sex, "A Tisket, A Tasket," plays.[32] What seemed an innocuous piece that played in 1950s cartoons[33] suggests that the basket might either represent drugs or a "daddy" who brings the care package to his lover. Not all the parables are naughty: the set list includes Miles Davis's "Move" from *Birth of the Cool* and several other 1940s jazz pieces.[34] Rich descriptions of sexual domains are part of the adolescent frame tale, confirming Kerouac's essentially romantic thesis. Cassady, naturally, struggles with his identity, and this constitutes the test of his adulthood. Torn between disgust for Joan's repeated suicide attempts and her irritating silence and impassiveness, and Harry's growing deterioration as a poolshark and pimp, Cassady builds his inclinations of responsibility and respectability, abandoning Harry when his drunkenness causes him to collapse and vomit in the basement kitchen.[35] No breach from the narrative plot and theme is attempted: women are silent throughout, passively supporting their men. Is a gendered chance missed in all of this? The answer, and not surprisingly so, calls our attention to social responsibility's making. Neal is rugged, but limits his adult pretensions, so depending upon the tale and specific encounters as the framework that could lead him into an ideal marital beginning. At the end, he coolly inserts terms friendly to the letter, with a raspy denunciation of Harry: "I thank you for the libation. But I have a happily ever after to get started."[36]

Cassady's demeanor expresses maturity when the police interrogate and jail him due to the fact that Mary is a minor; he simply pleads with the Chief of Police: "I didn't do anything."[37] Other scenes re-appraise prosperity and health, and result in Cassady's decisive vindication. As the snow-filled days approach Christmas, Neal stares meaningfully into a shop on a snowy evening with a cigarette in his mouth, enviously eyeing the patrons. He is not sickened from it, yet exposure to the city's materialistic culture anticipates Kerouac's depressive staining of it in *Visions of Cody*. Even at his worst moments of doubt, Jane is cognizant of the dream of success. Now having completed high school, Neal as literary progenitor enjoyed the moments of introspection and engagement of a purely external world that did not indoctrinate its unschooled, poor young men.

I think, therefore, the best operating thought about *The Last Time I Committed Suicide* owes itself to the letter: a private examination of the world formed the basis for reflections on one's identity and even on one's times. A common problem of adaptation, therefore, has to do with the context's form. True, Beat writings dispersed ideas, buckling under the weight of its indifference to the political-intellectual machinations of the 1950s. It is important to note that we alight upon a very different Beat Generation, that Cassady might have escaped his downfall in the end, and perhaps that his talents would have been recognized lest he voluntarily drop them in favor of his better-educated friends.

The letter's rhetorical pose, too, stripped publication of its exclusivity. I believe, then, that this film could spell out an early eclipse where Cassady reaped the rewards of being a unique social figure. We will now turn to the instances of public commentaries that grasp Kerouac's insightful, pragmatic development of literary form, consciousness, and polity. Graphing the author's story, then, reveals a continuing, messianic context, writing's internal turmoil, and resonant self-realizations, when compared to the deeply fabled joy and romanticism found at the footsteps inhering America's greatest self-discoveries.

Documentary Films on Jack Kerouac

What Happened to Kerouac? Richard Lerner's Post Symbolisms, and Collaborative Writings of Beat History

Richard Lerner's 96-minute long collage of interviews, Super 8 films, TV appearances, and author readings appears in 1982's *What Happened to Kerouac?*, with add-ons and features that comprise a 246-minute DVD. It featured poststructuralist historical studies that favor today's audiences. As visual and audio clips elongate and distend Kerouac's discoveries of text, and their superficial replication, they inspire us to use visual and aural perceptions to construct a history consistent with an audience's values and opinions. The film's visual strategy is sure and relaxed in gauging the viewer's eye, happily replaying against the Beat Generation's sophisticated, introspective written angles hinting at revolution. The cast of friends and commentators, in short, use imageries and spoken forms to give steep inferences about Kerouac's humanity, innocence, confessions, albeit painful, to audiences. These, in turn, cross-examine the author's biographical motivations.

We would be overly dismissive if we ignore the central find of this documentary example. As a whole, the film included a rich, artfully rendered archaeology of facts and finds that contraindicated anxiety versus the letters and manuscripts found in university libraries. Naturally, the idea that audiences could learn a literary movement's ideological and idiomatic focus from film revives biographical studies and today's prejudices that tend to ignore complex studies. In the New Americanist context, audiences type these shards to be idea-productive or culture-productive, whereas in letters and drafts we could understand Kerouac's emotions and fears about writing's chancy trajectories. At a glance, discovery's positive fortune is appealingly visible and rich, in a learning that augments, changes, or theorizes the misunderstood American movement. This stokes more patriotic fears of its contagious exercise, with more than the author's projection of the words themselves begetting modern tempest. Books of literary criticism after Deborah Baker's publication of *A Blue Hand* in 2008, too, point to the letter's special, un-scrutinized mystic intensity, and to the greater knowledge we are to gain by reading them. Kerouac's written proliferation of contexts, when paired with the documentary's visual inspirations and spoken forms, add greater image-text discussion of the idea as social metaphor, indicating the graphic sensibilities and historic continuity. The format is available and helpful for history and literature teachers, allowing them to "challenge [student] beliefs about the past that are commonly explained in textbook versions of history with a singular correct answer [...] but for which there are multiple and competing answers or complex perspectives."[38]

When comparing literature to film, an important question has to do with Beat authenticity, or the confluence of systemic experiences that constituted the author's art and ethics. We can then derive the impacts of these upon viewers, building the author's depression to state his romantic objectives depressively. This key, introspective technique had built the Beat nucleus's social integrity. Thus, letters and unpublished drafts force forward questions about the Beat imagination's limits and even of Kerouac's peculiar studies. We can no longer derive these from written text: as a whole, new visual and spoken contributions seemed etched in stone, and primary viewing is not for viewers with less interest in the Beat Generation's peculiar social mysticism, lineage, and myth-making. The written form supposes formidable challenges to Kerouac's pretentious excavations, though strong adversarial undercurrents push him to write the novel as an antidote and answer to modernity's ballooning sickness. Take, for instance, Kerouac's confessions about his friendship with Ed White, who opts for studies in the Sorbonne, in 1949:

> I only know, myself, that I don't believe what these two men said of my life and my work, and that if I were to believe then there would be nothing left to do but die. They want us to die. All eroticitizens will want you to die (Celine would be better off dead).[39]

Although Kerouac's insistent scribblings mark and question summative philosophical commentaries about his sexual normality, questions about his philosophical origins are the most decisive. We might then revisit his inner-city experiences, or his social circle as it consisted of girlfriends and boyfriends; we could even ask ourselves if his depression includes post-nuclear revelations that broaden his cultural horizons. Yet in all cases, the commentaries lie within the author's rhetorical and physical control: he is the lone architect and so voices questions, not answers, in 1949. By comparison, *The Unknown Kerouac* describes a much more pragmatically sure referent, and so are mature contemplations that cross into the boundaries of criticism and analysis advancing romantic antidotes to the military-industrial treason that abducts mankind:

> I *know* now that an anarchy will come in America in this decade or the next ... a rockbottom strange virility like the one in the dream and yet tremendously opposed to the virility idea of the 1900's, some kind of Dostoyevskian change is due—and it will be sado-masochistic, bisexual, futuristic.[40]

Tracing human action to its original wound means attention to the anxiety of influence. What also underlies the letter, however, is the agency of words and concepts. From standpoints that confirmed Kerouac's rigorous control, they spell out his specific purpose and the straightforward anticipation of a moral quest for masculine, naturalist valor and honor. Thus, we used the author's private comments to spell out an essential Being. Northrop Frye adds the crucial detail to narrative socialist realism:

> More important is the fact that every poet has his private mythology, his own spectroscopic band or peculiar formation of symbols, of much of which he is drama and novels, the same psychological analysis may be extended to the interplay of characters, though of course literary psychology would analyze the behavior of such only in relation to literary convention.[41]

Frye's rhetorical bias is appropriate for Kerouac's written form, which was opinionated and so assumed for itself a peculiar history which documentaries may help us understand. It should be said that our understandings of content are a key foil in the historical film's making and should be carefully judged. Yet this ought to be done with a stress on the historical reality. Historical moments breathe life into their presentation through screenings of voice, place, and characters: they are objective when recasting the author's humanity, and do not repeat illusions of grandeur associated with Kerouac's writings and notorious persona. In short, the film screens dramas of his life and authorship. We might add, then, that counterculture was not a mythic stew of peculiar, cultist strains that people should not mix with. It held within it deep, written histories, and was ably traced to its modernist roots in the 1930s and 1940s, when poor men and women first appraise life's technological absurdity. I believe that, in the biographical assessment, many shards of thoughtful information are relayed in parts of this film, accentuating the main character's strength and even the probability of his ideations. Rare readings by him, too, enshrine authorial place, dictating his specific artistic languor that gave ideation and voice to jubilant literary discoveries during the late 1940s.

When we visit the biographical film in context, we must say that the 1940s and 50s were a period of tremendous writing, contemplation, and immersion in numerous avenues of Western philosophical knowledge—a period that countered Heidegger-influenced man's regress toward a single consciousness composed of modern man's ethical and graphic completion. Kerouac, Ginsberg and Burroughs wrote numerous meditations on life and experience, using peripheral literary and philosophical models to justify parallel inquiries from the street, and from small American towns, speaking to his adolescent nature. Inquiries, then, forecast contemplation's influential angles, and so readings of Kerouac's unpublished materials guarantee romantic self-conceptions.

Based on this introduction to the evocation of art as form, the film's first chapters include the group's more cosmetic moments of intellectual dynamism. Beat writer Gregory Corso notes the fact that "four writers a generation do not make,"[42] and then lectures on the subject of Madison Avenue and its obsession with the birth of new, youthful talent in the artistic world. This is followed by a visit from Jan Kerouac, his daughter, that results in Kerouac's admonition to "write about Mexico"[43] and is followed by girlfriend Edie Parker's recollection of the "six sauerkraut hot dogs" she shared with him at their love affair's beginning.[44] Yet the most thoughtful, plainest dictum came from Kerouac's last protégé, Michael McClure. Balding and wearing a dull-looking sweater, McClure notes that Kerouac "was the only person more self-conscious than me."[45] We concede the obvious note of modernist glory, an introspection shading all modes of Kerouac's written expression. Nonetheless, we also note the film's decisive power as a historical agent. Screenings of living friends and adversaries constitute an essential Beat moment, testifying to the group's form and bearing no isolating marks.

Kerouac, too, gives us his steepest viewing perspective when he appears on *The William Buckley Show*, where he opts for a hilarious, drunken episode touting the idea that the Vietnam War was being waged because the Vietnamese "wanted jeeps"[46] and where he suddenly interjects that Senator Joseph McCarthy was a "flat-faced Fuji with the Floyd, Floyd."[47] More poignantly, Kerouac appears on *The Steve Allen Show*, in 1959, giving a "cool" reading of *On the Road*. It would not appease the New Criticism scholars. The inlays of poetic references to Walt Whitman and Thomas Wolfe, and repeated identification of the prose as "poetry," interrupt the un-romantic reality that this was prose, deriving its aesthetic powers from non-visionary characteristics. Still, dreamlike, visionary remembrances of Kerouac's early travels spoke of the breadth of his poetic simplicity and private tenor, thus advancing epiphany's burdensome stress upon him as he travelled gas stations and highway diners on the American interstates. Kerouac's reading raises the form of his visionary truths against sense-impressions recalling America's prosperity, humors, and simplicity. It should be said, then, that film wields a much wider transformation, and that rare footage or interview pieces impose a practical criticism that, in turn, suggests knowledge's non-written composition.

The film includes an all-star cast of literary notables and friends, and the resulting commentaries elucidated Kerouac's mastery of form and the personal, carefully guarded locations of his *hubris*. What I think is most memorable, however, are the confident and nuanced enunciations of the writer's memory. These aphoristic summarizations of text, in turn, invite viewing instances that suppose his character's essential dictums of truth, pointing to the strength of living interpretations that are mainstream or fringe. Herbert Huncke's clever gay comedy operates around Kerouac's shooting Benzedrine: aged and with a regressing chin, he laughs about his dope buddy, pensively recalling a time where he "picked up."[48] Edie gives the most useful note about marijuana: Kerouac smoked it for the first time with saxophonist Lester Young when he split a cab with him to Minton's.[49] Contemporary Beat authors stress Kerouac's isolation, telling of authorial stresses that confirmed genius. They, too, relay to us moments of reclusion that negate more jingoistic social portraits of the counterculture's godfather presiding over millions of would-be freaks and dropouts. Still, biographical shards of the late author's decline and death were less than those that returned to his literary origins, and narrative shots, biographic shards. At a different moment, interviewed speculations, too, spoke in favor of the literary movement's momentum, answering foes such as Norman Mailer and friends like Amiri Baraka (Le Roi Jones), who co-edited *Yugen* with Hettie Jones during the 1950s and 60s.[50] The writers, in particular, breathe confidence about their moment. It was everyday, drawn from jazz and the road, but infuse their words with the necessary energy of man's transcendent escape from modern sickness. No effort was made to attenuate Kerouac's mastery of forms and his impromptu referencing, two characteristics that anchor deep memories of place and experiences that we are still reluctant to say are part of historical and cultural knowledge.

Linda Hutcheon's cinematic axiom was at least ambitious enough to cover the intersection of film with biography, or maybe the instance of its diffusion and regeneration: "as *a process of creation*, the act of adaptation always involves both (re-) interpretation and then (re-) creation."[51] She then adds the concepts of intertextuality, repetition, and variation.[52] It must be said that Lerner's biographical form is much more carefully controlled, so as to avert tangling with the peculiar Beat mystique that Kerouac concocts. But we would do best to appraise the basic theme: Beat writers enjoyed the health and prosperity of a literary movement that gained recognition whilst other modernist writers languished in total obscurity, both in terms of readership and in classrooms. Fran Landesman, who observed Kerouac's worsening condition and found that Kerouac, being Catholic, could not commit suicide and thus wished to drink himself to death, strikes the fatal blow.[53] Otherwise, claims of true comprehension are diluted in the heady steam of grand re-creation and glorification, so as to state the true modernist art. There are no literary titans who criticize or negate any part of the literary work's creation, nor any Beat writers that could foment strong working perspectives about brilliance's real origin. Biography's absence, in turn, set up the historical film to testify to the legend's living force, and even in Steve Allen's cursory wit that dresses up *On the Road* with a straight-ahead piano riff and far-ranging transcendental motifs. This meeting was not easily negotiated in mainstream, Ozzie and Harriet-styled America: Kerouac's reading then, poses America's prosperity to be the necessary, final minutes of man's reasoned self-realization. In *The Quest for Epic in Contemporary American Fiction*, Catherine Morley writes of the formalist technique that supposes that fiction's conversations and stories must redeem common American histories:

> In other words, "myth and symbol" models still pervasive in contemporary American studies are, in part, the remnants of a national identity politics of the 1950s which sought to represent American culture as an organic whole, developed along the lines of consensus and convergence, and celebrating the unity rather than diversity of American identity in the face of the Cold War.[54]

Given the testament to mainstream modernism as man's essential story, we might peruse the filmed Kerouac from a position of rhetorical solidness—poised, essentially, to knock out the mainstream cocoon and owing his grasp, youth, and surefooted dispersion to class-based understandings of human experience that sequence his friends' easygoing storytelling and pop-flavored humor. The drift of feeling can also be recognized in the Super 8 films that screened wanderings of Times Square and car rides through the country replaying bop music. It, too, augments the visible spectacle and called our attention to "dreaming" as the true social agent—obviously, frowned upon in Protestant, White America. The Steve Allen Show's feature reflected its sure, comfortable visual angles and acuity, devoid of controversy or political criticism that may weaken prophetic transcriptions of Kerouac's fate and depression in American social instances:

> All the stories I wrote were true, cause I believed what I saw. I was travelling west one time, at the junction of the state line of Colorado, its arid western wand, in the state line of poor Utah [...] I saw in the clouds huge, and massed above the desert of everfall, the great image of God, with four fingers pointed straight at me, through halos and rolls and folds of light existence in the gleaming spirit in his right hand.[55]

Kerouac's live reading is useful for teaching American history in two ways: one, it narrated his spiritual transmigrations and their free, syntactic threading of TV narrative form; and two, it advances him to be an acolyte, one that socialist realism could not muster into its estimations of today's culture and place. "Angelic" distensions of "the story"—which the images and recollections of partying, adventure, idealism ensure—focus in antithetical directions that diffuse necessary race/class discoveries of conscious experience. They instead comprise a radically individuated self, sure that vision is a systemic antidote to man's social- and institution-borne ills. Painting Kerouac as prophet is thus a muted act of re-creation: it is set up through his friends' persistent attestations to the writer's internal brilliance, then given live performance without any historical introduction. *On the Road's* significance as a stand-alone example of faith and wisdom, too, is not challenged in this film: author after author, too, attest to Kerouac's peculiar intellectual vigilance and excesses, telling that he was inconsistent with more expedient historical characterizations that limit or deflate his ostensible cultural impact. Drugs, sex, and mysticism were and are meaningful, commanding a mainstream focus that cannot be tainted. I believe, then, that writers and friends faithfully tend to cultural portraits in the hope of reclaiming the dead ground, voicing man's apocalypse that shuttered his introspections and his capacity to learn from the outside world. But what matters most was Kerouac's protected living impulse: we might note, by contrast, that John Dos Passos's *U.S.A.* (1930)[56] and William Faulkner's *The Sound and the Fury* (1929)[57] state America's social decline by telling its romantic eclipse. Kerouac's reading itself is without pretense, calmly and sweetly orchestrating the author's pain when divining the American experience. This, it is true, is appropriate to the form of many Beat biographies. Nowhere does the writing's romantic breadth give any hint of long-standing pathologies and sickness that might cause us to reject the Beat visionary as an instance of social change. The reading, too, contrasts with live Kerouac appearances that were more comically suited, concurring with the tone of his jazz reminiscences that include radio broadcast appearances. Lerner films the national audience's understanding, producing a dynamic sense at odds with numerous takes on the erratic writer's life and times.

The Beat Generation's screenplay of Kerouac's life, attributes, and peculiar moment of genius suits criticisms of his manner and form, both of which got him into serious trouble with the existing literary order. In *Advertisements for Myself,* Norman Mailer poignantly executes a crude, below-the-belt destruction of Beat mystique:

> Who cares about impotence if one finds within it the breath of a vision? The beatnik, then, is obviously more sentimental—he needs a God who will understand all and forgive all [...] But then, the hipster is still in life; strong on his will, he takes on the dissipation of the drugs in order to dig more life for himself, he is wrestling with the destiny of his nervous system, he is Faustian. The beatnik contemplates eternity, finds it beautiful, likes to believe it is waiting to receive him. He wants to get out of reality more than he wants to change it, and at the end of the alley is a mental hospital.[58]

In the context of the cultural realism found in the 1950s, we may add that several Kerouac meditations offered us a sexless purity, and that drugs in particular created visions that obliterated man's practical necessity. Mailer's straight pathology, then, states the growing counterculture's root weaknesses. Yet, we may ably defend the Beats: they captured a natural aesthetic and a cultural diffusion that could build multi-ethnic regeneration of the American experience. Corso attests to the basic street-like strengths of a prodigal male: "[...] when he found out I was a faggot, he went double after me."[59] Yet it is aged, doddering, and raunchy Herbert Huncke who lay down the tempting motif of male beauty and strength: "he was handsome, Arrow Collar handsome."[60] From this light, Huncke's robust, spontaneity-friendly portrayal cancels out much of the film's debate about Kerouac's alcoholic deterioration, suggesting that the body and appearance, when giving its real strength and generosity, could outdo contentions that they represented a sickened, weakened state of physical well-being. Appearance and strength also anticipate questions that pertain to the critical portrait that evinced weakness and sickness. Whether gay or straight, Kerouac was depicted with visible beauty. Simple biographical commentaries, too, challenge theoretical and scholarly boundaries that literary theory has imposed: all of a sudden, what was the mark of deep, irregular and multi-historical meditations on man's perverse seriousness could be explained through personal histories, everyday life and its engagement, and simple steps of self-indoctrination and apprenticeship to the larger world's whims. Kerouac's loyalty to his peers and to the visible, agile spirit of his friendships, too, effaces the impassive tenor of negative criticism coinciding with the young citizen's effort to decipher and reject cultural norms that shutter their rational-intellectual development in fast-changing America.

With Lerner's contemporary biography having passed the test, we then turn to the introduction of the Kerouac's possible humanism, as they foretell the winds and waves of psychedelic discovery that might alter lifestyle, fashion, society, morals and finally, truth. "Political Fallout of the Beat Generation" was screened at the Naropa Institute in 1982: it was the first televised example of a movement's collective recognition and was followed with footage of Ginsberg's and Burroughs's lecture tours, focused on their protégé relationships with Kerouac. Written examples in drafts and unpublished novels and letters foretell of a dynamic discovery and the sweeping might of modern intellectual change. Kerouac wrote November 14, 1951: "I'm on the verge of some kind of crazy discovery that'll tear my head off for good—or make me great. The system of writing I use when sketching is tranced fixation upon an object before me."[61] In fact, numerous letters to Cassady and Ginsberg deftly promoted the ecstatic bubble, or the fact that something tremendous if purely indifferent to theory and political realities had now found its true expression. In reality, Kerouac had considerable trouble spelling out the structure of what vision and meditation caused inside of him. "Political Fallout," then, underscores timeless moral and psychic themes that asked for neither deep indoctrinations nor mainstream answers. This was the essential substance of psychedelic-influenced writings, and what was often overlooked in Kerouac's gusto-high hallucinations: the text's integrity and meaning, and more broadly its antecedents projecting insight and revolution. When placed near the critical magnifying glass, little of its doctrine actually held up, and romanticism bequeaths its depression and passive interrogations instead of true text that herald symbolic powers galvanizing young minds into action. With this glimpse perhaps closing their eyes somewhat, "Political Fallout" did much to introduce the idea of practical change, and the systemic negation of that change through irreverence and comedy that limit our modern absorption of key themes of confession and teaching. Timothy Leary's quest for LSD knowledge is positively put off in his comments' empty tedium; Ginsberg calls him off, turning the questions to Yippie activist Abbie Hoffman.[62]

I believe that the squaring off of beatniks with the hippie generation serves to remind us of the plain honesty of writing's transactions.

Notwithstanding the attempts of Burroughs and Ginsberg to learn and develop the rock generation, hippie transformations of written ideas and their meaning were instances that Kerouac least favored. More likely, the format's practical indifference and ambiguity cause us to lessen the essential pains of seeking vision and knowledge. For the hippies, Beat messages were translatable in terms friendly to their own existence. But we add the shade of understanding: if Kerouac was too complex, we may read his transcendences in terms of simple polity, a motion to recast cultural norms and expectations in terms friendlier to what we derive more easily—pleasure. I think, too, that this was an insistent metaphor for the maturing Ginsberg, who wrote about legalizing cannabis as early as 1962 and published LSD-soaked "Wales Visitation" after its 1966 criminalization.[63]

The primary attention is given to Yippie activist Abbie Hoffman, and it is his reminiscence of beatnik power and influence on modern liberalism, civil rights, and dissidents from the 1960s thereafter, that builds the greatest momentum. Sporting curly grey hair and from within a manly figure, Hoffman contrasted with the four men who spent their time quibbling amongst themselves. "Political Fallout" voices a once aggressive social powerbroker that now was far out of focus, finding that their energies were, by now, spent. There was no political power or crass continuity among the freaks, and theoretical determinations of writing and social movements missed the mark. When William S. Burroughs opts for the view that the Beats sponsored "a cultural protest against conventional modes of dress and behavior,"[64] it is safe to say the symposium's scholarly emphasis elicited depressed, silent participants who held no spoken power. Burroughs looks reluctant to grant the Beats any kind of meaningful, cultural-intellectual power in the United States. His appearance in civilian dress, and depressive rejection of Ginsberg and Hoffman, points to the Beat Generation's schizophrenic sets of communities, and not because of any pluralist majority that realized true change. Hoffman gives no literary introductions, though he recites poetry and prophecies at several points, then explaining how limericks became part of his schoolwork.[65] But the tryst with academic learning is special: Hoffman patiently explained the necessity of liberal, democratic social change due to the decay and redundancy of modern middle-class culture during the 1950s and 60s. He does not miss the opportunity for projecting the Beats' erstwhile political talent, and boasts about liberal reinventions and new, dynamic contexts in the Left social movement. The statement is apt if tart and simple: "Absolute power corrupts absolutely."[66] In short, the Left's intellectual archaeologies surpass their authorial meditations that limited and judged the text's value as an idea. Hoffman warms up to the camera and audience's presence: he recalls mankind's broadening horizons and diverse perspectives that "turn on" liberal activism.

Liberalism's classic defense, then, professes the social form's virtue and nobility. There were many examples of real social change, some of them taking place far from New York, that Hoffman attests to the Beats' written testaments and the fluidity of their living ideas.[67] But we might draw Hutcheon's point to the metaphysics of power, if only because Hoffman takes noticeable advantage of the impromptu leadership abandoning political power's illusory moment, and its general societal effect. Without Ginsberg's repeated guidance, the other three lecturers' commentaries fall apart, distancing them from the audience. Hoffman intercepts this visible drift in the moment's energies, to attach liberal political theory in terms that are optimistically broad and bravely synthesize mass democratic political struggling in America. "Power," in this instance, was part of Burroughs's negative studies and forced Ginsberg to voice the messenger's pose as being dynamic and liberal, so as to paint the writing's political presence. Yet neither held any strong governance over the Beat philosophy's treasures, which could certainly develop into political and pragmatic expressions of social class and education. The sustained comment, "Decoration of UNWORLDLY LOVE THAT HAS NO HOPE FOR THE WORLD AND CANNOT CHANGE THE WORLD THROUGH ITS DESIRE,"[68] attracts Hoffman's irreverent tracing of "Howl" to its New York origins. Thus, the sole exclamation from the Beat's loudest poet had surrendered the moment's charge to its more vocal, and considerably more plebeian-sounding, gladiators. Hoffman then jokingly synopsizes the deeply reticent, illegible Romantic dream by poking fun at Ginsberg's CCNY classroom where students threw potato salad, grossing out Ginsberg even more by saying, "well anybody from New York knows that you get a big corn beef sandwich, so once you finished that you don't feel like eatin' anything anymore."[69] Snickering aside, one must assess the Beat movement's mobility by supposing its imagination to move the hands of personages and groups far from the literary circle, and even farther from indoctrination's specific moment. I believe this is Hoffman's unique talent, to save the fallout from a rapidly decelerating cultural movement whose impulses are absorbed and dismissed in the emerging scene. Hoffman's freedom of reference seizes prophecy's arm from beneath its moral and geographic limitations. It also re-writes the idea of resistance to mean a youthful idealism that could be understood and transferred to any underclass group, or even everyday American imaginations.

Working-class identity underscores the deviance from *bourgeois* intonations common to Beat cosmologies: all of them came from educated, middle-class backgrounds. The preferred loudness of Hoffman's explication and thoughtful sermon is rhetorically far from Beat rhetoric, complicating and extending Beat thinking into avenues of social and moral experiences rhetorically more potent and mainstream than the oft-rued illusions of literary and historical grandeur. Hoffman's lengthy tirade includes manifold examples of how Beat simplicity, democratism, and cultural fluidities prolonged the *déclassé* minute of self-identification, dropping refinement's necessary reticence and abstraction when spelling out the crux of the idea's practical engagement. Henceforth, the Beats could be equated with the common talk of plain, everyday, disenfranchised people. Allen Ginsberg's academic performance and the contents of his lecture on the divine and Eastern mysticism are on par with earlier interviews and written statements assembling crazed, polytheistic readings of Hindu scripture as the counterculture's fact and artifact. The tone and spirit of Ginsberg's moderate voice and careful, inward reflection repeats Blake's central imagery. More, the screening of an elderly, bearded and balding older man projects both fulfillment in the form and its possible alienation from more youthful impulses. Polarized snapshots of the men, who were all still using drugs, revealed counterculture's real practical and administrative problems as evidence of *why it failed to sustain its agenda versus the silent majority*. I do believe, too, that Ginsberg's religious fervor was concentrated and strong in the early 60s. It should be observed that the self-styled prophet of Hindu-Buddhist idealism and self-regenerations held in his words the power to surpass queer biographical strictures that form part of his subject negotiations of poetry, history, and existence. I also read primary and unpublished works from that idea, that masculine writing bore no contradiction in form, or in examples, borrowed from the author's sexual life. When reading Ginsberg's poems, we appreciate their masculine sense: these inveigh the modern Era's power, the romantic sweetness of its bards and acolytes, their broad and unifying perspective on Ginsberg's life, and the gnawing, horrid, and visible sickness that haunted gentle memories of health and prosperity. Given that, I believe that Ginsberg's reading at Naropa spoke of the divine messenger even whilst cautioning audiences that Beat inhered a specific set of prophecies tied to vision, and so was divine. Concentrations of fact, therefore, appease audiences who fail to locate semblances of the group's nebulous, untested social power.

Lerner's film included no remarkable cinematic examples of visual or aural strategies, nor any explorations of the altered mind: truly, Lerner deliberately misses the chance to reopen speculations about the archival depth of the narcotic and psychological form. Still, the collage of interviews and biographical tale-telling offer a meaningful reassessment owed to the persistence and health of American consciousness and its poetic simplicity and beauty. Portraits of Kerouac's adulthood accentuate the literary hero's crowning at the footsteps of his peculiar minute of representation. The comments and histories, too, build the composite figure, including authorial snapshots and witticisms that ushered in a special purpose. Still, the health and confidence of Kerouac's friends and literary adversaries brings us closer to the nuance and subjective suggestion of grand narrative meaning. Their relaxed, thoughtful re-readings of the times, too, mirror growing confidence in the Beat Generation legacy.

Jack Kerouac as *King of the Beats*

John Antonelli's 83-minute DVD features many of the same interviews and TV clips found in Lerner's longer anthology. Still, the haunting specter of Kerouac's deep authorial anxiety is given a technically savvy and biography-deep introduction, so as to intersect the greater critical angle that invoked literary theory. Intersections between Kerouac's material and intellectual spheres operate the angle that brought his work most into question. Antonelli's film satisfies our craving for the essential re-conception, as it replays Super 8 films and readings to extend the narrator's rich, sumptuous re-castings of narrative voice in the small-town and big-city America of our dreams. Material techniques, in short, extend our viewing of its errata: Norman Mailer synopsized the agonies of spirit and word when he first tasted success, as he returned to America after *The Naked and the Dead*'s 1948 publication:

> I dread the return to America where every word I say will have too much importance, too much misinterpretation.[70]

Norman Mailer's paranoiac self-perception may force us to explain to ourselves what a modernist writer's biography, and studies of a modernist author, will cause us to recall about his fundamental character. In anticipation of the author's moral perspective, we are likely to plunder his life's content to assure ourselves that we might then carry away something natural, intuitive, or real to re-hoist his legend. These efforts inscribe our material boundaries to the novel's reading, and speak to the interviewer's sympathy with instances of the author's daily consciousness as one bearing a true, organic fruit in its expression, and in resulting extensions of the viewer's sonic, physical, and emotional approval. To these ends, *The King of the Beats* features interviews with Bruce Morrissette, Edie Parker, William Burroughs, Allen Ginsberg, Herbert Huncke, and Carolyn Cassady. Readings of Kerouac's works are contrasted with visual screenings of place and history that feature a star cast and a simple narrative portraying casual, daily American immersions and the contrast between prophecies and mainstream boredom that, in turn, imperfectly capture the spoken word's register. Music by Zoot Sims, Duke Ellington and Charlie Mingus complicate the foil, running the Beat dreaming reel through instances of hot jazz and big band jazz that were more Negro, and so less travelled in American studies. Scenes also include stops in a roadside bar, a Mexican taco- and beer-house, a candy store in Lowell, and Leo Kerouac's death scene.[71] Sensory renditions both confirm and contest the text's authenticity: they do not draw up engagements of man's serious emotions or speak to his suffering, instead sequencing the viewing eye to draw the ecstasies of Kerouac's brilliant memory. It should be noted that many scholars roundly state that these derivations of form spoke a greater poetic charm and uniqueness than found in the contrived metaphor of stardom and literary paternalism confirmed in complex literary and analytic studies. Tactility, sympathy, and confession were, after all, the stuff of Kerouac's poetic idealism: one cannot hinder the deep family, regional, and communitarian ties in his literary beginning, nor surface theory and philosophy to be a form of study eternally true to the Yeats-inspired metaphor for the writing spirit's purer sense-concentration.

Serious readings from the interviewers interrupt the sense-impressions of Kerouac's vocal presentations and his innocent, cavalier attitudes about his travels and revelries in post–World War II America. These examples re-anoint Kerouac's fictional realism while placing biography's social seriousness in context. John Clellon Holmes and Herbert Huncke place the emphatic stress on Times Square in New York, Jack's apparent refuge from his disbelieving father who disowned his pretense to become a writer. Holmes notes aptly and succinctly that he "was trying to discover what was unique about people of his age."[72] As the camera segues into shots of a women's wig shop in lower Manhattan in the 1960s, Herbert Huncke identifies Kerouac's skills as a "people watcher"—the impromptu comment meant to project the contested social idea of New York City neighborhoods and streets. In so doing, Huncke thoughtfully attaches legitimate social metaphors to drugged pretenses for dreaming and to the author's rejection of the official-imperial "system." Edie Parker and Allen Ginsberg dismantle myths about Kerouac's peculiar, private literary genesis in small, clever shots which solemnize and agonize the narcotic-influenced mind and its output: Edie notes that Kerouac first smoked pot with Lester Young, as Ginsberg recalled the "exhausted" Kerouac who worked at his typewriter for "5–6 hours" at a time while high on Benzedrine.[73] The heretical model interrupts and cut down the authorial pretense towards the deeply introspective modernist genius's familiar pose, as Edie and Allen maintain the common subject's history, that of a person with working characteristics and basic narrative investigations that anyone could have had. The conflict tracked Kerouac's perilous journey, extending private feelings of compassion: fiction readings are sweet-sounding, maintaining Kerouac's use of silence and his private urge to describe street life in poetic detail. Edie sternly defends the literary group's honor, attested to the legitimate effort to make Black archaeologies through jazz and drugs happen in the writing of novels and stories. In another scene, Burroughs deliberately confirms co-authorship of 1944's *And the Hippos Were Boiled in Their Tanks*. In short, whereas Kerouac as omniscient narrator stars biographical knowledge that hastens the sweeping might of poetry's narrative and artistic conflicts, friends were just as quick to return to the street scene's making. Because of this, audiences may find many examples revealing Kerouac's underground actions and reflections to bear meaningful ferment, as though he had divined relationships between the two worlds.

I would add that the narrative technique inferred from Super 8 simulations wasn't brilliant—as the reader of *Maggie Cassidy* enunciates "the moon, starting to show distant, defined unseen possibilities" in the "glitter of the night" and in "eternal blazes of stars,"[74] the camera rolls through Lowell homes, telling of a boy's relished gaze at candy stores, poolhalls, meat shops, and apartment houses. In so doing, Kerouac shadows the night's brilliant, somnolent isolation against the day's boundless discoveries and strophic innocence. This camera eye is less accurate when *On the Road* visits Mexico, yet extended the moment's continuity against the more caricature-like tale telling of shapeless tortillas, Mexican hipsters, and Oriental silence.[75] *On the Road*'s replay includes a stop in a diner, where a youthful Kerouac wearing a flannel shirt and carrying a knapsack takes a seat and reads. Set in a typical diner from the 1960s, the memory recalls a laughing old man, "you could hear his raspy cries clear across the Plains, across the whole brave world" and that "he didn't have a care in the world, and he had the highest regard for everybody."[76] Edie appears less kind about the author's angelic, heroic pose, saying that his "manhood" was blustery, where Neal Cassady's was natural and intuitive and eloquently told of the country's spirit.[77] She calls Neal a "modern day cowboy," but the main question still plagued Kerouac: what was Western naturalism's expressive voice, as Kerouac borrowed the metaphor and left incomplete its stance on social being? I believe, then, that Kerouac's reading establishes more natural semiotics of tone and introspection when retelling sense-impressions about an underground subculture. The tryst was imperfectly traced to *On the Road*, where Kerouac develops his poetic jewels despite the subculture's recurrent jealousies.

Super 8 film clips did much to rejuvenate the Beat social portrait in *Jack Kerouac: The King of the Beats* in that they portrayed a viable, jubilant, laughing culture of White youths interacting with everyday White, Black, and Latino cultures and subcultures. The full weight of the material portrait includes jazz gigs, beer-soaked evenings at taco houses, and races through the San Francisco streets at nighttime. Scenes of popular culture in the West and its familiar, plebeian aesthetics and "cool" outlook on travel and recreation raise the moment of youth, and its carefree engagements of "city" and "scene."

After all, are we as likely to give White, educated youths to perform underclass social transactions and experiences? Still, the jazz gigs in particular showcase White-Black sharing of the cultural, and gave a distinct epistemological chance at one's self-understanding. Readings of Leo Kerouac's death, too, give us the chance to reflect on biography as a part of life and the life and death of perceivable subjectivity, a closed door that had forced the other ones to open. In these regards, they allow the poetic end of the spectrum to grow and figure into the author's subjective grasp of reality. Contrastively, interviews in *The King of the Beats* protect the wide, gregarious nature of the group's ideation and communion, without interfering with the spoken words themselves. The proliferation of material, vocal and biographical signs simulates further readings that include drugs and mysticism, themes that were and are difficult to learn in all 20th century American generations.

Film Adaptations of Kerouac's Novels and Contemporary Beat Narratives

The Subterraneans, Gender and Young Adult Beginnings

Ranald MacDougall's 89-minute replay of Jack Kerouac's novel, *The Subterraneans*, first appeared in theaters in 1960 and starred the handsome, buoyant George Peppard as Leo Percepied, Kerouac's character. It took chancy administrative looks at the New Orleans–based subplot starring a white, French woman, Leslie Caron, as Mardou Fox, a Black lover in Kerouac's novel. The aggressive, contentious ramble, optimism, and crash of a young adult culture—bent on changing society through its wild impulses and occasional gusts of chance and poetic brilliance, anchors the much more thoughtful subplot of degenerated, shiftless, and poor miscreants possessed of the impractical and unsatisfying dream of catching transcendence in an industrial society. *The Subterraneans*, in league with aggressive verbal dramas such as David Ives' "Sure Thing," accents the shiftlessness and abrupt lack of purpose, love, and rhetorical control of the fundamental problems and ambitions in daily life. Polarizing the game of chance with the deep, troubling underworld and its scattering of legitimate society, the Beats are inferior and diminished, and their roguish playing and tale-telling sets up the ambivalence and daily chaos of a rejected mind and its more garish, funny attributes. Reading "bar culture" from an eclectic standpoint tells us more about the literary group's impractical, depressive game: it, too, sets up the lack of concern and the certainty of suppression as major characteristics of the Beat subject's navigations of "the scene" and home. A precursor to Dylan's ominous "Like a Rolling Stone," *The Subterraneans* masks critical Blackness through the spindle of anti-theistic, anti-moral replays of Beat "dreaming," in some senses closer to Arthur Miller's absolute deprecation and comic rendition of youth in *Death of A Salesman*. At the same time, the vibrant street culture duplicates the setting in *Heart Beat*, suggesting care and contemplation when faced with avenues of one's growing boggle of depressive criticism of "the powers that be." *The Subterraneans* resurrects Percepied's deep hubris versus the created Mardou, who exudes European characteristics that may tether the frame tale to previous counterculture, including the abstract, un-theistic surrealists.

Jack Kerouac's letters to Neal Cassady reveal the positive errata that MacDougall's film depends upon: these gaps are quite significant, and the starring of a White *femme fatale* erases the positive grist of this possibility, supplanting it with a comedy of errors and juvenile detailing of the modern subject's diminution. Kerouac wrote positively if not exuberantly to Neal Cassady on October 6, 1950: "I'm going to write one book in nigger dialect, another in bum dialect, another in hip musician dialect, another in French-Canadian-English dialect, another in American-Mexican dialect, another in cool dialect, and I might write one day a slim little volume by an effeminate queer."[78] One could transpose the obvious: "bum" translates into *On the Road*, "hip" may either mean *Subterraneans*, French-Canadian may be *Desolation Angels*, "American-Mexican" may be *Tristessa*, and "cool" may refer to *Subterraneans* as well, walking the streets of New Orleans looking for the Beat Generation. But the affective translation of a woman's character is authentically focused on Kerouac's pondering the African-American muse: "Ain't nobody loved me like I loved myself, except my mother and she's dead.My daddy, he done gone away so long ago ain't nobody remember what he look like."[79]

On December 28, 1950, Kerouac added his impulses toward sincerity in his private confessions:

> I am writing this confession entire to YOU because I want it to be a true and not a false and subtle confession; therefore, if this be to my advantage in the end, that is, a purer work result from it, you have every right to believe that I am doing this because it is not to my advantage to write a bad work whether published or not [...].[80]

Kerouac's anxiety, or rather the bereft form that speaks to his friend's jealousy and quiet criticism of intention, repeats the proposed depth of his inquiry. He means to tackle the rational and emotional grounds of multi-ethnic, multi-lingual adventures, meshing critical whiteness with the ambivalence of ethnic and street languages that could unpackage the collective mythology. But the myriad of reflections could not translate onto a 1960 film: the character of Mardou, plus her Black identity and independent navigations, would not be present in a film adaptation. It should also be noted that no Beat writer effectively engineered White translation of minority consciousness at all: Kerouac, Ginsberg, and Burroughs maintain separate White identities and verbal limitation of syntax that depersonalize the minority, who holds neither testament nor internal dialogue that we could read. White control of minority communication, neighborhood, religion, and vocation are absolute in Kerouac's works: even *Tristessa*, Kerouac's most forward work in this regard, clips Tristessa's spoken form to deny her artistic vision. When we figure in these factors, we must realize that the DVD ought to at least speak to the group's real tensions and the *ethos* of a partly diminished scene. In this regard, I believe that *The Subterraneans* is an adept adaptation, building scene, conflicts, geography, the arts, and social conflict that allow us to take a meaningful look at the diminished adolescent subject, who mutes and solemnizes their tryst with destiny. The powerful, studied ambivalence of one's direction in life, and even the true purpose of one's friendships and relationships, suggests a modern direction revealing the subject's polarity and his uncertain translation of true contexts.

Replacing an African-American woman with a French girl, deprived of her mother and betrayed to the authorities when young in Vichy France, is only part of the 20th century cinema that frequently substituted White characters or even sparred "blackface" to accommodate racial differences in facial and mannerly appearance. Mardou makes her biographic case: she is a persecuted victim of World War II, suffers bouts of insanity, and speaks her emotional terrors and whims to a psychiatrist at a clinic. These adjustments of character correspond to the persecuted Black woman as victim, and may call our attention to novels as recent as Edwidge Danticat's *The Farming of Bones*: they also testify to the erratic brilliance of writing, love, and social Being. But MacDougall's plot is clear: Mardou cannot control her emotions, has lifts of pure joy and freedom against the crushing emotional responsibility of marital relationships, and has no money: in the end, she runs naked in the street to a homeless shelter, barely escaping the police.[81] Thus, *The Subterraneans* repeats White female anxieties and motifs of self-confinement: the "American Dream" runs opposite the inflamed passions, erratic brilliance, and supreme jealousy that centers on a generation of artists out to make a buck and change the air of one's middle-class doom. Replacing New Orleans with sunnier, liberal-themed San Francisco is pulled off with energetic verve: the Beats read aloud at cafes and are writers, painters, and barkeepers and the descriptive artwork of cafes and salons is powered by jazz artists including Art Farmer and Gerry Mulligan. The air of possibility, and imagery and plot, too, speak to changing times where the exotic, the Orient, the stream of witticisms and splintering of consciousness, power the inflamed passions and sudden poetic jewels that offset impoverished and diminished financial lives.

Tracing a tradition of featuring challenged feminine agency and young adult conflict is ambitious, with Mardou inscribing and repeating Janie Starks' takedown of Joe in Zora Neale Hurston's *Their Eyes Were Watching God*, "writers write things down" and "boys stay with their mothers,"[82] complicates the frame tale, dissipating patriarchy and Percepied's strong rejections of female pretense. Agony is replaced with real, characteristic expressions of male and female identity: Leo's persona interferes with the seriousness of love, chances are immediate and fast-changing, and Mardou's confessions and personality alike speak baldly and descriptively of repressed female histories that could cross-examine the male pretense of writing in the post–World War II America. Of course, Mardou's unadorned confessions and poetic cleverness operate versus Percepied's strong, well-nourished male responsibility. Tensions between love of another, and love of the Beat Generation, nurture frequent female criticisms of male content and prophetic conceptualizations of the Era and of responsibility. It is not without realist criticism that Percepied is allowed to continue his work: he is criticized by another writer for "smoking dope and drinking" and for "waiting until you feel something to write."[83] Further, many are the films that supplant ambition with love, persistent throughout succeeding generations. But the display of the Generation's talents, intrigue, and "the scene" with its loud revolutionaries, con artists, and reticent street poets who defrock and deride newcomers, may tell us the group's power. *The Subterraneans* does much to display the group's productive talent and notoriety, very much advancing the changing Era and its rich cultural and intellectual focus. Still, projecting love and intimacy with a psychiatric patient aggravates patriarchy: the dream of love, and the dream of artistic transcendence, is stalked by the loss of sanity and the cold, brute power of institutions and their case history. Percepied's depressive misunderstanding, then, speaks to a broad list of American novels with women protagonists, and to the depth of adversarial messages meant to stifle male creativity and progeny. When love, mirth, discovery, and reflection are matched against writing's controlling genesis as a form of work, they speak to male-female adversity in makings of culture. This conflict informs a wealth of films that include women and children who protest of mankind's true responsibility to family and to initiations of one's social and contemplative life.

Also very noteworthy is the inclusion of Kerouac's mother, Gabriella, in a San Francisco home: by the time of the movie's release, Jack and Gabriella had a home in Florida and Kerouac had stopped much of his travels. Charlotte Percepied's nonchalant restatement of societal authority and responsibility, versus Leo's acrid dismissals of his worth and accelerated statement of pretense, joins *The Subterraneans* to realist narrations: a successful, yet impoverished writer betrays the emotions of his pretense, and the far-fetched idea of curing society through his erratic discipline. At the dinner table, Charlotte calmly states their situation's basic fact:

> **CHARLOTTE:** You were reviewed in *The Saturday Review*, weren't you? And I still have to support you.
> **LEO:** I bought you a television set, didn't I? With the money from the railroad, didn't I? It's not like I eat my head off around here.
> **CHARLOTTE:** Someday you'll have a family of your own, and you'll know what that's like. Although you'll never find a nice, clean-living girl.[84]

Still, Leo's soliloquy where he fumes about his pretense is real, and during its time very sympathetically advances modern intellectualism's pluralist, masculine point of self-infliction and progressing addition to the American Dream:

> I want every bit of life my body and brain can hold, mother, I have to go and find it. Life is a gift, mother. You have to run after it, reach it, grab it, grapple with it, swallow it in chunks, or you die. There's not enough time to read all the great books, see all the great paintings, to think all the great thoughts or just meet everybody. But you've got to try. I've got to try.[85]

Asides such as these were not meant to ingratiate Gabriella in real life: these confessions appeared in Kerouac's letters to Cassady and pushed loudly for the grand form of experimentation and eclectic living. Their exhalation in front of Charlotte mean to situate dinner-table conversations into the American hearth, consistent with Biff's promises to Willy in *Death of a Salesman* or George's promise to Lennie to own land in *Of Mice and Men*. "Going away" and "exploring" are suspect in this discussion from the 1950s onward: Leo speaks without institutions, breeding, or patronage. But this speech decisively signals the coming generation and its testament to living democracy: from one's ideas, and engagements of one, is the perilous and burdened development of Soul and Scene. I think this is the strongest resonance: MacDougall did not condemn the Beat Generation, and gave voice to its recurring complaint against the tide of proto-materialist, corporate-sponsored makings of American families. Discussions about drugs and the occult are dropped, entirely securing Percepied's legitimate form. It is noteworthy that times had changed: bar sets, too, in the North Beach clubs, attest to the form's virtuosity and popularity: as a stoned Percepied digs the jazz band, an African-American woman sings "Coffee Time," rolling forth the pure superficiality of the Beat's legal consumption.

More than most contemporary Beat-influenced films, then, *The Subterraneans* did much to pencil in the group's legitimacy and hence, legitimate inclusion in the American literary canon. Believable and burdened with a deep, gratifying social mission, yet checkered by the obvious errata of one's diminution, suppression, and intoxications, it succeeds where countless other films and TV serials in the 1960s and 70s fail: the goals and daily involvement of the writer is still meaningful, the possibility for understanding truth and humanity in fast-changing times populates and directs a significant urban culture in modern times. That is to say, much of *The Subterraneans* ignores and rejects dark realist cynicism about freaks and would-be prophets: terror, addiction, and crime are cropped to highlight legitimate and real ambitions. Further, as a young adult comedy, the screenplay technique appears progressive, and a prosperous materialism and concrete speculation accompanies the generation's followers. As a film that considers the "meaning of life" or "how to get through life," *The Subterraneans* accelerates class tension and promises the unholy, the antithetical, the suspected, as the herald of love and belonging.

Beat Angel, Spontaneous Historiography, and the Messenger and His Healing Power

Beat Angel is a thoughtful film for a number of reasons. It stars Vincent Balestri as the spirit of a deceased Kerouac, who returns to the Earth on the 30th anniversary of his death, the film stars a young and murky, sardonic writer-editor with the name Gerard Tripp. Tripp is sour to all of Balestri's thoughtful maneuverings of Kerouac's unheard writing. The thought that Kerouac could spontaneously read his unpublished contents at a slam poetry reading spooks Tripp, who then agonizes over his career's presumable demise and then mulls over a job as publishing editor. *Beat Angel* includes a cast of would-be Beat writers that are disillusioned postindustrial trolls who re-tell their histories and who suffer their daily, unimaginative chores. The cast finds redemption and liberation in Kerouac's angelic realism, or rather in its conscious advancement and re-reading that depicts writing's brilliance against the backdrop of the his glum, fetishized life. *Beat Angel* offers us neither a deep ethnography nor real sociopolitical grit to spell out the movement's real-life doldrums. Viewers are brought into the city's depressed urban characteristics and the familiar, generation-crossing themes of angst, dislocation, and the everyday tedium that checks our deeper ambitions behind the bar stool. Poetry readings at the event, too, are checkered and feature several down-and-out exclamations that spoke no attention to poetry's form. We, then, conclude without the form's eclipsed and irrelevant functioning that the steps of today's stereotypes signaled culture's loss and perspective's absence. We could even go so far as to limit and neutralize the venom and accented *difference* of mid–20th century literary production, even when it had projected semantic and rhetorical comprehension of the humanist's self-expression. Checkered, imperfect readings allow us a special configuration of poesy's angelic truth in the wake of modern man's destruction. True, the poems read at the event hold no statement about the literary group's collective social organization; and true, Balestri shirks most of the contemporary ground so as to mount poetic and visionary truth as constitutive of an inestimable, ineffably resonant form in all historical periods. Yet a concluding theme is centrally located in the text's authority: Beat writing and its deep, introspective seriousness were misread, and therefore films that re-examine their living force will go astray, cheapening the romantic acolyte's undying messages. When frozen in time, these key ideas promise us an unreachable, impracticable ecstasy that words, concepts, and histories may not trace to its true origin.

I would add that my experience as a conference-goer and presenter included several readings that changed my approach to the classroom and to Beat Generation literature in its reflection. Papers and comments at Southwest Texas Popular Culture Association in Albuquerque included a large host of graduate students interested in Beat literature's form and the group's social necessity. Graduate students depended upon readings of Beat poetry and fiction, but had also introduced untraveled spheres such as women, Black American, and European examples of Beat writings and activism. In 2008 Mindy Clegg, then a Georgia State University undergraduate student, presented on punk readings of the Beats: I did not know that the Beats could be read well outside their traditional subculture, and few were the number of times that I had seen anything manifest in the films that included poetry readings. In other words, I did not see much graphic or textual potency in today's re-readings of Beat literature, nor could I suppose their works as affecting postindustrial arts, music and their adaptations of rhetoric and philosophical abstraction. I felt, oddly enough, that my readings of Jack Kerouac's novels during the 1990s were acridly wakened because of pop movies including 1994's *Forrest Gump*, of note due to its narrow, immaculate stereotypes about rock's history, context, humors, and songs. Unsurprisingly, anything to do with the hippies and their historical value was mocked as the immature fruition of modern man's unfocused, indolent anxieties. Historical films, ranging in issue-derived context from Richard Nixon's presidency in *Nixon* to stand-alone spiritual indoctrinations of the modern Black man in *Malcolm X*, belittled and derided the standing point of the hippie's active perspectives on life and its social being as it gained points of recognition in the inner city's dens of sin, drugs, sex, and revolution.

I think that, then, *Beat Angel* purports itself to a dramatic and heroic re-reading of social and literary context. The contemporary world and social setting grows far outside Kerouac's confines, constructed out of themes, concepts, and social substrata that the young, moody Kerouac had phased out of existence. Now, from beneath a curious similitude of his depressed consciousness, they would hear his visionary supplication and understand it. Nonetheless, the advancement of a historical great as a voice of conscience or guidance to youths in today's society is commonplace and overly figured from social didacticism. As time travel appeared in American film as early as the 1920s in the silent film, *A Connecticut Yankee in King Arthur's Court*, and recurred significantly in American film genres, viewers address form's true geopolitics to construct the literary acolyte's more thoughtful, practical vision through writings, performance, and belonging. The inflation of simple moral messages meant to stir today's public, and so its residual conflicts in space, time, and agency. Examples of the time-traveling messenger are popular among youths and in middle-class cultures: they allow us, in turn, to assess our own schemes of personal and moral growth. When, for instance, Mahatma Gandhi preaches to a Mumbai gangster in 2006's *Lage Raho Munna Bhai*, prophetic connections are simple enough to resurrect iconic moral truth and guiding power to offer true governance of goodness in any society.[86] I believe, too, that instances in Indian film relayed the obvious truth that Indian movies, commercials, and TV shows copied American film and media examples, in anything from the most used clichés to fashion, plot, point of view, geography, geopolitics, and music. Because of this, the historical figure as messenger is a popular, oracular concept compensating the dearth of strong character-audience relationships in real-time for artists who opposed socialist realism.

I believe that, too, our attention may raise the Beat Generation's contemporary relevance, and our understanding of their historical past and meanings. Naturally, the idea that a young man from the 1950s with his intellectual and active engagements could proselytize and comfort today's younger generations is ridiculous. It is certain that the vastly greater technological and materialistic development of man's conscious existence, and responsibilities to the mechanics of today's interactive world, spawned greater confidence and involvement, and with the intensity and conformity of the mind's intellectual development. It is equally absurd to say that a person from the mid–20th century would, in his perceived literary complexity, relate to humans of this time period except while operating through progressive stereotypes. Thus, the film's angle of rhetorical development through conversation is nixed. It is impossible for a person from long ago to understand and to relate the terms of today's world: at least, confident angles of reflection and inspiration are less likely. Perhaps this is why visions, acolytes, and angels in contemporary film express teaching methods derived from individual histories, accomplishments, perspective, and knowledge. There is no shortage of teachable rigor in *Beat Angel*. Still, the second question is reflexive, supposing the brilliance of Kerouac's inquiries, owed to its hyperbolic meaning: how does one internalize Kerouac's rhetorical consciousness, and render it into an able writing in the world of today? After all, TV clips, interviews and films had kept it in the distant past: our readings, too, were stodgy and stamped with the print of pure theory, a passive anesthetic versus the turning gears of today's consciousness and interactive behaviors that, in their security and legality, call into question the Beat Generation's active ferment.

Today's empirical and spiritual consciousness would be more complicated and likely dislocate modernist attentions when tending to language and visual forms It must be admitted that, though admirable and a true instance of contemporary American perspectives about poetry, few of the read poems at "Kerouac's Death Day" celebration in a local bar inhere strong examples of Kerouac's much-garbled imagination and spirit.[87] Angst and disillusionment stem from Tripp's angry ramblings, as he is increasingly given to sneering rejections of Kerouac's spiritual and romantic studies of pastoral truth.[88] Tripp's supreme cynicism applied pop strategies of artificial, emotional constrictions of writer-text relationships in the form of Gerard Kerouac, Jack's elder brother, to the technique for using the messenger as a voice of conscience. When Tripp dismisses Balestri, he then falls into a nightmare and wanders his apartment amidst fear and self-possession when confronted with angels and haunted by Balestri's repeated admonition: "don't lose your mind!"[89] The simple, perceptible truth, when related to a writer's self-organization of his consciousness, dreams, and mental acuity, is parlayed into a dreaming liberation spelling out nature's abundance and the poetry's youthful vigor. It, too, compensates for the sour, crabby Tripp who scolds Kerouac's achievement. Parables of the main character's name or the inscription of written truths cause us to doubt this transformation: still, Balestri's vantage point attunes itself to Tripp's visible and deep depression, and to his idealism's cruel death.

Kerouac's presence, too, sustains the agony of Beat self-reflection thirty years into the future, at the millennium's beginning. The narrated tale and its parables agonizes the real possibility that Beat consciousness and narrative had bore no practical, modern necessity. *Beat Angel* also finds Beat Generation's devotees and patrons recalling their disappointment at the resultant depression and dejection about their involvement in the movement. Scholars and pundits, then, had concluded that the literature itself taught us the spirit's failed evocation.

I would add that, from my cold, academic reading of today's pop music culture, the fact that there is even hostility to the spirit of the ideas as art works against today's commercial angles and stereotypes. Conversely, the depth of Beat critique of contemporary forms and character encourage divergent readings and a knowledge base that could resurrect art's public and prophetic powers, highlighting the human spirit's triumph. The root translation of Beats as written ideation is a simple antidote to post-millennium similitude: in practice and in the sophistication of language that breeds liberal *difference*, and even in terms of the social imagination that builds subculture, activism, and *praxis*, were the Beat ideologically far from pretenses found in today's communities? After all, the key of uniqueness favors and checkers a student's writing options, and the development of social his/her involvement. It, too, causes them remember their specific social origins and thoughts as politically legitimate and necessary. Re-opening the artificial privilege of history, then, may cause us to track our development versus changing institutions, and to re-appraise our spiritual and cultural selves, re-opening Jacques Derrida's closed door through film narrations that layer and build writing into new forms.

I believe, finally, that academic culture has nixed liberal intellectual development of place and identity. Because of this, adaptation of the graphic and visual descriptions of Beat place ought to be rich and situate characters and places as those that are believable and which carried the didactic message ably. Mary, Carol, and Gerard all bear the marks of older age and depression, and the silent engagement of the world: Beat patrons range from cowboys to flirts to hippies, and locales are beset with short interludes of Gerard's dreams that include a whispered prayer in Latin and another where Kerouac exhorts Gerard to give up his job and trek to Mount Hozomeen, to receive his vision at the summit.[90] Yet urban scenes and neighborhoods echoed the isolation and depressive coldness of the impoverished America. In contrast, the bar is filled with young faces ready for a good time, breathing its traditional health without spoken or visual examples that favor today's culture. It should be noted that techniques for applying more silence in the film's audio and for reducing the volume of the actor's conversations and the sounds in the screenplay were commonplace in the 00's. By comparison, soundtracks and screenplays in the 1970s, 80s and 90s did not use silence as effectively, creating contrast between the subject's actions and fulfillment. Darkened visual angles of isolation and communion formed part of the author's dramatic messianism at the moment of his re-introduction. When paired with the haunting, narrow, and thoughtful intrusions of both biography and spirit, they promise the light and freedom that were part of Kerouac's purgatorial thesis. "The scene" is still popular, and good times could be had through drugs, booze, sex, and poetry. Nonetheless, the affect of a generation's visible distrust and alienation marks the rhetorical move toward angelic prose and its uplifting, graceful spinning of tale-telling and comic intensity to cast off the characters' mental and personal shackles.

Tripp's polarized consciousness affects his grass-roots challenge and the *faux pas* of his cosmetic rejection of literary inspiration. He, too, illustrates male crises that were prefaced from a seemingly incomprehensible, antagonistic antecedent that predated his own accomplishments. Within his pale, unresponsive drunken tedium, Tripp imagines the non-recognition of his own ideals, beliefs, and self-estimations of poetic and personal greatness. I believe that here was a crucial point of inspection for all leading characters. All of them, sensing something beatific in Balestri's antics and self-styled autobiography, approach and then challenge Kerouac in expressions of virtue and self-realization when they are their own, no longer suburban dependents with false aesthetic immersions. It should be said that these subplots, insofar as they relate to one's identity, protect Kerouac's role as messenger and teacher. The touch of wisdom, pleasure, and dreaming reflections visibly liberate Mary, Carol, and Gerard: in the dark hush of nighttime treks and behind the railroad train at its evening journey, suggesting the parable of learning to enrich the character's self-understandings.

Chubby, balding, yet bearing the telltale facial countenance and childish, ecstatic breath of didactic realism and trans-generation, Vincent Balestri gives the opening stanza's commentary to signal the literary metaphor's truth-transcendence of earthly life and thus the signature expression of the movement's timeless, and romantic, if vaudevillian, stream of messages that staged comedy, intensity, beauty, and clever limericks of Kerouac's travels and discoveries as he walked in the streets, lounges, and cafes of mid–20th century America. The beginning scene ushers in the silence and space amidst Kerouac's living room, filled with empty furniture and black-and-white TV blaring "The Galloping Gourmet" on the screen. Balestri intones, "Nirvana, the Catholic way. Whenever you get an idea and you're ready to create, your favorite TV show is on. I never wrote down that idea."[91] The screen then turns to the chef, dressed in a tight vest: "hack your way through a piece of rock,"[92] when Kerouac begins vomiting blood. Stated historically, the scene's sequence inscribes Kerouac's direct transference of ideas and content to Gerard, and accomplished their vicarious material disgorgement, a last exit from purgatorial life. We are given illusions of materialistic glamor and prosperity as key agents in death's redemption of the living Soul. Aesthetic simplicity tightens Balestri's expression of the true depth of perceptual revelation and indoctrination: "I closed my eyes and let go.[93]" When Balestri returns as a guest at Kerouac's Death Day reading at a crowded bar, it is in part to rescue the dying embers and sickened hearts of that which could have been Beat. As a languishing audience went through the motions of disregard in a fight over a poetess's plastic overtures, Balestri takes the stage and adeptly performed his timeless emblems found in the text. He picks up the guidance of fighter Jack Johnson, and the blowing vernacular power of much-adored jazz saxophonist Charlie Parker, to once again inspire the Beat faithful in their minute of true discord. Hemming his free verse that rethreads spontaneous prose with the gimmick for using American art forms to tell of the nation's life and in the beat of its truly jubilant, jazzed spirit, Balestri performs the untold tryst with Parker as the triumphant moment of Kerouac's childish glories:

> I was in a club in New York City. A hundred people in the room, Boom! The doors flew open, child of pot being escorted onto the stage, He had to be escorted, because he was Negro, he couldn't walk around the neighborhood. When he got onto the stage, he had a lot of suffering in his heart, He started to look around the room, look into people's eyes, Look in for something humble, something truly humble! And what he said, hey I have to tell you otherwise. He lookin' at him in de eye, and he started to blow the melody. [...]
>
> And I have a lot of sufferin' in my heart! And I gotta blow this sufferin' out of my horn-hole, into your eyes, into your heart, then there'll be no more sufferin', [...].[94]

Of course, improvised, history-friendly strophes did accomplish the soothing of a tense crowd, but concrete portraits of Bird and Johnson described the Black man's passions and suffering in accordance with Kerouac's self-constructed emotional metrics and prophetic ascensions to truth. Still, as the reading goes on, the paraphrase closely models Dean Moriarty's spell with the sax player in *On the Road*.[95] Interpreting Beat history through performance cements both authenticity and morality, but Balestri as Kerouac shares his childhood trance, and the underground's deeper translations of underclass forms. It seems obvious that White teenagers sought this trans-valuation through Parker, and that the learning curve for understanding Blackness as truth was risky and nebulous for even the main Beat writers. But Balestri performs at a crucial minute, seeing his community losing the emblem of the movement's heralded truth and loving bonds of unity. This was not new: counterculture's racial and class tensions had been introduced in films as early as 1970's *Zabriskie Point*. Magic realism and its syntactic metaphors were linked to man's imagination, and to the spirit's velocity that could arise from his suffering:

> Parker started blowing these suffering notes! Sayin, I like you! I can see your heart! Lemme blow some suffering outta my heart, ohh yeah! He inhaled, he lookin' at me I'm lookin' at him. I noticed he started to sweat on his forehead, I noticed I was sweating in my forehead, we're sweating in the exact same part of the forehead, And if you know it you know time you know everything's really fine. Blow![96]

Balestri succeeds in reviving the Beat Generation's collective intensity—the succeeding sequences, where he accounts for his football, military, and publishing oddities, are performed comically and ably distorted serious intellectual truths. Subplots that tread Beat history are simple and clever: at one point, Balestri simply sings, "Please Publish Me," a funny and apparently thoughtless piece. Paradoxically, when he receives the phone call to publish *Road*, he isn't interested in its success.[97] At another point, somehow sewn in with the awkward blaring of a classical piece, Kerouac stares into the hallway of his apartment at a bald-headed, mustachioed man who is the publisher. Standing in Kerouac's doorway, the man then strikes down parts of his overly long, scandalous book that, among other things, included objectionable material such as pot-smoking queers who masturbate, unmarried women, and cockroaches.[98] I think that skits that run the tape of the author's crucial dialogues with fame and recognition offset the tedium of the much-covered anxiety of writing and its analysis: perhaps, we may visit the human frame tale with greater understanding in its everyday, depressive simplicity, so understanding that subversive arts were tradition, and that its issues corresponded to the stiff, conservative authoritarianism belittling their sins and follies.

Tripp partially informs his bar-frequenting public of his divorce with writing and its mysteries when he denounces Kerouac's memory: "Kerouac was the most overrated writer of the [20th] century. Worst excuse for a hack who ever masturbated on a sheet of paper. What a loser! Killed himself with booze."[99] With long hair and a sardonic, fortyish grumpiness, Tripp belabors his newfound company with Balestri. A simple point of narrative and social organization came from Sigmund Freud, who wrote in *The Ego and the Id*: "to most people who have had a philosophical education, the idea of anything mental that is not also conscious is so inconceivable that it seems to them absurd and refutable simply by logic."[100] In socioeconomic context, Tripp's rebuttal is not welcome for the artist circuit. Today's hipster generation bore the frustrations of materialistic excess, technological suppression of ideation, and the War on Drugs as a persistent neutralizing agent that had suppressed pot-induced revelation as being an impractical, imperceptible mystic indifference. It includes hordes of punks and college kids who re-read the movement for inspiration found themselves lost in the postmodern polarity, with feelings and impulses that could not escape the monolith's stereotyping mouth and its sterilizing powers at the millennium's beginning. Yet Tripp's *faux* rejection of the Beat emblems reconciles mankind and masculinity to more piecemeal issues, and not to those of the left vanguard: it seems ridiculous to give up life, love, career, and egoistic self-assessments to an apparition who died thirty years ago. Still, as he tries to ask Carol for sex, Tripp exclaims his wish for recognition, poles apart from Carol's positive wish for discovery and enlightenment.[101] Ironically, separating men and women because of messages of inspiration and truth is risky ground, as if to say that a generation's specific, concrete values and their wishes for success, knowledge, and self-realization through sex and friendship plays out against the backdrop of their non-recognition and unheard minutes of *jouissance*. In this way, Tripp favors the mainstream world and pretenses toward meritocracy, and positivist values causing him to reject Kerouac's noisy, silly *oeuvre* of petulant, witty sayings and private histories that drive much of the action in his letters.

Still, Freud did not develop a comprehensive study of drugs and alcohol, and missing the chance at broader conscious expositions that the Beats craved and overstated. Through pot and alcohol, writers and friends spun subjective truth's pragmatic and visionary dimensions, and thus the interactive navigations of one's emotions, thoughts, and feelings. The group passes the time with a couple of joints by the roadside at night: Carol, feeling depressed, recalls her stint as a painter in college, and the patronage of a professor only interested in sex.[102]

If we tread the most pedestrian of grounds when examining literature and its impact, we will find that drugs and alcohol allowed subconscious and conscious metaphors to meet in American discussions of everyday life, problems, and emotional attachments to one's story. Logic, then, interlocks with mankind's private estimations of Self, a mirage-like dialogue that could unlock a more easily spoken self-understanding. Mary, for instance, attempts to read from *The Subterraneans* with her arms around Balestri as they slow dance: "I just feel like taking off all my clothes, fucking like a cat on all paws. Who am I what I am what I should be how should I live die."[103]

Balestri tells Mary that she, not he, wrote the passage. She then kisses him, as if to state time's consubstantial transcendence and thus the Self's concrete grounding of anti-rational testaments that spoke of truth and self-realization. Psychologically speaking, the technique for liberating a silent woman who felt "left out" restates the underground's proselytizing minute. We, who are the rock generation's children, depend upon these carefully located, yet simplistic, revisions of modern man's ordering of truth and experience to reclaim our living senses. I would state the parable's meaningfulness only because pot-winded ramblings seldom manage any tangible political power for young, marginal citizens. More simply put, illusions of self-immersion and nondescript truths, then, bequeath a living community that still depends upon its organization of followers. It was not true that pot had changed modern consciousness, but rather that it operated within specific social parameters of self-examination and understanding. It is also true, given the proto-European forms that impact modern American society, that many potheads visit their truest visions and self-interrogations depressively and silently, deriving no political or pragmatic impetus.

In concretely social terms, poetry readings captured the new generation's distinct *ethos* and, very significantly, its *pathos* at a clear moment of sweeping eclipse and discontent. To say that, after three successive rock generations and six decades of popular media, that poets and writers saw neither appreciable functionality nor dense and "real" reclamations of the Beat movement's tradition is only a small part of what made Balestri's entry so poignant. Prominently, the reborn Kerouac gives the living world his sympathy and decisive feeling, a crowning of wisdom that became increasingly distant and contrived, and clearly false, in the midst of money-driven popular entertainment culture that had pressed millions of everyday people into the insincere, superficial stasis of vainglory and illusory pop icons with their spoken exhortations. *Beat Angel* promises a dynamic revival, and a concrete purpose for a precarious, albeit more affluent, society.

Walter Salles' *On the Road* and Postmodern Cosmetic Technique

Todd Tietchen does deserve credit for re-opening ethnic and underground re-development of the Beat story. *The Unknown Kerouac* introduced the multi-ethnic form of self-inundations, the text's geographic multiplicities to advance an endless, comically sure American imagination, and starred the writer-hero who could dismantle theory's mainstream, materialistic scaffolding to favor the American working man's more truthful romanticism. Clearly, Tietchen took advantage of the adolescent Kerouac's many points of verbal and imaginative origin. Depression and alienation, too, are anchored in such a way as to highlight discoveries that promised ecstatic liberation through the "story." In the heat of that discovery, in 1951, as Kerouac worked on three novels, he had stumbled through the illusory colossus of man's rhetorical sickness and found that his non-recognition yielded a recurrent revelation: "Loneliness forever and the earth again, and I know that I'll never love or be loved again—on this pompous globe."[104] Roughly a month later, the depressive seed and *shtick* of the underground scene was apocalyptically re-written, as a test of post-atomic sense and sensibility: "now I'm about to try the most dangerous experiment of my life, the same tranced fixation upon the object which will now be the successive chronological 'visions' of Neal."[105] Re-writing depression and loneliness into visionary genius meant to unearth more essential American themes that were tied to one's social being. Proof of the validity and creative impulse of Kerouac's messages and "visions," however, lay within the explosive imaginative technique requiring occasional gusts of strength from headwinds foretelling his aesthetic beyond, an unkempt and undefined cosmic strength powering the liberated nouns and adjectives without rhetorical and social limitations. My question is a canonical one when turning to Salles' much-awaited DVD: if it was clear that *On the Road* envisioned considerable re-writing and surefooted attachments to postmodern stereotypes and *kitsch*, did Beat reconstructions correctly relay the social dynamic that spoke so loudly of revolution? Character, setting, and voice thus operate amidst the most fragile determinant: the word's estimable power, and what it stirred up in our psychic and moral consciousness.

Garrett Hedlund as Dean Moriarty drew the following sketch in *The Hollywood Reporter*: "Hedlund is as hunky as the young Brad Pitt, and like Pitt, he's a wily, charge-up actor."[106] The tall and muscular figure that navigated the road and fulfilled tales of comedy and sexual lust was not adapted to the screenplay from the novel. Many examples redraw conversation and reflection to reflect our understandings of conspiracy, the military-industrial establishment, family, and lastly Moriarty's good-natured drifting that made him so appealing. At one point, the vagrant pose of one's acquisition of true context and also of one's rebellious ingenuity is managed curtly and robustly, "if you're goin' to Mexico, I know a little Es-pan-ol."[107] Authority is screened only a few times: authority's presence is cropped to reflect conspiratorial ideas about man's conscious neutralization. When Dean admonishes Sal about the coming America that espoused authoritarian thinking, it is at odds with the novel's hilarious and inventive character, who exclaims when pulled over by an angry policeman: "Offisah, Offisah I was just buttoning my fly!"[108] Sex scenes include juicy pornographic revelries that favor graphic sexualities more provocative than those of the novel: the heavy fellatio would occur in Mexico with Dean and on the road with Marylou, and penises and cunts are potent and visible, a mobile, proselytizing testament to the Beat movement's health and perverse strength. Fortunately for avant-garde viewers who craved smut, *Road's* scenes are on par with today's soft-core porn that takes advantage of the audience's visual inclusion in sex acts and sexuality.

On the Road's visual angles, too, are altered to suit the needs of today's viewings. Jazz gigs and Bull Lee's reflections are matched against the nation's health, prosperity, and fulfillment. There are no heavy duels with America's persistent racial consciousness, nor any difficulty in doing what the novel did: place severe and scolding reflections in the hands of Kerouac's gay friends and in those of Cassady's lovers and family. The screenplay also repeated today's health and prosperity. There is hunger in only a few instances, and the Beats' homosexual acts are airbrushed of either moral quarrels or substantive discussion of mid–20th century America's sexual prohibitions. It should be said that Black fiction such as Gloria Naylor's *Bailey's Café*, and Richard Wright's *Uncle Tom's Children*, took aggressive chances when exposing 20th century America's sexual and drug prohibitions that feature underclass plight and instability, artfully staging tales and geographies that foretold crime's conscious growth and wider influence upon Black Americans. In the cafés, restaurants, bars, and tenements, and then finally "on the road" with his buddies, Sam Riley uses the backdrop of time and geography to be the positive foil for his novel, accenting living dynamism and power against corrupt, crumbling Victorian moral and social institutions. Sam exudes the silent meditation and deliberation against his friend's much greater fluidity. He is an appendage to Beat dreaming, and solo adventures echoed modernism's greater masculinity as it absorbed underground's elements that would become his sustenance. When Moriarty finds a wino and retorts to Sal, "Now, consider his soul,"[109] he accomplished the introduction to Kerouac's ethical and cultural consideration of American Selfhood. Salles' film, in context, offers Riley a wide imaginative chance to mount the serious pains and isolation of generational meditations and their wielding of social power. Shadowing Kerouac with Cassady operates adulthood's synopsis of life to beget more mature, masculine prose. Riley's checkered, oddly driven *métier* narrated memory and specific, concrete truths against the film's psychic chaos and the main character's self-diminution. At first, he is less resilient and alive than the prodigal muse who can fuck literally anybody. This means that he had to capture specific minutes of adolescent realization and reflection whilst ruminating on modernism's growth and maturity.

Modernism's idealistic moment, stitched and sewn on the pristine, wide-open, and joy-filled American road, had now faced its authorial shadow, and hence his poisoned and depressive manipulation of experiences that told him his mortality and inhumanity. In this way, Hedlund's glamor and subversion are put to the test: when Marylou drops Sal in a San Francisco hotel and relieves him of his wallet, Riley lives for two days off of cigarettes from a garbage tin.[110] Adolescent adventuring reaches a delicious minute of underclass grandeur and self-fulfillment when Sal finds Terry and elopes with her to her family's camp in Bakersfield. Again, narrative and character tensions are ignored because Sal's mediations were essential and testified to the writer's health, vigor and sexy innocence in passages documenting humanity's interdependence and warmth. When Terry is on the cotton farm, Sal easily radiates the smiling, thoughtless minutes of intimacy, family, and cross-cultural belonging without any pretense. Hence, authorship is interrupted to surprise audiences with the *mélange* of adolescent post-speculations: part of Kerouac's mystique and beauty involved his human appreciations, *to restate one's romantic inquiries and self-expression*. Riley is a supporting actor who allows life to go on, and who never coerces it. This well-versed presence in the narration is staged through an aggressive, happy ascent of scenes toward the final expression of a generation's power. In this way, we are led to think that life in their times were happy and that modern American man's residual depression could be altered or cured easily. Warmth, humanity, and the resilience of community and characters are key to the historical film's enunciations of true context. With the possible exception of films depicting war and dystopia, citizens of totalitarianism and injustice are socially active and interactive, and decisive moments of self-approbation starred young characters and their more vigorous purpose. Popular historical films that featured Denzel Washington in *Malcolm X* (1992), Ben Kingsley in *Gandhi* (1982), and Whoopi Goldberg in *Ghosts of the Mississippi* (1996) tell us histories that engender self-development's living societal energy and public attentions to man's social necessity. Audiences might also intone the converse, that many history-themed films explored pre-democratic and pre-modern monarchical eras to distend the body of man's normal and active social relationships: arrests, punishment, racism and crimes of honor worked against the obvious, burning living impulse toward spirited freedom. Riley, who is an Englishman dithers and meditates on an unwritten romantic space that comprises Nature, street, song, and subculture, audiences are encouraged to underscore the healthy grit of his youthful reflection and the sudden, jubilant leaps to truth and sensitivity. These, in Salles' improvised meditations on the novel's rough draft, recast the landmark intellectual discoveries to mean metaphors of interdependence and integrity.

I believe that Beat writers addressed racial politics unevenly, instead favoring the abandonment of political forms as the means to advance the Black man's identity, citizenship, and inclusion in American culture.

Historically, our studies of Jim Crow models were far from gracious when assigning racial content. Portrayals of Black Americans in the 1930s, 40s and 50s were racially slanted to view their permanent subjection and diminution in modern social spheres: this is why we expect true sociopolitical content to be restated to be part of African-American historical cinema. Well after blackface vanished from American films, Hollywood's racist screenplays and imageries told the Black man's complete cultural, psychic, and spiritual inferiority when compared to White men and women. Jazz's true depth was not explored, available only in moving cuts that interrupt dialogue, carrying the Beat social scene's incomplete projections. The opening chapter of *On the Road* begins with a "jumpin' and jivin'" club appearance featuring a speedy, wild-sounding tenor saxophonist.[111] In the place of Kerouac's deep, post-monarchical excavations of jazz's formal language and its visible communitarian motifs, audiences are only shown a crowd of Black men and women dancing and visibly appreciative of the music that could drive them to dance. This scene ignores jazz's formal presentation, instead telling of it as a simpler form of music and entertainment that spoke to pleasing stereotypes. Jazz's deep spiritual resonances, pain, and sufferings are never touched—though clearly, it was a point of operative focus in the novels of Ralph Ellison, Gloria Naylor and Alice Walker. Partying dispersed the spiritual-supernatural angle, shadowing the elucidation of meaning from beneath primitive art forms such as jazz that played free of technological or intellectual derivations. At a Battery Park apartment later that night, and after a dozen joints have been smoked, a Black man fucks his girlfriend and then admits to Dean that he was fucked by a White man.[112] No attempts are made to capture the Black community's politics or conversations, yet we must remember that Kerouac did not introduce jazz cosmology until *Road*. The songs, too, give us very little authentic tasting and sensing, with "Ko-Ko" and "I've Got the World on a String" replacing a deep, occult-sounding and crazy music meditation that did not get onto jazz records until the early 1950s because of White censorship of Black artistic content. Artists such as Charlie Parker and Miles Davis, for instance, were often limited to three-minute pieces without wild drumming or lengthy instrumental solos, during the 1940s. But the point is simple: Salles did not present the viability of African-American social and moral consciousness, instead tying Riley to dreams of White creation, not Black creation.

Jacques Derrida was circumspect in the handling of a key moment of narrative crisis in Europe and European America. When confronted with the question of the word's comparative authenticity in literate and pre-literate cultures, he quoted archenemy Claude Levi-Strauss, then writing that Strauss's opinion was that deception did not exist for pre-literate societies[113]: "It is just that [Strauss's] anthropological discourse is produced through concepts, schemata, and values that are, systematically and genealogically, accomplices of this theology and this metaphysics."[114]

The summative point for modernist literature was clear: writing's artifact, or rather the subjective grasp of consciousness and experience through words and themes, belonged more to the author and his specific investigation of the truth. Honesty thus did not exist because of the writing hand of White configurations friendly with Western man's essential inquiries. Film changed that in *Road's* private generational context. In the most basic sense, Salles screens *On the Road* without a guiding, omniscient narrator, and replaced the novel's paragraphs with spoken conversations, complicating the time period's viewing and its engagement of the social order. In other instances, many key conversations are dropped: this was thoughtful because of the Beat writers' recurrent tensions, and those concerning their families. We are left to study the character's emotions and the narration in the simplest perceptible manner. For example, Dean's relationship with Camille is abruptly cropped and destroyed: instead, the result is two scenes in which Dean refuses to stay home with Camille and their son, instead smoking marijuana and going to a jazz bar in downtown San Francisco.[115] The next morning, Camille orders Dean out of the house, and a sad-faced Neal picks up his one bag as the baby cries and screams for him. The following scene highlights Camille's lonely, motherly silence, as she is unsure of her decision and is without the dream of family and inclusion that meant a great deal to her.[116] We are led to recognize the screenplay's basic values of construction: it is a small apartment, and Neal blows off Camille to go to a frivolous gig with funny scatting in place of any tremendous, shaking story of music's power.[117] The jazz scene's wealth and jocund navigations of experience contrast with Camille's specially located isolation. Without engaging the dreamy, romantic literary exclamations and gasps that nurture the Beats as part of a serious culture, attentions to resonant perceptual and visual cues that restate adolescence's mortality and alienation. They also project a loneliness that Salles did not cure in the cast.

I believe that, however, the shining example of Salles' production and his re-writing of *On the Road* was that it captured grand narrative stanzas of adolescent understanding. We would at least be wise to say, in hindsight, that the film adopts numerous strategies common to contemporary film, and so rewrites the novel's aura. Conversely, there appears a new, visual mystique that avoids confessional realism: shots of the group's insanity force Salles to guard the writing from the analytic eye. Few historical films have captured this essential happiness, and the film as a whole diminishes instances of authority and family. More likely, beatnik partying, sex, and tomfoolery narrated a revived, jubilant defiance of modern social norms. Main characters are filmed in a brashly expert narration that challenges the English classroom to force teachers and students to drop their Victorian simulations that confirm repression of the scene's primary meanings. Marylou and Carlo are catalysts, adopting gay and straight sex to the conservative multitude and for their heroes, Sal and Dean. Marylou's oral sex act sends a frightened man off the desert road[118]; meanwhile, Carlo parties with Marylou in a sexless moment interrupted by cries of "up your ass!"[119] In short the demi-gorgon of American sexual conservatism is exorcised at impromptu and slated community gatherings on the road or in New York. The actors breathe a confident happiness that translates the idea that such revolutions of thought and being are applicable to the sketchy, confusing today's adolescent subcultures. All of them exhibit hubris, but the characters' living minutes exclaim subversion's strength and agility versus the dry official culture that neutralized the modern social scene with its stereotypical behaviors and language. Of course, films portrayed adolescent characters in several film adaptations of the novel, and include the sumptuous courtship in *Ethan Frome*,[120] depressive Negro estimations of justice in 1986's *Native Son*[121]; films such as 1985's *The Color Purple*[122] that detail the graphic of violation and abuse, and those such as 2013's *Anna Karenina*[123] and 1995's *The Scarlet Letter*[124] which privilege the touching, breathing organism that lay beneath sexual prohibitions and marital guilt. Yet few films had tried to tell an adolescent's story along with his estimated values and impromptu confessions and beliefs. From the 1950s, it was popular to narrate young heralds of an incomplete message was not understood by the common man. *On the Road* thus accomplished its basic task—to document a strong, broad engine of adolescent rebellion, and the intuitive sureness of college students in their defining moral moment.

    Walter Salles chose to cast Sal Paradise in the cloak of a passive, silent character. Salles denied him the role of omniscient narrator, and further suppressed most of the spoken narration of the writing until the very end, when Sal greets a visibly shaken and uncertain Dean in the New York winter.[125] It is only at the last minute that we visit the personality and range of Sal as an omniscient and benevolent creator. We would, then, attach or infer nothing from the instances of contemplation, only pacifying ourselves into watching happy and fluent junkies in the absence of meaning, thus remaining indifferent to the narrative scenes. Examples of Jack Kerouac as cultural messenger, too, were protected from the outside world's persistent inroads: there are no cross-examinations from the mainstream, nor the advent of postmodern fiction that sought to dislocate and denature the symbolic emblems of Kerouac's "beatitude." I wish to point out the obvious: *On the Road*'s primary features are the literary group's shiftlessness and depression, and so Salles attack the primary axis of rebellion and instances of its true necessity. Instead, the robust healthiness and easy transferences of place, character, and context manifest the Beat movement to be a triumphant juggernaut and a well-natured, confident adolescent group possessed of his materialistic, physical, and social advantages in post–World War II America.

On the Road projected no new archaeological findings about either Kerouac or his times: the coverage was very skimpy and reflected its main interest in the characters and production. Whether this is postmodern-friendly or not, limitations placed on Sal shrunk modernist discussions and didactic influences on the human subject. I believe that these factors have remained in the form of today's literary film: still, adaptations may preach the work's content in the hope that audiences would consider history's value as it coexisted with today's simpler ethics. Silencing Sal accomplishes the basic task: gone were mankind's literary pontifications, and duly advanced was the common man's altruistic valor and his gregarious, pluralistic spirit as it could be imagined in the late 1940s. Input from critics, students, and citizenry was of course clear: mankind would be painted with the specific tones of his common, every day, sensible attributes. *On the Road* spoke the Beat Generation's confused, dislocating methodologies as they extended and accelerated their impact during the 1950s and 60s. In virtually all instances, Sal is silent, mute, and unappreciated versus the prodigal and wacky Dean. The parable, of a rivalry among friends, repeats juvenile modernist rhetoric and thus asks of us what could be the outcome of underclass friendships.

In truth, *On the Road* performs the replacement of literature with pop history very adeptly, harboring no pretense to attach scholarship to the juicy, wild tale that seemed to maintain few or no boundaries. It is, classically, a postmodern film that uses and nurtures skillfully derived male and female stereotypes to beget man's expression of his social norms. Text, too, was roughly translated out of the writing's semiotic inflections of its shrouded, sheltered voice and into the generalizing present: we are to trust bodies and speech above writing, or at least visible projections over screenplay. This move was expected: still, the postmodern materialist ethic that stressed man's physical nature above his romantic unreason was captured and nourished, repeating our rejection of Theodor Adorno's formal expectation that art echo dramatic conflicts within one's spirit. The key paean that reaches us again and again is that the story and characters are *believable* instead of alien to us—a key anxiety that calls our attention to film's production as a social agent.

Modernity and Eternity in *Big Sur*

Michael Polish's 2013 film, *Big Sur*—in large part filmed around the Pfeiffer Big Sur National Park's beach—re-screens Beat redevelopments of writing and thought as social ideas, a series of philosophical ruminations that fanned the flames of a modernist afterglow, and a visual immersions that transpose Kerouac's literary techniques onto audience screenings of color, contrast, and synchronous shots that bring forth the music's intent and the author's readings. Polish's film also transmits the literary work's oral virtue through taped recordings transforming our perceptual indoctrinations. The author's story, or rather the rambling and crashing vortices of his literary and philosophical imaginations as found in the 1962 novella, was lengthened and given more sensible, raw turmoil. Polish challenged Kerouac's health, sanity and happiness, accomplishing his expansive legend and the sweetness of his cultural-ascetic pretense through their mirror images. The film's production is airbrushed of legitimate ideological adversity, as it is thick with Buddhist nature-*haiku* poems and prophecies, parables, and the depressive, nightmarish graphic of the author's alcoholism. Polish tried to concentrate the text's raw data, to advance generational anxiety clearly and without the mediation of a competing ideological apparatus. His textual strategies were borne of the anxieties of both the 1960s and the modernist eras. What became a cinematic *coup de grace* appears simple in offing. Polish's film accomplished what Kerouac's novel doesn't—the Beat Generation's classic re-conception, on a scale that favored later Beat writers and those who address crucial biographical questions of influence.

It is very fair to note the fact that critics weren't enthralled by *Big Sur*, and did not give high marks to the modernist thematic development of Kerouac's literary genre that sometimes included jokes and meditative pauses. It was not new, it had been a part of Kerouac's form since the 1940s, and so had left critics wondering what Buddhism's true power could be in the wake of Kerouac's escapism that chronicled the generation's social-political decline in the 1960s. The film largely ignored, too, Kerouac's inability to amass a truly creative aesthetic force and languished in a form that was distant from implied fiction possibilities and memories that still posed their response to realism. The tryst was crucial as to *Sur's* modernist relevance: by comparison, *Tristessa* built a much greater and deeper narcotic and street sensibility consistent with the vagrant's pose. More adeptly, we advance the obvious premise: *Sur's* references to Buddhism had only built a casual, street-friendly route to the nondescript delirium and portals of enlightenment. This meditative gap, too, had been written before, in *On the Road*: "this was a manuscript of the night that we couldn't read."[126] We should understand, then, that Kerouac offered us a trail of imperfect translations that sprang from his mind. By comparison, *Tristessa* offered a very gritty, socially conscious, and strong grounding of Mexico's drug cultures with specific intonations of Kerouac's grandiose, morphologically concrete ramblings of it that scribbled morphine addiction across Mexico's neighborhoods, culture, and poesy. It was in this novel, on *par excellence* and with deep, reigning prophecies, that Kerouac testified his integration of drugs with modernist writing form as that which favored silence, individuality, and remote thoughts.[127] Thus, audiences arrived at the windswept beauty and Zen-like abstractness of *Sur* with greater, not lesser, demands for true comprehension of Kerouac's writing form as social messenger.

A major problem with *Big Sur* was the distantness of its pose and the weakness of its Buddhism. Because its literary symbols are so confused and intermixed, we cannot grasp the zigzagging Buddhist escape from modern man's painful sameness. Powerful and sweeping, *Big Sur* erases the virtues of learning and scholarship, and so stated decline to be a part of the Beat community's self-realization and part of its meditation on man's irrational symbolisms that intervened with true Selfhood. There is no opportunity to connect with America's political movements, and so the tale instead celebrates the Beats' final demise, in a move from public to private consideration. When Kerouac summarized his return to America after his opium nightmare at the end of *Desolation Angels* he ejects, "a new life for me,"[128] with no discussion of the revelation's meaning. Prophecy's absence, or rather its self-interrogations to weaken its active tense as it sharpened and grew through Jack Duluoz's aesthetic visions, would resolve the whirlwind, erratic Beat popularity in the waning light of *Road's* magnetism. Kerouac's visions unearth no political metaphors, instead blindly and joyously enjoying one's living minute.

The task of teaching film adaptations at American University of Afghanistan was often mixed: not only did student suggestions and eagerness collide with sharp criticism from conservative Muslims, but I would patently state the obvious price of exchange with any Asian student: if they did not think as idealistically and critically about the film's contents, what would be gained when learning the American epoch and its intellectual, literary and popular developments? Student criticisms restated moral probity and its self-evaluations: while they laughed at Harpo's follies in *The Color Purple*, they said it was "horrible" because of its graphic terror and maternal cruelty; by contrast, we screened Leonardo Di Caprio's role in 2013's *The Great Gatsby* with enthusiasm as it gloriously unveiled scenes and intrigue common to today's hip-hop and ambient scenes. Films such as 1966's *An American Dream* shored up crucial misconceptions about content, voicing student criticisms about our excesses: one student asked if Deborah was a hippie, while another wrote that the story was "distinct" and reflected Americans' lack of understanding of "love," as she raised radical feminine heroines. *Big Sur* brought controversy and some uncertainty due to its sex scenes: still, students commented that the actors were "brilliant" and "handsome," while noting Kerouac's drunkenness and rambling. Still, *Big Sur* did allow them to trace the philosophic diadem of naturalist reflection? In my view, "brilliance," and the sexy stream of plots, plus essays that tell of his ruined transcendence, manifests cognitive appreciation of counterculture's form as it could be exchanged with their more familiar adolescent/young adult narratives of discovery, learning, and conflict. I doubt that it is a misnomer that many Asian students are drawn to Western humanities that appear to feature "cool" realities: it is a common theme of minority classes where serious philosophical inquiries adapt more popular forms. Still, I will say that making a literary period one's own is an important part of the humanities experience: students commented positively on Barr's visions, while deriding his abuse of alcohol, much as they would figures that inhere the same imaginative problems. By comparison, Amitabh Bachchan's drunken swing through Mumbai streets with a Vat 69 bottle dangling from his hands told us the eternal tale of love, marriage, and friendship in 1977's *Hera Pheri*: the abundance of parables and sayings in the Bollywood tale, then, deepen our interest in the film, offering simpler prophecies and their meaning to young adult navigations of "street," "scene" and contemporary life. When telling about American history, film adaptations might then offset the novel's critical reception, and the novel's lack of rhetorical power.

We might at least investigate the novel's narrative content before giving unchallenged literary glory to *Big Sur*, written after the Beat Generation's apex and symbolic of its lingering and irreversible doom when contrasted with the broader American culture that retained its commodity fetishism and political nuclei spelling out anti-colonial critique. Allen Ginsberg defended all parts of Kerouac's inquiry, stating on October 10, 1991, that

> Each book by Jack Kerouac is unique, a telepathic diamond. With prose set in the middle of his mind, he reveals consciousness itself in all its syntactic elaboration, detailing the luminous emptiness of his paranoiac confusion. Such rich writing is nonpareil in later half XX Century, a synthesis of Proust, Celine, Thomas Wolfe, Hemingway, Genet, Thelonious Monk, Basho, Charlie Parker & Kerouac's own athletic sacred thought.[129]

I think that Ginsberg's commentary was apropos, and stated Kerouac's literary influences to measure rhetorical weight that documented his broad, humanistic pretense. Still, we must weigh in the raw evidence that weakens biography's power—Kerouac's attention to the "clean azzholes" and his discussion of crap directly repeated Japhy Ryder's inferences concerning mainstream American students in *Dharma Bums*.[130] Kerouac's stay at the lodging held by a "vulture family," too, was stripped of meaningful personal details that could spell out the weight anti-human parables or at least state the palpable, if remote, humanity of poor whites in America's Western territories.[131] Sparse and vague references to Kerouac's Buddhist and Taoist influences, and their specific moment of wisdom, are applied to pilgrimage and memory and calculate their strength through instances that tell of our knowledge of Kerouac's studies and of his peculiar sensitivities. They do not, in short, weigh against the specific Catholic confessions that constituted Kerouac's great grasp of America's true pluralism in the third generation of media and media-influenced popular culture. Kerouac dismissed his protégés' ambitions, proclaiming himself to be "sick and tired,"[132] thus destroying the supple ferment of natural imageries and reflections that caused man to break away from his materialist and moral confinement. The decisive moment must be reached apolitically, and without rehearsed pretense: thus, spontaneity limited moral messages of transcendence and supplanted them with a permanent authorial tedium, inward looking and not transferable. In a real sense, this was unfair to the audience discussion: many Afghan students chose the topic transcendental philosophy with intentions of proving the widespread ferment of Eastern aestheticism that include untouched Sufi poetry and criticism, while doffing Kerouac's visible excesses as they hadn't been used to extract the meanings of natural philosophy's link to truth and rhapsody. Afghan perspectives had been acute and thoughtful, working within the critical humanist structure of Islamic historical and intellectual comparisons, and speaking to the culture's modern ethics and internal judgment of prophecy's visual moments: there were as many comments that ran Barr's appearance and lust alongside notations of an interesting film beyond their immediate conversation, and so theory was marred with their recurrent reaction to pop film production and its glamor.

Therefore, I believe that comparative readings and suppositions favored Kerouac's written form, and so film adaptations derive insights and wisdom through the retelling of Nature's visual, aural, and imaginative dilemmas. On this night, the ENG 240 students reacted in many ways: they were protective of their modern deliberations that favored popular culture, music, and censorship, but intrigued by the content in ways that favor the visual angle. Unsure about the import of the evident debauchery and sickness, students praised the film's formal presentation of history within the iconic gaze of film narrative: sour in their criticisms of Kerouac's alcoholism, they were moved by the tense intellectual environs and the healthy release of modern dreaming in California. I believe that Asian social anxieties nudge forward this parable, so opening *Big Sur* to greater readings of the Beat family and its narrow engagements of Zen and Taoism.

We might tackle Polish's movie from the standpoint of the emerging Self as a moral and philosophical messenger, weighted down with the burdensome, nondescript void of postmodern indifference but tenaciously building memory and perception onto modern man's totalistic representation and expression of a special genius. In this light, *Big Sur* assembled the force and multiplicity of consciousness versus Beat cultural determinants. These collages that mixed visual cues with textual narrations, music, and the emotions found in the face, the subject found in the author's appearance, and the Kerouac's diminished tale in the vast wilderness and vaster California, cast forth modernism's wide hues of ideation. They, too, rebuilt horizons that hung over Kerouac's feelings of satisfaction when catching a glimpse of philosophy's collective aesthetic achievement, should audiences track the evolution of *Sur's* visual forms, readings, and anxiety from our comprehension of naturalist writing from Americans such as John Muir, Wallace Stevens, and Gary Snyder. Polish brought forth the text's many unstudied parables: these are richer and more inane in nature, a sign of the dying monolith's penitent escape. Examples of prose that are played during the film's first part state philosophy's pretense and were mixed with footage of Pfeiffer Big Sur's tremendous natural might. They, too, suggest more aggressive modern realizations from beneath Nature's shadows, or rather from Emerson's reflections that carefully paraphrased the deducible appearance of American male character. More thoughtfully, *Big Sur* did much to absorb and concentrate the movement's authentic impulses toward social change and spiritual freedom. Airbrushed of any competing social or institutional messages, Kerouac's mental angles build a strong, mobile composite that could tackle the headwinds and tailwinds of any gust of social change. He and his friends are confident and sure of their metaphors, teachings, and their inclusion in the vague, transparent postmodern idealism that began to flaunt its social and political messages when telling of man's undiscovered frontiers. We may hold no appreciable view of the movement's momentum, but happily and thoughtfully admire the characters' sexual swagger, their moral and aesthetic strengths, and their confident rejection of the system as tattered and waning in the light of Kerouac's visions and revelations. The audience is given a complex narration of counterculture's sensible moment and its refreshed geography in the California cities, beaches and houses: it is clear that the Beats were the idea-creators of counterculture's possible revolution, holding neither semantic nor epistemological constraints that pointed to an airbrushed and therefore nonexistent political and intellectual scene. I believe that this development of film medium meant that Polish's extraction of writing and being is successfully re-constructs Beat societal ethics: the massive idea-structure of the 1960s lay dormant, and introductions to San Francisco's street scene guard the signs of Beat cultural, artistic, and philosophical creation.

Audiences, then, focused on the movement's singular instance in the brush-stroke of its aesthetic realism, consistent with the naturalism and romanticism of 20th century American poets that included Wallace Stevens and John Muir. The absence of drugs in *Big Sur* does not challenge the novel's morphology or mythology, yet street hawking is persistent. The movie, with its carousing inmates of the postmodern gloom, builds its anxiety from motifs of confinement that appeared in novels such as Ken Kesey's *One Flew Over the Cuckoo's Nest* (1962), and thus affixed modernism's penitent gaze. But more important was the test of the movement's symbolic rhetoric: Polish imagines the beginnings of a greater vision of text that brought together East naturalism with Western insanity and anti-mainstream poetic realism that pushed psychosis and sickness. *Big Sur* developed reflection's visible power and art's problematic staging of internal turmoil as it borrows from the steam of its dilemma amidst the swaying tide of American culture and philosophy.

I think that the thoughtful fission of literature and film, as it included examples from Kerouac's letters and rough drafts, gave a resilient thematic base for re-examinations of modernist authenticity when we contrast American narrative ingenuity with the world's broader narrative traditions. The resulting thematic collision, then, causes us to interpret literary film from the multi-textual construction of narrative and its manifestation of ideas so as to represent collages of the American experience during the mid–20th century. In my last book, I noted the conflicting trend to be the instance of cultural difference, when comparing the largely American Beats with expatriate writer Paul Bowles: "Ginsberg, Burroughs and Kerouac never attempted to adopt a patriarchal tone because of the mismatch of their ideas with American reality."[133] The precise minute of authorial fission makes our inquiry more complete and revealing: Bowles stated the Orient to be nontransparent, and so presumed a stronger and deeper artifact of man's cultural difference that could strengthen Orient influences. Patriarchy, when applied to narrative, suited Kerouac's originality and exoticism, projecting his benevolent control. By comparison, the Beats shattered narrative order and so arranged spoken words, writings, images and scenes to foreword a much greater interdependence with more modernist text references and with unexplored, yet visually clear and nascent, possibilities. Still, the literary imagination did not attach revolution's political possibilities to its published form, and this unfocused the idea that we could understand the Beat cultural engine as scholars. We might then presume the relative absence of synthesis, and hence the special, adorned artifact that sat wholly within the author's subjective sense. A challenging example to Polish's re-creation and adaptation came from Kerouac's 1960 Buddhist poem anthology, *Book of Haikus*. Authorial voice and style renders the directness of this challenge: a leaflet features a swaying tree and Kerouac's admission that he "was a boy" for sixteen years, and that "the finale will be a hermit."[134] The poem itself is mired in familiar modernist aesthetic dislocation that repeats film's anxious presence: "Nodding against the wall, the flowers sneeze."[135] But Kerouac attacks his post–Wolfean delirium from beneath a productive and painful alienation, suggesting the passiveness and feeling of modernism's prolonged sickness in the technological-real world: "I had an eerie sensation in Paris, of having lived there before, suffered greatly there, it was too familiar and painful."[136]

The unpublished letter, with its juvenile tracings of authorial interest in poetry and society, confirms Kerouac's state of flux in mastering the art of philosophy. It, too, abnegates "the system" and its enshrinement of rational and empirical dialogue when understanding humanity. Traditional, rustic-flavored defiance of the mainstream was arranged against the depressive intonations of Europe's moral and intellectual history, a sickness of the soul that text could not rationally subdue. Could then, a movie version of a Buddhist-imbued flight to Nature assemble the writer's hand at storytelling, and thus its tenacity and timelessness? After all, readings boast their loud presentation and contrasted the artist's ecstatic strophes with hitherto unstudied attunements to traditional motifs of voice and presence. Could we, then, derive Kerouac's understandings of Chinese mysticism and poetic idealism when merging text, image, geography, music, and lifestyle? The opportunities for a person fully attuned to Hutcheon's focus on re-creation are many and creative, but written interjections must draw real sociopolitical and institutional arguments against Buddhist meditations, and with no trappings of true Eastern mysticism. The modernist parable reifies and destroys modernist beginnings mired in authenticity and narrative voice. Audiences can then synthesize text and imagination together, as it suits the greatness of American democracy and its untold quest for self-realization and *dharma* in the emerging Era of the 1960s and, when filled with the hordes of thrill-seekers and rebels looking for young man's political self-organization as they reject existing American history.

My sense is that *Big Sur* as a film documenting Beat meditations on existence took enormous cultural chances that a straight readings cause us to deny. Kerouac's moving, sometimes chilling, depression and visible paralysis in Jean Marc-Barr's middle-aged manner and complexion stirred the post–Buddhist picture more than anything in Kerouac's crucial repertoire. Buddhist and Taoist scripture are not repeated, truncating sly moments of philosophical wisdom and transcendence to accent the psychiatric picture of alcoholism and sickness. Several scenes find Barr in tears, shaking, pathetic in his small-figured private ramblings of the soul: when Ferlinghetti walks out on him, he cries his regret silently.[137] Buddhist archaeologies are cut out, with Kerouac instead reading *The History of Philosophy* and crucifying Herman Hesse's character development in *Steppenwolf*, synopsizing Hesse to be a pretentious fraud who "thought he was a big Nietzsche."[138] Yet simple visual strategies augment the once-buoyant Western intellectualism's vicious and paranoid eclipse, offsetting the peacefulness and absorptive moments unveiling the wide ocean, the tide's swelling, and an elderly replica of Beat synergy and ribaldry who still calls upon Nature's symbolic answers. Kerouac's premature noting of death, and his theme of abstinence with "no booze no drugs nor bouts with beatniks or junkies"[139] are quickly condensed into the sudden, vicious paralysis of his anonymous decline: the parallel betrays the author's diminished herald, "no one will know."[140] Yet the generation's decline was spelled out gravely and accentuated modernism's eclipse from inside the brain: "I had been fooling myself all my life thinking there was a next thing to do to keep the show going, but I was just a clown."[141] Kerouac's thoughts arrived on a sudden burst of wisdom, in the aftermath of a harrowing meditation on work that pales in comparison to the jovial, happy confidence of Chuang Tzu's "free and easy wandering" in the forests: "The sea seems to tell me, 'go to your desire. Don't hang around here for fun for joy or love or some sort of girl. Why not go to your desire and laugh?'"[142]

At many points in the film's opening chapter, Barr is stunned because of his spellbinding vision at Sur's beach, staring intently onto the ocean, and suddenly racing through the creek riddled with fear and uncertainty. Determined to read books by Herman Hesse, Thomas Wolfe and Ralph Waldo Emerson, Barr's initial meditations polarize the Beat influence and thus draw an avalanche of questions that aim for political truth. The Beat way of life supposes a new turn in its direction, staking out its partial home amidst the written turmoil that understood Kerouac's sickness to have grown from the excess of symbolic, material and cultural influences that burden his mind and easygoing confessions. Thus, the haunted parable ushers Kerouac away from isolation into more enjoyable, sense-derived wanderings of Beat parties and the poetry-spiked nightlife, sex with girlfriends, and idle speculation about America's pale institutions and capitalist determinism. A young and exuberant Neal Cassady, now out of San Quentin Jail and now working at a tire shop, whittles down to Kerouac's passion for life, love, and his spirit's liberation. Barr's specific vision advances the study of Kerouac's possibilities against philosophy's lingering tedium, and one that had fanned the flames of his insanity. Messages that anticipate contemporary film's screenplays range from a party where a groupie exclaims "fuck that ballerina shit!" and where Lew Welch tells patrons to "fuck off" when the partygoers crash his Zen meditations, to a seamy love affair with Cassady's girlfriend, Vulture Girl, and Kerouac's private exclamations about his lack of commitment and erasure of man's social traditions.[143] Somnolent music by jazz guitarist Bill Frisell hangs scenes of physical and psychic *pathos* amidst gusts of pleasure and relaxation that restated the Beat dictum in classically Buddhist terms. The Beats were freed of constraints of the mind, language and society. Thus, Polish develops the Kerouac's special tenacity and the undying abstraction of ideas and revelries holding the details of its very special, peculiar and crippling sickness, one that Polish deliberately builds in graphic terms showcasing weakness and diminution away from fame and adulations back at home. Poet Michael McClure's attempt to attain *protégé* status with Kerouac is narrowed down to a depressive template: "I work in language and you're an idea man."[144] I think that Kerouac's alcoholism and private depression burdened the Buddhist tale: still, Barr's visible satisfaction at eternity's breadth and the freedom of it is found at the tale's end, with a prim yet satisfying smile and a confidence in the literary movement's strength and the mobile wisdom of it. More than anything, *Big Sur* supplants authorial isolation with the good-natured, adept, and pure intonation of collective being that travels California easily and with form's sureness and its happy, spoken promise to live and know. There are no monumental battles, then, that poetry and *dharma* and "the void" could not solve.

The presence of voluptuous *belles* and groupies, too, anchored the Beat movement at an equinox of transient, commercialized times, and structure the author's meaningful return to the literary scene. Female protégés thus constitute a primary adaptation technique since few critics endorsed the spirit of Beat writings and were even less likely to do so after *On the Road's* publication. This was perhaps due to Kerouac's drifting, romantic eclipse, and because he and groupies no longer operated from the same generational circuit of underclass power that made them naughty, dangerous, and susceptible to institutional control. Kerouac snatches Vulture Girl into his arms and fucks her, with Neal standing there with his mouth agape and crying.[145] Barr's attentions to Carolyn Cassady, to Billie, and Romana, a Romanian poetess and singer, extolled the luscious story of California girls who crave a good time, and the beauty and sweetness of poetry. Yet groupies were part of Beat Generation ethnographies and archaeology as bearers of poetic truth, and so display no corrupting influences of the much larger mainstream, commercial society. The film's seamlessness, with Beat followers operating a fluid philosophy that did not hold attachments or agendas, develops from the game of chance with pretty girls. It, too, allows Kerouac's redemption from alcohol, to restate the literary progenitor's health and the upswing of Buddhist ramblings of freedom. The collusion of material and autobiographical pictures constituted part of the group's delusion, challenging the format for partying, taking drugs, and studying ancient books that bore aesthetic and moral metaphors. After all, mescaline and LSD were put to the biographical test in *The Doors*, and marijuana catalogs Dennis Hopper and Jack Nicholson's dramatic sexual adventuring and graphically adorned, yet torrid, downfall in 1969's *Easy Rider*. In 2013, the idea that meditation and *satori* would be put to the test, so as to derive the living force of truth, was clearly a mature idea that still had not been examined in any textual form in popular American films, and voiced monologue were often cropped or drastically limited in film versions of American novels as recent as Alice Walker's *The Color Purple*. We could also ask the question, "why?" as my Afghan students did: for many, a brilliant chance was lost because of drug and alcohol abuse. Spelling out the subversive work's intricacies and parables is given subsidiary encouragement, with a casual Carolyn exhorting Kerouac that he is "nobody's fool."[146] Of course, controversial material should endure criticism from the more morally conservative non–Western world, thus figuring in the Orient's practical wisdom when applied to today's high-tech Asian societies that behold serious cultural, lifestyle, and intellectual tensions that reconceive youth's internalization of Western liberal freedoms. At American University of Afghanistan, I read three student essays that referenced Ralph Waldo Emerson, while both girls and boys admired the handsome actors and actresses in American movies. Anxiety, then, makes us dispute our concept of teaching. Polish, however, handled this challenge by imbuing consummate support and recognition of the author's intellectual and moral talents. I believe that key themes of artistry and thought counter-strokes film's tedium, where the mind's virtues are replayed with difficulty and where the might of mainstream society's preference for crime, institutions and didactic middle-class stereotypes accented its much greater base of power. The same scheming is found in Oliver Stone's movie *The Doors* where "Riders on the Storm" is the last track, supposing the eternal vision of truth versus Morrison's drugged insanity and depression.[147]

In short, threads of meaning in Polish's *Big Sur* appear to be resonant and healthy when telling of realizations of man's essential goodness. The screenplay, too, is far from poseur and reads in terms favorable to the literary group's health and optimism. It, too, contrasts with alcoholic reminiscences and so invigorates the movement's tenacious cross-country organization and their clever, clear imagination that returned viewers to the health and simplicity of counterculture's perspectives and places. More than anything, the collective family portrait stars the contextual interrelationship with Kerouac's private meditations. Beat groupie "families" may also breathe the special thought of compassion against interviews and TV appearances that appear to mute any kind of background relevance. The Beats would happen, and be happening, away from the stage of activists, protesters, and Yippie politicians who abnegated all or part of the movement's collective idea. Family would also connect the Beats with its rock ancillaries in the decades to come. Still, I think that the group's purity necessitated the transference of their ideas, and maybe even the youthful gaze and synopsis that could easily adapt to more commercial intonations of youth, found in *The Doors, One Flew Over the Cuckoo's Nest*, and *Drugstore Cowboy*. I believe that these films include a considerable visual and rhetorical archaeology that extends adventuring and the Beat Generation's estimable utility. Social dramas that extend the private meditation to lifestyle and culture are, then, ably maintained in a manner that many literary authors were reluctantly given in film.

Two

Allen Ginsberg
The Films and Romanticism's True Test

Critical discussions of bop poet Allen Ginsberg are focused on a wide archaeology and complicate more genteel portraits that build his sentimentality and ascensions to radical protest power. Ginsberg's gay criticism starred the unique relationship of a Jewish-American boy to British poet William Blake; other criticism presented the writer's specific orality, and his attention to writing that rebuilt poetry's Victorian, Occidental prejudices. Key instances of his deeply romantic excavations of hallucinogenic consciousness through pot, psilocybin, and LSD, as well as his pursuit of rock stars to broaden his prophecies' semiotic horizons, cause audiences and students to stir the winds of social and class criticism. Lastly, audiences are given the simple, generous tale of love and tactile feelings as found in poems about his family, narrowing closer to understanding his mother Naomi, whom his father, Lou, confined to a psychiatric ward after their divorce in 1943. Let us establish one navigable truth: it was Ginsberg, not Kerouac, who unveiled the Beat Generation's dramatic, conscious moment on the world stage. It was he whom is read from the generalist sense in undergraduate American classrooms. Orality and "voice," in the post–Derridian sense, then confuses and misdirects the literary group's sexual power: Beats are gay, straight, hypermasculine, ascetic, and so had rewrote America's human stories, defacing stereotypes that could confine and limit family and social histories. We reach the moment's realization of authorial purpose without deducing its obvious seeds of male control. Kerouac, a heterosexual male, kept essential control of Beat prophecies, and hence the films' corollary thrust is to derive Beat origins from either family or the circumstances and actions around the group's first nucleus at Columbia University. Films replay the scope and affectation of Ginsberg's boyhood origins, and specific intonations and pathways agonizing his narrative persona. As a whole, they speak to the tenacity and strength of middle-class character when treading the occult, secret societies, and revolution's beginnings. At the same time, Ginsberg's puerile minutes constituted part of his ability as a Kerouac protégé: they, too, enforce public expressions of femininity and dependence versus a wilder, louder, more obnoxious transference of voice which made him controversial. Without the benefit of a deep, concentrated political consciousness, we then turn to Ginsberg's dimensions as a man, not as a prophet, who was an apologist for his times.

The task for re-inventing Ginsberg through film was ambitious, mixing memory, chronology, the literary group as social agent, and finally what could be deduced from Beat testaments including his best-known poem, "Howl." Identifying writing instances to be the living metaphors for social change directly challenged the modernist canon. Therefore, the films clear Ginsberg of his Hindu/Buddhist religious self-conception, stressing what it meant to be revolutionary and un-academic during the Jim Crow years. If we missed chances at shadowing Ginsberg's perceptions and strict regimen while he built the social and political themes of self-immolation, we might instead deduce the form of a grand re-invention of adolescence and of modern man's coming of age after World War II. Hence, we perform the juggling or mixing of imaginative cards of what writing could signal for battling within 20th century America's ethical and cultural continuum. Videography and cartoons aside, social realism begot Ginsberg's specific romantic challenge and operated all the depth of his loud and defiant vocal critique. Ginsberg's anti-war, anti-establishment, anti–American poems were in print twelve years before songs credited to Beatles singer and guitarist John Lennon introduced the New Left's agenda.[1] Power, irreverence and revolution were thus found in the effeminate man who "comes out" to spell out worldwide prophecy versus the model of effete, misdirected youths holding no power in America's moral and economic spheres. Without tending to the film's self-censorship of content, it is important to answer the basic question: if scripturally profuse works such as "Howl" could be taught, what dynamic causes us to integrate fringe and dissident rancor with democracy's development of young adult morals? I believe that the film adaptation narratives, 2012's *Kill Your Darlings* and 2010's *Howl*, fulfilled this role intelligently. The films tell stories of Ginsberg's adolescent conflicts, using visual technologies, imaginative colorations, and screenplay to repeat visual content in terms friendly to adolescent film. This means that they echo intense challenges drawn from our understandings of today's reality. *Kill Your Darlings* sprang from the same thematic debacle and imaginative form as did 1989's *Dead Poets Society*, while *Howl* traced the form of coming-of-age stories and surpassed them, grafting cartoon interludes and sublime dreaming sequences onto poetry readings and "Howl's" obscenity trial to target our memories and feelings.

Howl adopts a more engaging thrust than even the poetic call-to-arms of 2010's *Freedom Writers,* sparing audiences the classroom's stiff, debilitating rhetorical tunneling of thought and of its noxious, racist angles of cultural-realist deliberation. *Howl,* in turn, heralds idealism and freedom that had undone its socioeconomic shackles confining poetry to romantic obscurity, to speak to man's communitarian needs. My sense is that the idea's subversive contexts forces teachers to explain how rendering Western civilization a *declassed* metaphor can stimulate the writing and vocation of undergraduates who have purchased the idea that society's institutions, culture, and authority suppose all of adult life's possibilities. The lone existing documentary, Jerry Aaronson's *The Life and Times of Allen Ginsberg,* returns us to poetic form and to the countercultural spotlight, extending Beat political-social power away from their private, carefully guarded escape from American normalcy, extending the form and idealist dramatics with energies and *karm*a-like developments filling the pages of Kerouac's journals. From these representations' aggressive verdure, audiences might trace the poet's specific steps of prophetic introduction and the depths of his humanity and *hubris,* to bring forth the romantic verve that elder poets and writers fought endlessly for during the 20th century's last decades.

Beat Narratives Starring Ginsberg

Kill Your Darlings and the Sentimental Film

Key canonical and biographical factors, recurrent in biographies and works of literary criticism, influenced and rhetorically developed the writing of Beat Generation writers. Biographical measurements of the Self that demanded critical inspection began with Kerouac's dropping out of Columbia University to serve in the Merchant Marine in 1943. College life and its peculiar setting initiated the form of the Beat nucleus that we commonly known to be Jack Kerouac, Allen Ginsberg, and William S. Burroughs, with lesser roles given to Gregory Corso, Lucien Carr, Herbert Huncke, John Clellon Holmes and Lawrence Ferlinghetti. The geographic realities and engagements of learning, and criminal rejections of academia, in turn stirred the evolution of drafts, readings, re-readings and so on. I think that these are not the key themes for examining Ginsberg in *Kill Your Darlings.* Still, we often perceive knowledge and literature as media that elicits our sentimentality, or rather the anxiety of one's ethics and one's poetics. Place, and its special moments of introspection, draws the portrait of a shy, penitent Ginsberg who dreams of literary transcendences. *Kill Your Darlings* establishes the Beat Generation's gut pretension—crime. Nonetheless, it would behoove us to dig up the persistent social metaphors in the construction of romantic genius. We ought to at least say that modern man's labyrinthine adventures and trials beget moldings of romantic manhood, hence a man's outlook on changing moral and intellectual times. Without boast or pretension, then, Allen Ginsberg faces New York's criminal actors, its psychiatric henchmen, the academic oppressors, and gentle citizens who suggest warmer possibilities. De-constructing Ginsberg's passions meant attaching the spoken truth of urban-intellectual parables that paired jazz with more meaningful minutes of disarray that grew democracy in its fight against modern life's specific anesthetic, its essential, surrogate sameness that foretold sentimentality's death. Much in the spirit of 1989's *Dead Poets Society*, *Kill Your Darlings* takes administrative chances to understand America's social ethics, as they projected the characteristic struggle between good, or upright, and evil, or misunderstood, at knowledge's edge during World War II's last years.

Critical receptions of the film included those that underscored adolescent narration's collective uncertainty, and the writer's uneven thrusting to bring together Ginsberg's perceptions, engagement, and agonies. Simply put, Daniel Radcliffe as Ginsberg hooks up with Lucien Carr, who murdered David Kammerer in a lengthy, oftentimes spooky love triangle causing Ginsberg to join the tryst of parties, slum-travelling, and love affairs punctured with the grist of an undefined, uncharacteristic change in human culture and its actions. The liaison is told to destroy middle-class pretense and Ginsberg's innocent, carefully guarded nature. The classic tale is where family and community are replaced with young socialites searching for dramatic, unkempt tales of psychic and poetic intensity, graduating the puerile fold into a more cynical adulthood, where crime was a key maker in melding Ginsberg's astonishing subjectivity. Damon Wise of *The Guardian* offers the most apt praise: "[It] creates a true sense of energy and passion."[2] Many will assess the film from the moral high ground: as the film starred several Columbia University acolytes, it challenged the class structure and the class-ensconced membership at a power-granting institution. *Kill Your Darlings* instead offers us the juvenile and vagrant possibilities for youths colored with the light of revolution and campy, thoughtless revelries that reveal the underground's profound discoveries. The second review was perhaps more studied and poignant: "[It] is inquisitive about [the Beat Generation's] worth, and the genius of its characters is never assumed."[3] Of course, Burroughs did not sustain this point, noting, "It was Kammerer's doing, really, Kammerer's obsession that provoked the killing."[4]

Still, the sunny solstice of Ginsberg's adult moment will draw the obvious adolescent tale and unleash its questing adventure: Beat lions were hardly established, and thus the nature of their learning was in question. Thus, they are narrated in stereotypical terms, friendly with the idea of a new generation possessing its independent values and symbolic appraisals of their worth in a true narrative. Rhetorically speaking, this vindication in turn spells out the republic's decline, and thus the gnawing need for new conceptions of it to build its galvanizing force for coming generations. I believe that this pretense, to acquire and wield knowledge, was best suited to Ginsberg's anticipatory, facile, and innocent minutes of confusion.

The general comment gained from Ginsberg's father, and from Lucien and his friends, was that man's aesthetic and moral purity scarred the Beats into repeatedly choosing the middle-class man's private moments of subterfuge. Modernist ambiguity was, then, an open door that could repeatedly, if psychotically, denude institutions and their tradition of the stranglehold on knowledge and liberal perspectives during the years following World War II. Professor Steeves' pointed interrogations of Ginsberg inhered the special minutes of the poet's doom: obedience, conformity, and submission were the democratic man's new traits, and America's young were commanded to heed them without any rational understanding. The dour, authoritarian teacher shadows book learning and strophic imagination in 80s movie plots such as in Roger Waters' biography of Pinkie in *The Wall*[5] and again with Robin Williams's students in *Dead Poets Society*.[6] Adolescent themes of disenfranchisement, where academicians gain control of the poet's word and its exercise, catapult Ginsberg through levels of pure ambivalence comprising the making of the intellectual man's destabilization, and so his sweetened, far-fetched romantic testaments versus American materialistic conformity. Special emphasis, too, is given to the screenplay's deeper cultural textures that build the technique for adolescent disclosures about love, knowledge, and society: literary genius puts its ideas to the test using the guise of authority as the persistent villain. As powerful administrative forces constantly seek to destroy the literary group's fundamental ideas with new concepts, ideas, and avenues of life and libation, a more schizophrenic, freed Pax Americana includes discoveries that told a much greater, inclusive social responsibility contesting authoritarian dictations of truth.

Ably, John Bunn's screenplay spelled out the contrast between middle-class dream and renegade daredevil, and maybe the specific moment of crisis that slowly and sporadically would hit the pages of poems in the Beat Generation's early years. The middle-class dream is shadowed in a sunset meeting of Lou and Allen on the porch of Lou's Hoboken home when Allen gets his acceptance letter from Columbia. "Home" is then robbed of its sanity and idyllic American, middle-class outlook six weeks later, when Lou divorces Naomi and sends her into a psychiatric ward. Social mobility rises from the lanky, swarthy, and scheming Carr's takedown of this dream: he serenades Ginsberg atop a desk table, extolling Henry Miller's ode to "a big, cancerous cock," then moving to present his schemes at a liquor- and drug-soaked party at lover David Kammerer's apartment. The speed and calculation of Carr's acquisition is supple, using images and scenes to stimulate sudden conversions and carnality, such as the spoken "Go!" to a Black woman who wants to approach a different man than the one she is seated with.[7] The screened technique, where the scene stops and all motions are temporarily frozen, famously if cavalierly introduces Val Kilmer in *The Doors*, marking a special, imaginative technique in the ballroom dancing scene of Joe Wright's 2012 film, *Anna Karenina*.[8] Thought's suspension through instances of sex and partying references modernist text that stopped time and sound in John Steinbeck's *Of Mice and Men*,[9] fomenting a decisive generational minute of pure comprehension of one's spirit and Self. I believe that these factors assaulted Ginsberg's untested familial and citizen strengths. This was deliberately done, so as to say that Ginsberg could have concocted a very different engagement of conscious semiotics through his poems. The idea that family and love were ripped from him contrasts with the waiting presence and lift of strophes and stanzas, at one point forcing a frustrated Ginsberg to glare angrily at Carr and spit out: "Give me your fucking math!"[10] Literary criticism of poetry's form did not bear the same visible clashes, with Carr curtly denying any studied impact from Ginsberg's true attestation of form: "As far as language went, their communality of language was more in terms of bop-prosody and all this kind of bullshit."[11]

Truth be told, *Kill Your Darlings* managed adolescent psychology and community to stage the movement's first incarnation as being drowned in crime, insanity, and failure. With no attempts to supersede the group's hallucinogenic momentum, only one instance is rewarding to the eye: Carr, Kerouac and Ginsberg's theft of books in the Main Library that are the "sacraments" in the "church."[12] The adolescent riddle's baldness and braveness is ensured because of Ginsberg's gay impotence: he cons a librarian to have sex with him, only for her to find out that he cannot be aroused, and her loudly exclaiming that she suspected as much from a Jewish boy. Kerouac engineers future thefts from the New York Public Library, but is an outsider in the film, living with Edie and giving the literary vagrants a place to stay. Still, the use of supporting actors as background is far more engaging, calculated and generationally sure than with similar escapades and trickery in *Dead Poets Society*[13]: the idea that the Beat movement carried an authorial seriousness is engaged not through poetry, but in the wake of angst and tensions that could turn it into radical ruminations and self-reflections that extract the raw substance of modern man's revolution. This, too, coincides with technology-friendly films and expositing a "coming of age." The riddle, where the hero performs things known to be bad and destructive to the mainstream *ethos*, was part of the character of Winston Smith, commanded to break the rules and expect no rewards in George Orwell's *1984*.[14] The public debacle, embarrassing and sudden, of the stolen books replaced with erotic materials, parallels other seeming victories for the system's most forgotten instances: The Black Panthers, for instance, held up the California Senate in 1967 in *Panther*, our only TV-screened instance that issues a decisive advantage to rebellion from behind aristocratic governmental shadows.[15]

Kill Your Darlings did nothing to address the movement's rhetorical power in the grasp of its romantic adventure: more tightly, we would call it an instance of the Beat Generation's failure to realize true transcendences that would change the ethics of a rapidly growing democracy in the minutes of its greatest power. The generational message may be simplified along the lines of socialist realism: to fight for democracy, one left home and with it the simpler trappings of his loves and sensory happiness, to learn ideologies and theories that forever made him unrecognizable in the precious, savored moment of middle-class, familial humanism. I would say that the loose, happy friendships were interrupted, and gay love was clipped to avoid the intonations of sex's deducible power in Ginsberg's rhetorical and spiritual development. Still, the introduction of a sensitive, much argued urban aesthetic is a meaningful and decisive narrative of transformation. The change from teen to adult ensured that a more populist assessment would carry forth poetry's light and pain into deeper, more penitent reflections, and that the Left's idealistic values had risen from its colonial, pre-modern shackles that attached disintegration and sickness to the much-adored frame tale of modern man's rebellion.

Howl and the Remaking of the Classical Romanticist Tale

Most American undergraduates read very short instances of Beat literature, and Beat writers are ignored in the classroom because the sentiment of their writings weighed their collective political-social agency against the mainstream American story and social scene. "Howl" is purposefully challenging to them—Ginsberg is gay, a drug addict, and a Marxist-influenced radical whose later ambitions included destroying the system in favor of growing hippie idealism. The crunching frustration of Ginsberg's generational debacle, "I saw the best minds of my generation destroyed by madness, starving, hysterical, naked"[16]—allows Robert Epstein and Jeffery

Friedman the rhetorical width to examine Ginsberg in terms of his family, prophecies, and self-inventions through dreams, memories, and even its cartoon tales. As many Beat films greatly expanded narrative story's visual technique, viewers deduce that the producers examine several facets—most notably, family and sexuality, two anxious factors in the makings of literary genius and its true relevance. We might view Ginsberg's reading at the Six Gallery in 1955 as a kind of coming out party—not simply with regards to being gay, but also when underscoring the deception and betrayal that all the audience members may trace to universal truth's precision. My effort is to document how interviews, cartoon narrations, and the trial itself all approximate Ginsberg's construction of rhetorical and moral purpose—the anxious Ginsberg fights with mid 20th century cultural controls and the indifference of late Victorian moral controls. We, as readers of modernist poetry, might then judge sensory, conversational, and institutional anchors as constitutive art and its true symbolism. Audiences thus forge a greater breadth than for Kerouac and Burroughs, since Ginsberg's more authentic persona exhumes his awesome struggles with society and with himself as a penitent moral and literary messenger.

Linda Hutcheon offers a guiding point of semiotic and narrative introduction. *A Theory of Adaptation* spoke to the necessary, dislocative technique: "What both the New Critics and the poststructuralists alike were protesting, in their very different ways, was having recourse to authorial intent as the *sole* arbiter and guarantee of meaning and value in a work of art."[17] Hutcheon's formal statement of literature's unheralded disintegration has, I think, produced wave after wave of scholars who unearth works from the library in the quest for authenticity and authorial purpose. Still, techniques that re-imagine the historical work of literature suppose their imaginative re-development *contra* literary critics bent on enshrining the moment's pure, un-contrived distinction from our ordinary grasp of truth. Our study of "Howl," then, is a labor of contemporary translation through sense-impressions and the conditioned state of historical re-visitation. Hutcheon continued to stress the moment's binary impulse that causes us to register anxiety and anxiousness when constructing prose's spoken expostulations of modern man's "poetry": "In focusing primarily on the textual dimension, of course, it is the *critic* who has the authority, not the author or adapter."[18]

Assuming our reluctance to ensure this point—after all, it is the author who composes the weight of literary metaphor and its context—we may express thoughtfully our minute of incomprehension. This is, at least, important in the light of the author's travels through dream, drugs, sex, and abstraction—key themes that keep us separated from Beat characters. That reluctance, though superficially meaningful, causes us to restrict writing due of its necessary interpretive relationship with persistent labyrinths of mankind's cultural and experiential choice. Yet controversial dialogues about drugs, sex, and revolution breathe specific, semiotic gatherings of man's pluralistic tendencies. How, then, can we imagine what a democracy was, and how do we situate biography against modern man's constructive purpose? Stating "the critic" as the final, ultimate authority multiplies authorial readings, too—there are many imaginative and textual angles to assimilate before we say that a historical or biographical film has caused us to learn more about the dynamic moment of history's controversies. We are likely to deduce even more paths to knowledge if we study anxiety's deepening of the literary wounds that, in realist terms, require us to re-assess the supremacy of American ethics. In short, we as critics held a greater power, and angles of perception were widened to suit true transferences of Leftist agency. I believe that literary and cultural criticism can then use both archival and imaginative critique to increase the moment's presumptive power, accentuating re-writings of the literary canon in terms friendly to students in the classroom holding incomplete ideas of what literary fulfillment is. Hutcheon, then, posed the teacher's technique for being helpful when encouraging student perspectives, thus accentuating his/her genuine breath of studied understandings of American history. Complicating narrative's location in its perceived and simulated angles of perception, too, in modernist notions of story and Self, proclaim the author's liberation from his/her isolation and non-recognition. I believe that the majority of historical films do this, but Ginsberg as an example narrated a wide, complex American history, borrowing a greater license to preach and proselytize from the critics. A screenplay's skill, or the visual technique's concrete divergence, causes us to emphasize humanity's dynamic rebirths, in turn receiving criticism's cross-examining challenges that sought to retain all the elements of literary control, and hence that of the story's power. The greater moment of study bears fruit as it interrupts and disarms theory, opening studies of historical language and technique as it broadens scholarly aptitude. The Beat Generation operated from a special ferment—heretical, profane, and juvenile, they envisaged a broader technique in film, so as to pervert or destroy the annals of literary modernism's reticent, sure calculations of the American family, scene, and education.

    Robert Epstein's 84-minute collage includes a fictional interview with the young, shadowy Ginsberg in his New York City apartment, and a skeletal re-running of the obscenity trial versus the State Department. The plot then interweaves an imagistic reading of "Howl" at the Six Gallery, cartoon vision-narrations of the acolyte's dramatic engagement at the gates of Hell, screen-shot memories of Ginsberg's childhood and adolescence, protégé flicks that include early readings of *Reality Sandwiches* on park benches, and remembrances of Naomi's lonely wandering through divorce, incarceration in a psychiatric ward, and homeless poverty.[19] The true brilliance of Epstein's form owes itself to the fact that he features no controversial, non-canonical instances of Ginsberg's life history. Neatly cropped, the film supposes Ginsberg's rise to stardom to coincide with the cross of adulthood and his prophetic beginning at the Six Gallery in 1955 that opened the door to Blakean recognitions of modern manhood as voice, sight, reflection and evisceration suppose them. The complex image-text synthesis interweaves doubt and realization. It realized actor Joseph Franco's biographical pretense as it maintains temperament and screening eye that limits or redirects Ginsberg's pornographic impulses to poetry and prophecy, dislocating queer minutes of pure, subversive intensity favoring politics. Epstein's cartoon film is friendly with the camera's screening eye that rigorously presents the poem's tale and morphology to children and youths. It, too, accentuated the battling of good and evil in a modern, postindustrial setting. Epstein thus deserved credit for sweeping the Beat imagination of its lewd and comical undercurrents. "Howl's" cross of vindication, versus its legal prohibition, prescribes conversational and technical limitations to otherwise free exercises of Ginsberg's homosexual *forte*, a major point of his ballyhooed pretense to prophecy during the 1960s and 70s.

Gay relationships are neatly located in the spoken word, not in the graphic expose. Thus, focused criticisms of the author arranged its subversive political content when it associated family and prophecy amidst the urban ghetto's prolonged, exclamatory remarks at the Six Gallery reading that had presumed an awakening, one consistent in persona and messianic force with the much greater Civil Rights Movement. Collective statements of radicalized power signal filmed versions of the Left's aggressive, yet crucially admonitory, stasis in movies that transposed the Black Power Movement in *Panther*, The S.C.U.M. Manifesto that informs *I Shot Andy Warhol*,[20] the *brujo's* supernatural kingdom of *The Doors*,[21] and Mahatma Gandhi's pious-sounding exhortations to poor Indians in *Gandhi*.[22] Generational attentions, then, are uplifting and drew a depressive challenge to common forms that bolster the robust fulfillment and intellectual-world realizations of American supremacy. They also prolong and sustain the minute of a young, Jewish male's "coming out," and a spiraling rise to self-realization rising that draws its strength versus imperialism's colossal, unrealistic grip on world power. Epstein assembles the poem, the trial, the vision and visible memories to spell out Ginsberg's biographical pains as he walks and agonizes the modern world's quiet, tedious geographies and stiff-tongued sentimentality. Man's public self, found in voice and ideation, is concentrated in the adolescent debacle, which projects scripture from irreverent, disenfranchised youths and from the mental sickness they sought to cure. Therefore, classical arrangements of story and consciousness echo the divide between profanity and prophecy, stirring up canonical debate about American literature.

It is worth noting why it is more commonplace to use cartoons in films such as these, so as to advance man's comic, sociopolitical engagement of story and experience, versus those which stage theory, studies of modern history, and those of ancient epistemologies favoring mind-altering drugs and their parapsychology. The frame tale's story is colored with instances of geometric patterns and nature-mind rhapsodies, and the confluence of strophes and concepts that distil Ginsberg's pure, divine inspirations. The answer is simple and abundant: drugs, love, and God represented man's post-affections in a godless world that had enshrined capital and class status in Protestant, White America. Hence, man's persistent denaturing, and his irrational-soaked personal immersions in the fragmentary, polarizing dictations of truth, welcomed comic extensions and colorations of the human landscape, projecting a new gothic where romantic Mankind might languish, hide, dream, and pontificate. Cartoons project man's everyday humor and his plainness, even though they also aggravate art's failure to sketch man's subjective leaps of self-concentration. Psychedelic-influenced writings during the 1960s, including those of Ginsberg, presumed the exact functioning and wrote more ideal reflections of light, color, shape, and humanity. Scientific realism in the movies of William S. Burroughs inhere visions and spoken shards of the ideal state, yet we return to the fact that the Beats depend upon Black, urban, underclass, preliterate intensities of experience, writing from man's rejection of, and not his ascension to, status and recognition. In the case of Burroughs, this did not limit his journey toward knowledge. For Ginsberg, self-realizations were more painful, and religious romanticism languishes and suffers behind the joking, criminal, *fellatio*-riddled exterior that commandeers hippies to adopt Eastern wisdom and its tumultuous *praxis*. Revolution, in short, rose from self-identifications in the underworld's grip and from Beat followers political rejection and racisms denying Ginsberg strength and power. Epstein's film points to operative tensions with Kerouac, who enjoys a much greater fulfillment that did not need to be investigated: his appearances *Howl* include an apartment scene where he tries to get a blow job, and his innocent, contemplative, and sure presence at the Six Gallery reading.[23] Orality, too, presumed the form's rejection to be the instrument of one's life and personal growth: "Coming out" was attached to a long, wandering pattern of recognition and realization versus the lifeless, wicked phantom, Moloch. Ginsberg's gay moment does not interrupt his self-realization's epistemology: his ethnic, regional, and conscious grasp of experience was broad and projected the ascension of his voice to angelic triumph. Suddenly, gays are holy, holding the locket of innocence, hence of power, in heterosexual America. The tribute was thus self-reflexive: surrendering political agency to powerful male, heterosexual gods in the Hindu and Buddhist traditions stirred in Ginsberg a new fecundity of prophecies that divorce themselves from adolescent insecurity. Ginsberg's career is thus titled and centered on his persona's beginning minute: he is Western and European, not Indian, and so depends upon his youth.

Also, I believe that we would misunderstand Beat culture if we dismiss the completeness of Kerouac's demand for confession among his protégés, whether they were gay or straight. Thus, we presume that Beat intensities of form engendered a slew of narrative techniques that Epstein studies and codifies with skilled and poignant visual and cinematographic renditions of poetry as a narrative form. Where Aldous Huxley rigorously documents the religious and scriptural development of "non-human images" to coincide with LSD's "living geometries,"[24] Ginsberg's imaginative technique might shadow and promote the descending, haunting profane verse, queer pornographies, and drugged mendicancy and sickness that force him break his material dependences. In other words, drugs and dreams allowed Ginsberg to escape Victorian moral and social control. The sharp-looking Ginsberg knocks out the pretense of Beat, "There was just a bunch of guys tryin' to get published,"[25] then adds revolutionary and pornographic colorings into semiotic and graphic constitution of Beat Generation as the underground's literary engine:

> What I did was diddling around, finding a pretty shape. There's only been a few times when I've reached a state of complete control. Howl and one or two other poems. I wouldn't want my daddy to see what was[...] in there. So I assumed it wouldn't be published, so I'd write anything I want in there.[26]

Ginsberg's gabbing did not shorten Kerouac's very clear expectation that the form of writing be dislocated so as to liberate visions and aesthetic realism from its material-industrial shackles. He wrote about his discovery of the word *eschatological* in 1949, "Ah well, great minds obviously run the same course. Now, of course, it will be necessary for me to work out a new idea."[27] Mankind's moral necessity was quickly driven to its response from the rhetorical breadth of literary experiences and from within the new metaphor's intensity: "When do we break out of forms? When we know what a form is for."[28] Kerouac adds the decisive street input: "In America it is understood that marijuana is smoked by degraded sex-fiends in dens, by Negroes and Mexicans, and members of the hip generation, and jazz musicians, making them crazy."[29]

Beat geographies put in place the added syntactic stress on heresy and self-divination, key anchors in the Beat nucleus's popularity and promotion. Was Epstein's presentation faithful to the history of the Beat ideas? My response would consider Ginsberg to be both personal and prophetic: his reading, or at least in binary realizations of Self that applies cartooned visions to the stanzas of "Howl," depends upon a skilled writing of Beat history that "Howl" intersected with. Providing place and figure attends to the Beat imagination's specific locations of its power and urban authenticity: the angle of Ginsberg's resplendent anxieties lengthens the lingering minute's special intensity.

Franco's reading of "Howl" adapted and entrenched writing's vocalism: its focus reached for urban manhood's redemptive dreaming state, and its inclusion in resurgent moral dilemmas at midcentury. The treading of a tight narrative interfaces with the projection of ascending purpose, reflection, and self-immolation: thus, the screenplay augments the development of poetry as identity and biography. Franco stands in the light, isolation, and expectancy of the pulpit at the Six Gallery. Wearing glasses and dressed in the familiar college preppie format of slacks, shirt and glasses, he labors through his isolation as the underground American man making his ultimate speech and paean out to his loved, believing multitude. This is backed up through his confessions: when he ejects, "Really, I wrote Howl for Jack,"[30] the screen cuts to Ginsberg enunciating the free verse meter easily, "Benzedrine face screens trains skeletons arguing leaps rooftops howls"[31] as a tangle of images simulate the receding train against the silhouette of a woman boasting lipstick and a cigarette.[32] The screen shot moves to a crucified, bald Jesus emerging from the train's light,[33] extending the vagrant pietism that haunted Cody Pomeray in Chapter 1 of *Visions of Cody*. Divine light and one's angelic deliverance from the sins and illnesses of materialistic, postindustrial excess build *Howl*'s frame tale and nourish Kerouac's moment of the Soul as a pure, unfettered reflection. When the page's typewritten words rise into notes and a saxophone player spills out his gold light, the illusion narrates opposite scenes from the trial, the Six Gallery reading, and the interview.[34]

With young, college-age kids squatting on the club's ground, and a smiling and expectant Kerouac posing his glance thoughtfully at the words, it is also clear that *Howl* enshrined the undergraduate's penultimate moment of truth. The polarity is absolute: Ginsberg owns a divide where the health, innocence and stability of the world's greatest democracy lay in ruins because our leaders and notables had betrayed America's sacred trust in her institutions. Audiences are given a full historiography from Ginsberg's childhood haunts and home in Hoboken, thus stating one's middle-class innocence as the operative factor. The main character is shadowed in his ride in a stolen car that later betrays the Beat Generation's criminal enterprises in a crash. We are also pacified when registering shades of Ginsberg's temperament, with Naomi's poor isolation and shiftlessness turned into a photo of a senile, elderly Naomi loitering at a park. Scenes featuring Ginsberg's friendship with Kerouac innocently replay literary stereotypes. At one point, Ginsberg heatedly tries to read *Reality Sandwiches* to a disgusted Kerouac; at another, Kerouac arrives to receive his blowjob, but Marylou walks in holding a bag of groceries.[35] In truth, the film doctors most of the nudity and graphic sex out of the plot. This was, I believe, done to transform Ginsberg's gay fucking into gay writing that stated its "fuck" in the prose. By the time Ginsberg exclaims, "Cocksucker in Moloch!"[36] well beyond the time's conventional rhetoric, the film minute captured the Beat moral communion and its serious interrogation of America's moral centrism, and not its sexed disintegration. It was not to say that this fission between Kerouac's testament to his insanity and his excavations of form that dissolves and romanticizes them again would be deliberately taken up. It is much more likely that viewers will report they saw the torch's passing, from idealism and humor to moralism and protest. Again, "Howl" is the only Beat work that most undergraduates read in college: its loud denunciations of word and meaning attest to the perverse supremacy of materialism-moralism in today's ethical construction of Self. Thus, gay romanticism could either state the subject's romantic feeling and imageries of his mind and body, or explain in the most corrosive, scalding sociopolitical terms, where homosexuality grew and prospered due to modernism's decadent, godless and permanent rejection of love.

Instances of the obscenity trial of *Howl* state the literary movement's resultant optimism and so complicate socialist perspectives on Ginsberg's authorial origins and on the validity of his poetry. Bill Morgan's cataloging of Ginsberg's letters to Ferlinghetti in *Howl on Trial* is noteworthy for the ambivalence of purpose and the gutting of adolescent ruminations of the Self. In a January 15, 1957, letter, Ginsberg pushed him to drop the dedication to Lucien Carr, hastily ejecting, "if the whole thing is printed and bound already, have it done all over again and bill me for the second printing."[37] Yet biographical truth is simply put: optimism graced Ginsberg's writing form very early after the publication of *Howl and Other Poems*, and so much so that we revisit the Beat Generation's collective assessment in rhetorical terms friendly to massive, super-ethnic and super-ethnological rewritings of poetry closer to Kerouac's root aestheticisms that cried out for its home amidst its political idealism. Free transformations were adeptly promoted in 1970's *Indian Journals*. I think it is a worthy moment to star the movement's free translation as an instance of its massive re-development of culture and imagery into a massive, romantic, didactic engine. Gay romanticism quickly absorbs the East's mythic, poetic and narrative pretense to man's freedom and his multi-referential rejection of modern realism in a November 27, 1962, entry:

> "There are many much Babus in Bombay"—"Who your guru?"—"I have guru—In X-town." One (says Peter) was green vested with manycolored pockets & a green purse hanging that looked like a Vaishnav bead teller disguise—with which he'd left with green turban'd fellow. But the 4 or five rings on his friend's finger! And his own green ring, and one in black with a gold band around it, & one maybe in white.
> Then I waved my arm in a slow circle & fluttered my fingers like feet walking the long winding road to go.[38]

If quick adaptations such as these spell out the generation's adaptive technique, and therefore the mobility and unchallengeable strength of the primary theme's dictum, we are likely to assume that the Beat movement's political-cultural power had sprung from modernist immersion. Because of this, we stage parables against modern man's scaffolding of material and institutional signifiers, ensuring sameness and non-transference. Could we, then, operate the testament that knowledge, culture, and community will change, and even change so rapidly that we might jettison the class-sure Beats into a new dynamic of material self-appraisals? The trial itself is pared down to America's democratic essentials: the move is given added strength by the prosecution's testament that "Howl" wasn't literature at all, speaking of no governable experience.[39] University of California professor Mark Schorer fluently lays the ground for modernism's total re-evaluation from eyes and hands that were beyond the pale, projecting the underclass's agile, wieldable re-writing of democracy and modernity in optimal terms:

> Q. In other words, you don't have to understand the words to—
> A. You don't understand the individual words taken out of their context. You understand the whole impression that is being created and in this first part particularly, where I have already used the word surrealist to describe it. You can no more translate that back into logical prose English than you can say what a surrealistic painting means in words, because it's not prose. Poetry is a heightened form of language through use of figurative language and rhythm, sometimes rhyme.[40]

Schorer assumed the form of modernist teaching—the tradition for "Howl" was well established and is casually understandable. It is noteworthy that his rejection of canonical poetic conventions established the moment's power in place and experience. Tying the sign's visible and potent location to its legitimate theoretical moment, Schorer adroitly broadens man's perceivable horizons when suggesting the recurrence of Beat materiality, and thus that the chain of material and philosophic signs testify to a greater social being and more dynamic *elan* for telling democratic verse's cultural and psychic truths. The testimony is rendered smoothly—a waiting parable of experience that Schorer snatches from the annals of officialdom that hides its art in minutes of *bourgeois* fear and self-guilt. Teaching "Howl" thus assumed a much greater moment of possibility, and trysts with learning admitted its perceivable experience away from mainstream mankind's predominant institutions—law, education, church, and the workplace. Schorer's case—the case for freedom—easily rendered the movement's dynamic *métier* and so cultural and lifestyle explorations friendly to liberal political and societal ethics. Epstein's trial, in short, projects democratic pluralism as it gave the go-ahead for poetry's further explorations away from the West, the Church, and modern technology. In doing so, he summarizes the young generation's living ambition and its moral ascension away from Protestant conservatism.

In the truest of senses, the mélange of screenplay with cartoon re-narrations and family history that builds "Howl" and its reading parlays a sophisticated technique that sustains the voice's utterance and the urgency of that utterance. Synchronous with Ginsberg's private and meditated urge for expression and self-realization, *Howl*'s scenes demonstrate anxieties that weighed American man's origins and his education's error—thus, the need for a burdened soul to "come out" as a legitimate social messenger. Lest we harm the poem's Judeo-Christian origins, we would be wise to attain the poem's stated moment of vision to be a counter-force to the much more prominent "official" histories directing our spiritual responses. Stating a generation's frustration accomplishes the basic critical angle. The mind's dislocation, in doing so, refocuses a painful, romantically deep history and cold, mainstream authority as its eternal antagonist. Agonized genius and nonlinearity supposes the American experience to be dynamic, instructional, and holy. In these regards, examinations of doubt coincide with telltale realizations in the poem's fully angled, deeply referential performance. The heralding of Ginsberg's true sentimentality bears the stain of indoctrination, yet held many needed points of substantiation to engage the spirit of democracy. This meant taking up lingering, cinematic doubt that plagued great American figures in first-run biographical film characters such as Malcolm X in 1992's *Malcolm X* and Ray Charles in 2004's *Ray*, or even the ever emblematic Jim Morrison in 1991's *The Doors*,[41] all of whom resurface fundamental anxieties that build much of their social message's positive uplift.

The partial juxtaposition of poetry with the necessary and moderating power of fiction—where critical attentions are more prevalent and sustaining—in the casting of Allen Ginsberg, lends itself to criticism of the movement's origins and more provocative tailings of their voice and emphasis. Romanticism, then, was a carefully nested force craving the outside world's input, and so limits criticism's pervasive hold on culture and consciousness. It must be said that film narrations of Allen Ginsberg repeat the time period's sentimental focus. At a glance, they played without the rhetorically sweet frieze of Eastern travels and journals, ripped out from torrid excavations, modern-splitting examinations of drug imaginations, and unwashed, unkempt mysticism of incompletely narrated themes, ideas, gods and popular translations of the Middle East, India and China. They instead reach the wake of a sweetened understanding condensing its more radical-sounding overtures to favor Ginsberg's academic environs, lengthening his immersive shadow. I believe, then, that films weigh against Deborah Baker's examination of Ginsberg's guilt and anxiety in *A Blue Hand*.[42] The argument's reverse, building aggressive technique and straight, purely thematic answers to one's heretical contentions, suggest that family and community point to a mature focus that tracks and treads a genesis holding wide-ranging possibility in its true grasp. That being said, it is worthwhile to note that the films ignore wider critical analysis, thoughtfully tending to Ginsberg's persona, character, and youth, three operative forces that in the end replay maturity against the diminutive portrait of a boyish, insecure queer who confirms his more masculine counterparts' positive invention when directing the rise of new cultural performativity.

Ginsberg and Documentary Film

The Life and Times of Allen Ginsberg

Jerry Aaronson's 84-minute film, *The Life and Times of Allen Ginsberg*, offers a life-spanning biographical story linked with critical biographies about the Beat Generation. The film tracks the elder poet's stint with the hippie counterculture and rock music, includes analysis from musicians and literary friends, chronicled activism culminating in the Chicago protests of 1968, excerpted key and controversial interviews with William Buckley, and duly repeated instances of Ginsberg's poetry during the film. At a glance, Aaronson did not take biographical chances in many parts of the film, instead sustaining a coherent Self that had treaded the growth and interaction of liberal political climates in the United States and Europe. Nonetheless, Aaronson focused on instances that dredge up modernist sensibilities, and indeed upon the altered mind's sensitivity as the maker of truth and justice in today's aesthetic and moral universe. Commentaries by Amiri Baraka, Norman Mailer, Timothy Leary, Abbie Hoffman and Edith Ginsberg, Allen's stepmother, retell the sensitivity, beauty, and freshness of liberal perspectives. Though references to Jack Kerouac are limited, they too entrench the modernist example, advancing the collective portrait as central in Ginsberg's crucial *métier*.

Still, I believe that *The Life and Times* carried through interviews and videography its very capable estimation of the poet's romantic, hallucinogenic, and prophetic themes. Commentaries from friends and family approach poetry to recast modern, technological interferences with democracy, and the distortion and distension of poetry's traditionally masculine focus. It also builds the engaging portrait of Ginsberg's mother, Naomi, as a partial muse who instilled the matriarch's peculiar move towards middle-class romanticism, upholds and solemnizes the pain when seeing these encodings of Self ripped away when she was committed to a hospital. I feel that the language and cadences of Ginsberg's poems, too, feature a poet with considerable and mobile skill and with his enunciations and persistent, romantic spell upon the audience. Whether seated among hundreds of young listeners, recalling the brink of his transcendence at the Six Gallery reading in paintings, re-reading classics such as "Howl" and "Kaddish," chanting "Om Nama Shivaya" at the Chicago protests, or singing the lament for his father, Louis, the post–Beat Ginsberg weighed in considerable artistic skill and was an engaging poet in full command of his modern/ancient, romantic/technological sensibilities.[43] The word's power is evident in all of the readings: more, the film's visual technique and simulation, using Super 8 films and films of the protests and Congressional hearings, added the human portrait of a strong, populous, youthful and aggressive liberal movement that understood the spoken, Eastern word and its true relationship with protests, communities, and the moment's ethical realism. Visual technique also included films of Ginsberg among his Beat friends such as Neal Cassady and photographs that include Kerouac's New York apartment and nudes that recalled Ginsberg's introduction to his lifetime mate, Peter Orlovsky.[44] I believe that, since the narrative technique of commentaries was quite simple and didactic, that the film's living instances of Ginsberg anoint a special, peculiar dynamic that highlights the writer's romanticism and pursuit of compassion. Given also Beat scholarship's detailing of the author's homosexual origins, the film's general presentation directs us more fairly to a Ginsberg who was beset with lifelong anxieties and wish-fulfillments that came from a period of heavy, emotional suffering found in his poems. At the same time, Aaronson committed the biographical error of omitting Ginsberg's considerable East travels, deflating the ethnographic detail of his more aggressive hippie-era poems found in 1971's *The Fall of America*. Still, the activist's roughened portrait of the activist and public figure as liberal social messenger courted rock, student youth, and Eastern Europeans. Thus, strong hippie mobilizations favor the literary work's uniqueness, giving the poet many opportunities to expand his story as one that had sprung from a novel, complex base away from his friends.

Generally speaking, fresh narrative perspectives on poetry as an art form call our attention to the author's political values and to the integrity of those values. These conceptions of oneself link American poetry to the instances of societal change and maturity. Of course, Ginsberg inhered many unique bibliographic resonances. Nevertheless, reading leftist poetry from the standpoint of revolution, hallucinations, and modern man's vulgar and comic demise at the hands of mainstream insincerity and insensitivity usher in the poem's dislocating impact. Yet this is hardly the case with Ginsberg. He reads with thoughtful confidence and elocution that girds his palpable humanity, is well-received and, even in the most adversarial confrontations with the government-military "system," confident and expressive of romantic truths as they began with drugged or sexual mysticism. The best of these is found at a 1968 reading on William F. Buckley's *Firing Line*, where a bearded Ginsberg read his best version of LSD tripping, 1967's "Wales Visitation."[45] Pure, natural and sweet cadences of Nature, and of its intricacies and the decipherable, arithmetic arrangement of the elements and perceptions, are well received, pleasing the otherwise reactionary Buckley: he smiles, showing his false teeth in the middle.[46] We are given the American mainstream's ideal: with or without drugs, Americans understood Nature's simple, pure, and manifold apperceptions to comprise a timeless, manifold theme, and a unifying one which all of us could enjoy. It was not to state agreement: the Buckley interviews include the host's derision of drugs, prominently stating his supposition of their political irrelevance as something "naïve." I think that, too, stating the happy collision of liberal and conservative intellectual forces against the multitude of students as they were gassed and arrested in Chicago, and Ginsberg's nurturing role for the students, treads a dynamic engagement again confirming his political maneuvering and power.[47] At all stages, gradients of liberal learning and its relevance compose the notes of Ginsberg's resilience and beauty, and even the possible impact upon future generations that had not read modernist poetry without the canon's prescriptions. Still, techniques are simple, leading to Ginsberg's instruction of students at Naropa University. In these examples, contact and semantic recognition of one's conscious symbols, and hence the technique for the poet's syntactic dislocation of form, elicit the younger generation's smiles and approval.[48] I would say that these were not as easy to achieve as with the rock form, which seems far easier to understand, and had carried with it emblems of the senses and mind that speak with more vocalism.

Ironically, the film's references to Ginsberg's lover, Peter Orlovsky, were studiously limited and avoided the content of his works, travels, and adventures: we are instead pacified with their meeting's sweet, enjoyable memory and how it had communicated love's true message to Ginsberg. I think that viable points of comparison existed with films that included Ginsberg's peers. Films related to Paul Bowles, for example, retold the author's cold rejection of love and his antipathy and silence when approaching death: this remote human agency lengthened modernist shadows of doom and anti-realism in his world.[49] I believe, too, that biographical films covering Jack Kerouac miss a much greater chance in that love and belonging in a relationship omitted long periods of marriage, collapsing complex negotiations and antagonisms between him and his lovers. When a smiling, reticent Ginsberg admits that he felt "accepted as a human being for the first time,"[50] the authorial statement operates a distinct power. Love entrenches Ginsberg's penitent, meditative romanticism, and his emotional values and sympathies where other writers had retreated or lost the happiness and feeling for romantic knowledge and aesthetic truth. The crucial emblem of "love" transcended Bowles, who had said "it was an obsession,"[51] and Kerouac's decelerating bust of responsibility from the pages of *Desolation Angels* where the Beats were "bums/nothing but bums."[52]

Aside from the poet's stated values, biography intermixed Ginsberg's family tales and the nest of relationships with his father and mother to augment a considerably divergent academic and literary delivery. I think it should be emphasized that Beats had navigated the casual redirection from parents to friends, from adolescence to underground youth. They encouraged us to free ourselves from our communities and to interpret liberal activism and "world" perspective to mean the rejection of parental, middle-class American morality. Yet, the continuance of Ginsberg's compassion for his mother and father, finds its way into poetry and music, and Edith Ginsberg's terse recollections of the Beats' early days re-entrenched very different outcomes for leftist poetry. After all, it was Ginsberg who courts the counterculture's masses during its escalating clashes with American military-government power. Also, we might as easily readdress point of view—Ginsberg's deep biography breathed a deep textual and sensory reminiscence that recalled the movement's attachments to place and its social pretensions. Thus, viewers adapt narrative chances that suggest that his was a unique and self-ingratiating perspective, and one that had its own epistemological powers that could escape his elders' subordination and mentoring. I think the time has come to assess the perspective of independence and allow its thoughtful introduction of form. Of course, shuffling these intellectual and moral possibilities through film allow us to gauge whether the movement was dynamic and could sustain its professed values as postmodern materiality and stereotypes co-opt and transform communitarian emblems of the Self and their social indoctrinations. We might as easily sustain what Kerouac refused to do in "Man, Am I The Granddaddy o' the Hippies"[53]: namely, that cultural stereotypes and media eclipse modernism's beatific, waiting gaze, and thus that the purity of Ginsberg's message and demeanor would build the poet's ethical simplicity, and so his tenacious, seething invective that speaks from streets and through Nature's idylls.

Incisive commentaries by Imamu Amiri Baraka, Norman Mailer, Abbie Hoffman, and Timothy Leary nicely augmented the biographical frame tale, commending the artistry and nascence of the poet's world prophecies and the sweetness of his aesthetic revelries that had stemmed from radical essays and poems during the 1950s and 60s. Commentators recall the beauty of the poet's form and its public manner that gave its sting of importance. It is even more likely, then that they project greater windows of learning and mass democratic political development of narcotics subcultures in the United States. In a stricter biographical context, they project developments that cause writers and thinkers to be interdependent. Leary gave the most substantive generational inclusion of drugs' impact upon "new consciousness" and wider social and moral rhetoric:

> During the session we sat around the table and Allen started spitting out his concern at the misuse of drugs in America and the need to have a positive approach to uh, psychedelic drugs and uh, instigated in my mind a, uh, basically the politics of ecstasy, the notion that we would have to go around the country turning on influential artists, writers, poets, uh, philosophers, uh, so that they could report back to us what they were getting for their brain activity-made experiences, and uh, then could put out to the world the benefit of their trip.[54]

Leary's comments breathed its visible drug-influenced pathologies, and the burden of his hallucinogenic use when figuring their examples illustrative of drug theorizations and studies. Leary had lost some of the natural flair for spoken words and elocution, hacking his concept of "the politics of ecstasy" into an irrelevant stab that compared poorly with the more skilled orations of Ginsberg who, while suited and before the Congressional Committee, pointed out drug use's pragmatism while encouraging Americans to understand each other. The visible portrait confused audiences because of Leary's stance as a professor: "I knew I was never gonna be part of that system, being part of the liberated, bohemian artistic mind."[55] Leary's purposive statement ignored the depth of his investigations of psychedelic drugs and their theoretical understanding. Although Leary's ascription to crucial difference appears truthful, calling attention to the art of cultural being as a social messenger, viewers may doubt the cover up of what was a much deeper relationship. Still, the operative pragmatic comment suggests Ginsberg's fieldwork with artists and writers—the galvanizing cultural forces for the hippies during the 1960s. To say that psychedelic-influenced writings had fanned out into the broader community through literary analysis suggests its growth, sophistication, and direct challenge to existing epistemologies that extol mass democratic social force. The film tracks and proves the truth of this vehicle, with prayer, intoxication, and mass protest being coherent, meaningful, and directed at greater conscious realizations.

Mailer's commentary, narrowed down to the explication of poetic form, again targets Ginsberg's stream of political messages and his sharp estimations poetic form. Of "Howl," he surmised that:

> I do recall the poem had an immense effect on me and I felt at least that Ginsberg would make a poet, a genius. I hadn't read any poetry with that charge. I knew he was going to make a revolution in the consciousness of the time.[56]

Mailer's paternal tone, or rather the admission that more critical and dismissive commentary found in *Advertisements for Myself* omitted the writer's intellectual perusal of the vocal changes of the public figure as writer and its application to the mind and spirit at mid-century, allows him considerable distance. It must be said that Mailer, by the 1960s, had given societal relevance to the Beat Generation writers such as Michael McClure.[57] Ginsberg, then, might be an exception: his form's brilliance counters and erases Kerouac's serious, if rambling, experiments with form, retracing form's humanist origins. "Charge" thus mobilizes youth generations or simply emphasizes the romantic man's aggressive moment of explication: there would be relevance and impact from the form, without the stain of social pretensions that were for Mailer unguarded and untrue. Amiri Baraka, who co-wrote and edited *Yugen* with Ginsberg and Kerouac, also assented: "[Howl] had that anger in it. It attracted me, even before I knew that I was angry myself. It was the voice of young people protesting the disgusting, inhuman culture that we had grown with."[58] This admission was hard in coming: by then, Baraka was a pan-Africanist and a "Crow Jim" prophet of radical Black masculinity and his quest for *Umwelt*. He identifies his passion and vocal sympathy with the virtue of Beat perceptions, too, from a common identification of modern American culture's solstice. The moment's courage, or rather the courageous rise to prophecy through its self-expression, is nicely documented, re-introducing Baraka's own legend and suggesting that more could be learned from "Howl" when it spoke pertinent social messages. McClure advanced the counterculture's casual rhetoric about bourgeois critique: according to him, the 1950s "was a time of intense psychic pain because of the alienation and deep polarization."[59]

Commentaries include those with folk music star Joan Baez, who attests to protest's spontaneity and novelty, and Abbie Hoffman, who champions Ginsberg's commitment to achieving peace: these are overlaid with film reels of Bob Dylan shuffling signs that included words from his song, "The Times They Are A' Changin'."[60] Overall, I think that Ginsberg's poetic intensity and beauty are the most prized characteristics: those, along with the purported mission to save humanity, accelerate his writing's public expression and his attention to prophecies that gradually weld together the disparate countercultural factions such as environmentalists, human rights activists, drug reformers, and communalists.

The poems, when seen in today's context within the poet's aged, generous and blissful gaze far from Orlovsky and the press, established the form's legitimacy in a manner that the printed verse often fails to. The older Ginsberg is human in his aged, haggard reflections, but incisive when pulling together words and dactylic and iambic strophes. Nowhere was the form's emotional intensity, or the pearly beauty of iambic revelation that spoke to British Romanticist motifs of light and simplicity in poems about Naomi. Using occasional crossing of iambic and dactylic meter, Ginsberg intones while reading "Kaddish":

> O glorious news that bore me from the words,
> myth that taught me life and taught me music.
> Tortured and beaten in the skull,
> What mad hallucinations the damned that drove me
> Out of my skull
> Death which is the mother of the universe
>
> I decided I should shut up and be shy, be goofy
> And I found that people who were sweeter than we want
> And I listened and they tell me about it.[61]

I think the important rhetorical parable notes the movement away from meter to showcase the words and concepts, and the spoken voice's special attunement to their inclusion in form. Ginsberg's poetic tradition, elastic and timeless, absorbed modern impulses and graphic shards that often communicate modern paralysis and sickness. Emotions that were derived from tragedy, such as the separation of mother from son, repeat the same deep organic and sensory feelings that Kerouac attached to his father's death and constituting a greater, reflective mercy for Ginsberg and a tenderness that volubly advances the poetic form and its unique brilliance. Links with traditional modernist poetry were also strong: concrete and filled with sharp and painful motifs and their tale, the form calculated the emotion's pained release from modern unhappiness and insanity. We are given the ultimate sense that Ginsberg specially threaded his humanity, or rather his incomplete understanding of the world throughout his life.

This refreshed minute thus resurrects the romanticism's form, and its engagement of industrial non-recognition.

The Life and Times of Allen Ginsberg missed several biographical chances at realizing a more potent Eastern mythology and morphology. Still, it incorporates a broad range of syntactic and epochal elements into the greater interrogation of modernist form as it approaches decades of material-conservative resurgence. More than the aggressive documentation of the poet's relevance and significance as a public figure, the film anchored poetry and its rebirth in political-social navigations away from the private *salon*, while preserving the form's true intimacy. It is safe to say that Ginsberg, the most vocal and publicly notorious of the major Beat writers, wasn't the most read or adored: this, too, accentuated the verbal form, and its skillful navigations of modern experience.

Three

William S. Burroughs
The Films and His Postmodern Techniques of Reinvention

Critical studies of William S. Burroughs's films developed their thematic analyses from five roughly consistent themes of the author's self-indoctrination. I think that audiences will re-assess the impact of the study of narcotics and narcotic-influenced narratives, adopting themes of self-dislocation and reconstruction to gain more details about liberal politics. We also receive a strong treading of Burroughs's gay love life and the anxiety of ambition, whereby he became an outlaw to destroy love's simple, poetic utterance. Further, we absorb instances of Beat origins and their youthful exchanges that pushed Burroughs to find his social-political *métier* that we are more familiar with and in favor of. Strong interview appearances from Burroughs rock "family" attribute the communitarian idea from the Beat Generation's unspoken doldrums: protégé contributions to the narcotic statesman's testaments and prophetic pretense are many and fluent. Finally, films and documentaries are suited to the postmodern technique for re-formatting Burroughs's consciousness and character. Attentions to postmodern screening, music, and characterizations allow Burroughs the chance at cross-generational understandings, and to transform gothic techniques that speak of postmodern *clichés* encompassing poetry's urban consumption and adoption of social routines. I think that Burroughs's films took the same operative chances as did other postmodern-leaning films that duplicate literature's history and works of fiction: this method ensured the addict's special moment of consumption, hence his redemption.

I believe that it is an ideal time to give credit to Burroughs's adolescent imagination and the completeness of his epistemological studies, to document trends away from feeling and innocence and through the dynamic of a post-universe that speaks and overstates the author's criminal life and friendships. This shadow grew from Burroughs's mature pose as a criminal and narcotic adventurer, leaving no room for dramatic Orient re-conceptions that determine critical Eastern archaeology for decades. Because we, the viewers, did not take Burroughs's contributions to *knowledge* seriously at all, indeterminate emphases distort yet simplify transferences of youthful, imagination-studded meaning. It then calls into question the youth's moment of true agency, at a time when knowledge professed its materialistic, and therefore non-transparent, impact upon us, privileging its content away from the radical writer's specific thought. We could then ask, appropriately, what knowledge meant for its class consumption and narrative transference. Burroughs's life, marriage, and drug addiction call our attention to mankind's class sterilization, filling our imagination with the penitent, depressive weakness of drugged consciousness, social spheres, and narratives that blare its unkempt, barbaric wisdom. What would it mean, for occult knowledge to bear popular meaning and relevance? In our learning context, what did it mean for children to create knowledge and conscious narrative? Did youthful innocence hold in itself a chance to fight man's patriarchal sameness? Was tripping through crime and decadence a moment of sickness or one to spell freedom, and a renewed search for mankind's teleological origins? Archaeological questions of character and valor complicate our attempts to project a meaningful narcotics epistemology that repeats class subjugation.

Introductions to the specific crux of Burroughs's literary imagination intersect with ingenuity and innovation in his 1961 short story, "Over the Hills and Far Away." When we situate his discovery of psilocybin while in Tangier, and repeated overtures to the Reich Orgone Accumulator, plus the narco-epistemology and ethnographies to be found in 1959's *Naked Lunch* and 1989's *Interzone*, "Over the Hills and Far Away" maps literary forms that embodied thematic developments of modern super-consciousness to include art and imaginative themes analogous to science fiction. Specific intonations of discovery and agency were to be located in the thought—and imaginative—foci of an adolescent boy. The limerick of discovery is found in impoverished, innocent, and ruined Oriental territories:

> Johnny could hear bells tinkling as ragged boys drove goats through the square and he saw women with veils carrying tins of water on their heads and open stalls where men were making shoes and furniture by the light of kerosene lamps—but nobody seemed to see the machine—they can't see us unless I want them to [...].[1]

The closely guarded eye, or rather the eye's visual metaphor which begets modern man's social expression, was carefully linked with the innocence of thought and dreams, posing invention's practical, modernist innocence and the magic realism of man's irrational discoveries:

> The machine burst like a kaleidoscope inside his head; throwing out pieces of colored light that fell into shape like a jigsaw puzzle. A little man of about a foot high,

made of blue flames, jumped up and down inside cylinder. He wore gas-flames blue overalls the color of his sparkling eyes.[2]

Such readings gave considerable impact to biographical and adaptation films whose crucial moment is Burroughs's impetus for discoveries. Modernist ingenuity and creativity were located within the specific whims of a gifted child whose collective talents lay unrecognized in the form of romanticist dreaming. We are given enough material to build the theme of man's resolution from his daily and elemental problems due to Burroughs's childish ingenuity. The unbound, unafraid acolyte held within him more innate perceptions and thoughts that foretold years of concrete dialogues about man's capacity to manage his life and environment from his studies, papers and journals.

With this as background, it is just as likely that Burroughs's films entirely miss the mark. Instead, audiences were given long accounts of his battles with preconceived yet remote sickness, and even the dearth of true points of reference in his studies. Published sources did confirm the fact: works as liberal-themed as 1963's *The Yage Letters* and 1984's *The Burroughs File* found Central and South American geographies and signs that were meant to be humorous and vague. Yet we find that "Over The Hills And Far Away" suited Burroughs's true innocence against his landmark, underground symbolism. In short, the studied portrait sheds light on a thoughtful, ingenious elder man who attempts to change symbol-image-culture relationships in the modern world, tapping an essential innocence given to his favorites over the years. Modern man's identity as it was develops and is spoken through narcotics, too, depends on people as much as it did upon the developed chain of literary and cultural symbols that enshrined drug addiction to be a narrative social force.

Deliberately, it seemed, Burroughs was not the man people said he was, but the door for examining subjectivity allows us to project him to be a redeeming social force, far from the pages of *On the Road* or *Naked Lunch* and as a determinate social force that draws itself from the author's peculiar stance or rigor. We will begin with the operating narrative fiction from Burroughs's beginnings as a famous international author, amidst the ribald-flavored discoveries, literary tensions and growth that fan a very different import for the quintessential "Beat," who clambered into the world's antithetical realm away from Kerouac's paternal gaze.

The Making of *Naked Lunch* and *Interzone*

The *Beat Hotel* and the Movement's Second Nucleus

Beat Hotel includes Allen Govenar's 82-minute film that appeared in 2010, starring Burroughs, Ginsberg and Corso as the primary nucleus of

Beat literary and cultural production and so "queered" the novel moment of *Naked Lunch's* epic-like creation. Govenar's presentation of the Beat Hotel, patrons, and literary/avant-garde investigations of Paris communities and experiences spoke its broad didactic claims that profess gay counterculture to be a persistent liberal and underground force in the Western world. We might note the obvious theme: its writers and friends held no quarter with masculinity's mannerly, romantic inculcations of male erotic and societal power. This focus was debatable: Ginsberg confesses his protégé admirations of Kerouac from the frame-tale of an unadulterated romanticism, a convex exchange between the group's leader, who chose William Butler Yeats's "trance writing," and the protégé familiar with William Blake's more passive, reticent verses. *Beat Hotel* also includes interviews with biographer Barry Miles, photographer Harold Chapman, and contemporary Beat critics. Critics and colleagues expound the finished work's questionable origin, and deep interrelationships that weaken authorial meditations. When doing so, they detail the Beat circle's colonization of Paris, and translations of the modernist/surrealist cut-up technique in fiction assembling the idea's shards against the Beat circle's reviving, nurturing threads and special instances of patronage. More ambitious claims from critic Regina Weinreich suggest bold accentuations to the modernist form, inferring contrasts with the very limited instructional role given to Beat Generation literature in the American undergraduate classroom. I think that the strongest theme was the instructional form, even as other moments of thematic clarity recur and are developed in the hope of audience interest in renegade meditations and artistry. Methods of teaching the hotel's literature and history operate from simple, class-conscious investigations of middle-class anxieties and the ambivalence of place and narrative form. In short, the visual template did not erase or obfuscate the much broader and satisfying literary one, though augmented with camera footage, collages, interjections, and photograph examples of culture's place and conflicts. *Beat Hotel* decenters writing anxieties, explaining the group's consistent interdependences to simulate greater literary interaction. The film's international-savvy direction of modern/postmodern fictional techniques and relative communitarian agreement, too, contrasts with America's McCarthyist depression found in Kerouac's roaming montages of America and Mexico. *Beat Hotel* also includes visual navigations in the photography suggesting greater transferences of the idea's collective power. In doing so, it transcended depressive postmodern mental imageries consistent with Roland Barthes' division of photography and visual examples into the Self, which is individual and therefore anti-rational, and Society, which turns the visual idea's inference into class conflict. The surrealist parable of the mind, severed from its origins, ascends its way to anti-dogmatic possibilities. The visual motif joyously travelled advertisements, film and photography so as to bring forth new, irreverent freedoms that showcase the jubilant Beat talent to misrepresent the mind against brooding, gloomy realisms of France's appealing, though divided, citizenry.

The collaboration of notables and critics four decades after the fact built notions of transcendence, yet also advanced the archetypal claim that the gay Beats were pioneers of modern consciousness and culture. I believe that this angle deserved greater scrutiny because of the deep modern-postmodern interiority and this mechanism's shaping of family, knowledge, democratic spirit, sex, and consciousness. While *Beat Hotel* offered few instances of American social life, Michael McClure's hushed memory descends upon the dour, morbid similitude that corralled millions of Americans into obscurity. *Beat Hotel*, then, owes its critical value to contemporary interest in rebellion, posing specific questions about rebellion's utility and formal intensity. The genteel portrait of elderly writers and photographers include clever navigations stating the fringe's postindustrial adaptations of place, hinting at their postmodern humors and multi-directionality. The romanticism of place, culture, and community in the Beat Hotel anticipates the channeling of modern man's romantic impulses through conscious and unconscious contrast and turmoil that spun faster and built non-stereotypical investigations of biographies. Oliver Harris and Regina Weinreich attach biography's central fact when considering the writing. Not only was the archetype developed and re-developed over time, but also the novels of Burroughs and Kerouac (who were married and had children, and so were straight) were and are also interchangeable with gay studies and its mystic attentions. Harris notes, too, the more obvious parable: Burroughs did not finish *Naked Lunch* until Ginsberg agreed to edit it, though he narrowly stars the facts of its literary production.[3] Burroughs wrote *Naked Lunch* to express Burroughs's love for Ginsberg, not to politicize and criminalize the drug cultures of the world in a super-masculine simulation of intense literary anxiety borne of deep, controversial research about the Orient. "Queering" Burroughs strips him of his paternal characteristics—throughout the film he is depicted from beneath his addiction and isolation from the literary and mainstream world. Instead, commentators noted that *Naked Lunch* paraphrases Burroughs's "naked lust" for Ginsberg.[4] Momentum would also be given to Ginsberg's compatriot, Gregory Corso, against literary progeny's pose: narrations of the significance of "the bomb" or H-bomb appeared in a poem on white paper, shaped like a hydrogen bomb. The literary spectacle, where Corso eclipsed Ginsberg and wrote more torridly and unashamedly of man's tryst with destruction, supposes the Beat Generation's agility and comprehensive breadth. We might then praise and internalize its penitent rejections of the modernist novel as social and textual achievement.

Beat Hotel enjoins instructional limitations common to historical film, and so missed many chances at a meaningful development of the literary work's ideas. It also limited the visual and spoken angle that could retell the group's narrative and intellectual development in the world setting. Clearly, it missed the chance to film divine intonations and disfigurements of the group's distant, spoken Orientalism, filled as it was with raunchy stories of drug-soaked gay partying and thoughtful, if not merely abstract, hallucinatory moment. Relying upon photographic collections and paintings that were surrealistically dim and unadorned, the film includes more aggressive contrasts with materialistic-commercial Eras. Excursions into Paris presented the city's art, commercial art and advertising and the contrastive shot of diminished urban working-class citizens against the advertisements' visible pulse of health, sex, pleasure, and power. More internally, narcotic investigations of meaning and graphic intensity are missed, the exception being a few comic subplots where Burroughs's elder double cameos as a soothsayer and a visual prop: there are few examples of what gay pleasure or eroticism was for those who stayed at this hotel. There are no instances supposing any written content from the spiraling narcotic deluge of trips in the run-down hotel, even though commentators advertise the residents' smoking hashish: it must be said that film examples telling of the drug experiments of Paul Bowles and Brion Gysin amass much greater visual and temporal acuity.[5] Barry Miles's summative comment is thoughtful: Paris wasn't as liberal as it is today, though her racial and lifestyle freedoms were greater than those of middle-class America.[6] Still, I believe that one of the key traits of Beat fiction and poetry was its pleasure-soaked indolence, hence the visible languor in out-of-touch middle-class American youth. The operative stress, conversely, produces greater development of the Beats' subversive axis of consciousness and culture through sex and drugs. Thus, a chance was missed, and with more familiar rhetoric that referred drug addiction and sexual relations to short, critical commentaries from friends and critics who maintain that the Beats were marginal, in a state of constant peril, and, in the formalist view, inartistic.

Nonetheless, *Beat Hotel* manages the major operative chance well, stripping Kerouac of his authorial power and control of the literary group and pushing forward gay literary synthesis during the late 1950s. Without the meditative Paul Bowles to communicate with in Tangier, Ginsberg, Corso and Burroughs were free to pursue Western commercial and everyday contents, and to sermonize the forms of European art and its technique. They harbored the means for Orient literary production, suggesting anti-rational and occultist drawings of social spheres, but attributed their ideas and prophecies to the modern, industrial setting where commerce and technology changed mankind's visual and artistic imagination. Paris archaeologies target the spectacle of the modern mind's uniqueness: it was in Paris that greater authorship suggested more aggressive writing than from within the major Beats' guiding themes. In the context of interviews and footage, Corso performed a magic realist eclipse of Ginsberg, and commentators recount Burroughs's dependence on Ginsberg to re-write *Naked Lunch*. Literary progeny is attacked from many sides when screening the literary work's writing, editing, and authorship as future generations studied it. Burroughs's anxiety crosses him with sustained doubts about his work's quality, or even concerning the use of his studies. Weinreich's comment, that Burroughs sought "naked lust" with Ginsberg, confirms homoerotic studies that defaced authorial prophecies that lay beneath the author's guarded sexual anxiety. Still, *Beat Hotel* repeats discovery's true ambivalence: Black-and-white photographs, along with paintings, allow for more casual introductions to Paris's current scene, and its retention of the spirit of leftist revolution. More innocently, Chapman walks through the renovated hotel, and the proprietor proudly extolls the air conditioning.[7]

The portrait of the Rue Git-le-Couer's proprietor Madame Rocheau is warm and inviting in its quaint street etiquette and luster, and enriches the scene's novelty and sympathies favoring the Paris underground's historic preservation of one part of its special and carefully unveiled history. In fact, Rocheau's biography introduces the promise of a new Era, a street culture of artists, writers, pimps, prostitutes, addicts, police, and groupies who existed symbiotically and without official sanction from the government. The film took administrative chances when it noted the illegality of drug use and its hushed practice. When recalling the sale of hashish in the hotel, narrators omitted the fact that French narcotics law that did not prohibit cannabis until 1970: more, *Beat Hotel* did not mention the prevalence of marijuana in the cafes.[8] Govenar's contention that drugs were *not* legal in France hides the resident's ignorance when confronted with the police: though the United States criminalized pot with the Boggs Act in 1951, and Morocco instituted formal prohibition of cannabis in 1956, France had not and was known for its tolerance. But the confusion is more certain, calling attention to Burroughs as a heretical novelist who wrote about drugs and junk sickness, hence his narrower legal status. With the much-spoken example of existentialist philosophers Jean-Paul Sartre and Simon Beauvoir smoking reefers outside Paris cafes during the 1940s and 50s, it is likely that Burroughs was a rejected outcaste whose case history got him into legal trouble.[9] Barry Miles and Michelle Green both covered

Burroughs's 1958 arrest for hashish possession, documenting what was probably a studied profile: Burroughs had been linked to several criminal syndicates, smuggled the drug from Morocco and noted it in a letter to Gysin that was intercepted.[10] Rocheau appears in a white gown with a round, fat-looking face and slit eyes, smiling: she scrutinizes the customers to find Beat followers, giving rooms only to them.

If we consider the narrative contributions of Rudie, Chapman, Weinreich, Harris, and Miles in the American studies medium, we might ask questions about what East-West synthesis at midcentury meant for viewers with little or no knowledge of its crucial, more volatile tensions. In my last book I wrote concerning film and music, "Re-invention surpassed the colonist's moment of discovery and meaningful incomprehension: without boundaries, a new dynamic would operate centuries-old dogmas of performance."[11] Without drawing the easiest of conclusions—namely, that Michelle Green had not fully considered its possibility when she wrote *The Dream at the End of the World* in 1991, my sense is that audiences would contest and criticize the authentic purpose of East-West interrelationships in the cultural re-creations of the Other. Abstractly, they then understand the film's body of evidence and commentaries from modern standpoints about audiences as classroom subjects. After all, the complex similitude of modernist literary ideas inhered no true Orient symbiosis, and so jagged, uneven scripts tell more about American Leftist internal anxieties and, in turn, advance questionable research goals and intentions to purport mainstream countercultural use. Nick Browne adds, "establishing agency by either the authority of the character or of spectator corresponds in its alternative rhetorical forms to the articulation of the ambiguity of the double origin of the image."[12] I believe that it is this ambiguity, plus the rebuilding of crucial archaeologies through simple didactic forms and concrete evidence of the film's strengths, that allow the Beat Hotel's residents to escape the essential dictum that they stole exciting, fanciful shards of Oriental drama and junked sickness for their own political and social communications. In Paris, deep East-West semio-psychic rhythms were weighed and popularized: it was here that biography traced through photographs and films acquired its clear objectivity that underscores the truth-value of liberal experiments with graphic and philosophical subversion of the mind, psyche, and realistic Self in modern times. In this very essential moment, Chapman, Miles and Weinreich document a sustained change in thought, reconciling its discoveries with psychedelic techniques for writing about social rebellion—the subject of later Beat travels to Morocco, Japan, and India during the 1960s. Thus, if no empirical thread existed, at least Beat re-developments of context allow us to deduce "what we are to know" about street humanism and its study.

Nick Browne added, "the image can also be taken as originating from a point in a different kind of space, recognizably different in terms of habitability [...] it is from a fictional and changeable place implied by an origin contained in the image."[13] From this refreshed angle of discovery and learning, photographers in *The Beat Hotel* aggressively performed and documented their development of the Beat scene, adding sentiments of technology, underground, and poetry to counterculture's visual sampling techniques. At one point, Harold Chapman recalled films he shot with Gysin from beneath a shopping cart in the Rue Git-le-Coeur neighborhood[14]: at another, the form of painting friendly with cut-up developments of logic and subject is introduced through drawings of circular figures upon the grotesque human mask.[15] Numerous outtakes by Chapman and Rudie took advantage of the garish, sumptuous cartoons telling of our lust to consume cosmetic and fashion products amidst the façade of Paris's Catholic, working-class neighborhoods and communities, and even the consternation of French nuns when found in proximity to growing numbers of decrepit, sinful folk. It is as though a sustained comic exaggeration cements the beauty and multiplicity of new modernist perspectives that digest the art form's strategies of unconscious dislocation. Weinreich's example of Brion Gysin's Djemaa el Fnaa painting, c. 1961, re-introduced the cubist tradition with human, black bodies and white configurations of landscape: later, an aging reader of Harold Norse's description of the multiracial, addict-friendly hotel during its heyday reads aloud in the street outside the location.[16] Image, place, and time are collapsed in this film so as to breathe airs of continuity and consistency: literary and cultural imaginations are freed of its Eastern and Western constraints that held back the group's true notoriety. Although *The Beat Hotel* missed many thematic links to the growing psychedelic form, it is at least true that American counter-histories are given strength and interactions.

Govenar misses the chance at biographical instances of the lives and public testaments of Bill Burroughs, Allen Ginsberg, and Gregory Corso. Aside from a few photographs of their stay at the hotel, there are no live examples of interviews, lectures, and public presence in any form. We might recall the obvious form of American Studies-derived centrism when publishing literary greats—Kerouac was straight, and had appeared on many TV and radio appearances, where Ginsberg did not cross into the mainstream eye until the late 1960s and Burroughs until the early 1970s. The absence of indie film was indeed conspicuous—it limited and forcibly re-directed the gay counterculture's biographies. Paul Bowles operates from behind mysticism's looking glass—his gay life, when censored, allows him the opportunity to join multimedia presentations and to evince legitimate involvement in cultural and countercultural studies. Still, I will point out that the multimedia presentation is indeed ambitious and many-angled. It adds readings, short plots with impersonating figures, and biographical discussion that favor decentered Beat worlds far from the glossy mirage of an apparent genius. Still, it behooves us to recount the tale as it had come from onlookers, biographers, and critics: as angles for instructing Beat ethnography, knowledge, and political notoriety is very strong, we might usher in a greater criticism that builds the concept of a history which drew impact upon our ethical and cultural standards, even as it told its social, rather than individual, production.

Chapman recalls that he loved "to sit in a room with Corso talking—addressing, rather, telling his stories which obviously he told more than once with such vivid impact about driving a getaway care hitting the wall, going into prison discovering Shelley, everything that once would now read in his biography."[17] The broader statement re-assigns class mobility and conflicts that prevailed in the Beat circle, for Ginsberg had avoided jail and continued his studies at Columbia. Scholarship is wrenched from the hands of college freshman and "the best young minds" when the biographical segment turns to Corso's poem, "Bomb." Chapman's contextualization of poetic form is aggressive and startling, as if to declare a brand new humanism within the circle. Placing the H-Bomb-shaped poem on a long reel on a desk stated non-romantic assessments of man's mythological eclipse and the necessary power of destruction, "he didn't appear to be condemning the bomb,"[18] incurring angry criticism from antiwar protesters. At that moment, the camera scrolls to the poem's middle verses:

> O the happy stands
> Ethereal root and cheer and boo
> --------------------------------
> The spitball of Buddha
> Christ striking out,
> Luther stealing third.[19]

Corso's modernist historical-epic redevelopment, or the collusion of the poem's mythology with the motions and jubilant sport of modern life when seen as a suspenseful, haunting acceleration towards death, is significant. It restates the social ethics of the Beat Generation's basic problem: that of generating idealism that could mobilize America's youth versus the phantom of civilizational destruction. "Bomb" would be published a year before Ginsberg attempted the force of nuclear destruction in "Television Was A Baby Crawling Toward That Deathchamber," where he exclaimed, "AMERICA WILL BE REFUSED ETERNITY BY HER OWN MAD SON THE BOMB." The generational point favors the idea's greater exchange within the Beat literary nucleus, and the multi-directional form of semantic expositions in the modernist poem. Since Beat meditations on the coming nuclear holocaust include many authors' letters and works, we then say the movement wields much greater rhetorical and intellectual power. Literary progenitors, then, suppress content and its extra-Victorian social and academic direction. Conversely, audiences find the most obvious inference, namely that modernism held more acute perceptions of coming postmodern literature beginning with Thomas Pynchon's 1966 novel, *The Crying of Lot 49*.

We ought to recognize Govenar's true thoughtfulness in his presentation of Burroughs through contexts of writing, publishing, and mystique. Of course, this is because Govenar scarcely pays any reading attention to either the written work (with one exception, from *Queer* in which the narrator identifies "naked lust" as the Kerouac-discovered title) or any writings, letters, or interviews in which Burroughs represents himself, and the outcome for his ideas and perspectives.

Psychoanalytic narrowing of the spectator's role to develop a film's critical intensity might lead us to Beat biography from insights gained from its generational pose: surely, Burroughs fans and book collectors ought to give a closer look into his biographical tales and follies that influenced his narrative development. *The Beat Hotel* ignored published works, instead unveiling tales about El Hombre Invisible's secrecy, dependence, and isolation. It accomplishes the task of teaching discovery through both the artist's fame and place of residence, and through inventions and commentary meant to increase readership by transposing a new familiarity without books or critics. Though the 2009 publication of *Naked Lunch at 50* is prominently featured, analysis was tied to both the writing and editing of *Naked Lunch*, and to Burroughs's phantom-like ideas, humor, and mysteries. Reflexively, building the literary giant as it advanced cult fashions and mystery above the dirt of close readings, and attending to less-visited avenues of Burroughs's later literary works, collapses the moment's novelty. This, in turn, suggested there was more to the writer's developing thesis. Collaborative, shared power of investigations that appeared newer, less tied to generational stereotypes, and conducive to new perspectives that, in turn, orchestrate and exaggerate the literary work's social outlook. Harris identified the means of literary production to rise from Beat circles, confirming that it was the author's meditations and thought that produced the finished novel. He narrows his comments here to propose a greater intimacy with the minds and psyches of contemporary audiences: "*Naked Lunch* is generally considered to be the great 'secret' novel of the self-styled beat generation. It's still fresh, still has an edge."[20] Further, Burroughs's comment about Gysin, "I see in his paintings the psychic landscape of my own work,"[21] greatly expands possibilities that cannot be tied to the published work, or formalist analyses anchoring straight literary development that is due to his academic and vocational background. Greater moments of the gay writer's wanderings cause us to envision a much greater, modernly inclusive set of ideas and principles colluding with postmodernity and hybridity. There is the chance, too, to figure in perceptions favoring purer, more distinct imageries and hallucinations that wander the history of artistry's past and future Eras. Gysin's secret catalysis envisioned the dislocating chance that his idea-conceptions were imaginable from subjectivity's postmodern depth, with no dream-states and visions that instead tell us to recognize the vagabond genius that casts the acolyte's shadow while in Tangier, Paris, and London. The film's chance at seeing and thinking about something new or undiscovered offers multiple interventions of text and vision with today's scenarios that produce the Self's ascription to liberal political and psychosocial introspections. This movement of awareness, in turn, distances us from generational themes and rhetoric that crippled and stultified American prose during Senator McCarthy's "Red Scare" of the early 1950s:

> "Secret" and "psychic" unveiled the positive potential to read and understand Burroughs as a timeless force, one that cannot be restricted to the audience's ignorance of the time period's necessity and necessary political-social conflicts. Secret stands in noticeable opposition to Kerouac's jubilant tale of recognition and fame in *On the Road's* wake. Liminality, or even the liminality of responses that shadow discovery with uncertainty and spontaneity, ensures a more volatile American history, and one that could deduce human identity and suffering from more favorable thematic and perceptual points of self-immersion and learning. The film's patient instructional tone aside, *The Beat Hotel's* recovery of relationships and thought was based upon art and community, and anticipated Burroughs's return journey to Tangier in 1961, where he, Bowles, Ginsberg, and Leary discussed psilocybin's "conditioned mechanism,"[22] and where Burroughs set down the beginnings for his later works.

The Beat Hotel includes two scenes where patrons find a seated Burroughs, sitting in the room's corner and wearing a suit and tie. The seated figure bore no resemblance to Burroughs, instead showing a bald man who was heavier and less ministerial-looking. The drug-addicted prophet's lingering strophe of power lay in his voice, at one point intoning gravely: "follow no leader. Nobody is living; everybody is dead and the dead that think between the legs and ears."[23] The parable's true power cannot be biographically narrowed: Burroughs was impressed with modernist horrors and severe carnage sketched in Bowles's repeated destruction of the body, psyche, and spirit. His cavalierly Yankee adjustment of Bowles's graphic contexts spoke to man's sexual liberties and the happiness of his extra-moral transcendences that offer hope and are interchangeable with those of modern filmmakers and musicians who sang and told of man's liberation. The operative thrust zeroes in on the hotel's sexual freedom that opposes modern man's status, class, and educational determinations of the human spirit. Depressed ascents to joy and pleasure were not easily negotiated in Burroughs's primary works: *Naked Lunch* instead assumes the burlesque form that foretell Burroughs's gothic physical immersions that were anti-logical, destructive, and comically deranged so as to sustain terror and secrecy. I think that making Burroughs "cool" was not an easy task because of the author's visible sickness and his depressive, post-academic aura. It is more likely, then, that we will discover ourselves in the text when the writers' meditations give us positive transcendences of the worst junked sicknesses that we, who are warned not to meddle with drugs or gay sex, ignored because of *NL*'s peculiarity.

The generational moment, too, was sweetly arranged to testify to the movement's brilliance and sustained energy: documented are the photographic excursions and writings of older residents who, fifty years later, still could recognize the innovative sweep of the hotel's goings-on and the relevance of deeply meditated narrative ideas that jump-start 1960s counterculture. The work's presumptive seriousness is abolished: many scenes feature the critics and photographers finding street side bookstores on a sunny Paris day, perfectly exchangeable with any content favoring today's culture. When I attended the *Naked Lunch at 50* Conference in 2009, I was pleased to find that modern films and their discussion had anticipated a greater understanding of ideas that found their way into print. Still, with less knowledge about the authors and their works, I was just as likely to screen *Beat Hotel* for instances of discovery's pure innocence. Through the actors, the Beat movement is alive and mostly intact. There are, too, the casual introductions to, and investigations of, the street's history that document place's aliveness and undefined sympathy for re-visitations extracting more subjective content that today's students and writers could use for more radical social narratives and spoken forms.

The Junky's Christmas and the Modernist Ambiguity of Story

The chance to adapt historical fiction and drama is exciting, and ushers us into greater social and characteristic avenues that dramatize and tell of influential popular institutions, music, thought, and experience that change the short story's reading. Claymation techniques and characters, after all, supersede the awesome spectacle of dehumanization and denaturing of the body and life on Earth, as it was found in many stories in *The Burroughs File*: they accomplish the unreality of drug transactions, of translations of spirit, and of the special, marginal efficacy of language and consciousness at the mercy of the streets. As historical films depend on popular transferences to mainstream audience who watch with little or no understanding of Beat history, they assume the might of today's semiotic or narrative presences in song, conversations, manners, physique, and behaviors.

Because producer Francis Ford Coppola and Claymation directors Nick Donkin and Melodie McDaniel made use of these transferences in 1993's *The Junky's Christmas*, my appraisal of the film's narration assigned the postmodern technique of global revisions to suit today's urban geographies. The film features music by Hal Wilner and the Disposable Heroes of Hiphoprisy, and Claymation that echoed similar 90s films which featured people, cars, animals and buildings as living entities. It does the familiar job of retelling Burroughs's specific meditations on drug addiction in today's world, with the present as the story's guiding minute. Danny the Car Wiper is appropriately confused and bemused because of the absence of compassion for drug addicts at Christmas-time: Danny's clambering walk through city streets and apartments finds him unable to control his pain and frightening sickness.[24] When he finally gets a "quarter-half" from a doctor, he must still find an abandoned apartment to inject his fix. The story's sequence, ending in a light-drenched vision of Christian redemption playing "Glory to The Newborn King," extended our stereotypes about reflections on the bygone scene or even its more remote religious understandings. Burroughs was not an everyman, and did not intend to be one.[25] Use of today's hip-hop music and fashion tempt Burroughs to gauge ethnic re-makings of the underground tale. Sporting dreads and not distinct from today's street generations, the Drug War's future communities diversify the author's portrait, complicating his answer's logistics.[26] In the end, Danny outwits another drug addict and walks away with money in his pocket, but criminal deceptions operate during the brief moment, a studied introspection contrasting with Danny's deep purgatorial honesty about his drug addiction.[27] White and nonwhite communities aside, we are wiser to attach this formal grandeur, as though to say that elderly men from the lurking, meandering urban past understood complex, polyglot discourses of man's materialistic illusions alongside the city's ethnic, urban markings that were harsher, more aggressive, and less favorable to the nation than to its rural, idealistic beginnings.

The Junky's Christmas takes narrative advantage of the controversies about the drug user's elemental understandings of community. Christmas, and the story's Christian foregrounding, retreats to shadow desperation and sickness in the wake of joy and prosperity, and advanced the message that God loved all humans, even if they were addicts. The foil is casual, and the community's interdependence is tested at several points, assuring us that poor drug syndicates could and did survive the drug purge's cataclysm during unfriendly times. *Pathos* as the active messenger of truth is ensured when the reticent, gravelly-voiced author reads the story, beneath a Christmas tree at night. The supreme moment of reflection juxtaposes the quiet hush and resplendent suburban remove from the story's urban grittiness and sickness, as though the answers existed at the conflict's beginning, just as warnings and denunciations about the evils of drugs elicited man's fundamental compassion. When the local drug dealer declines to give drugs to Danny, but instead gives him $3, we are given the stereotype's classic moment of Reagan-Era indoctrination. Suited and behind sunglasses to offset the humanity of one's eyes and body, the dealer exercises "cool" compassion in the coldness of the city's non-recognition and non-affectation.[28] Still, the story's ethnic remaking appears casual, accenting the story's timeless moment: there will always be drug addicts, and anyone can understand God's truths. It need not be recounted that many liberal pundits over-spoke the scriptural metaphor whilst advancing its political values. Liberalism's corrosive and inventive techniques are commonplace, and junkies bore testament to everyday life's power over them. The moral principle, when applied against the weight of evidence and reason, preserves and protects the junkie's peculiar, yet inevitable, grip on actions and language, rebuilding Victorian social and moral codes. Subversions of these codes would aggravate mankind's social questions. May we teach drug addiction in our classrooms, as a true story that told us of a greater range of American experiences? I have found a broad range of responses, with some disbarring the idea on principle and others curious to examine fashion, voice, and cultural arts as the links that were engaging. Thus, a rewrite retains the story's arguable tenacity in changing times, as drugs are still popular and influential.

Documentary Films on William S. Burroughs

Burroughs: The Movie, "Ladies and Gentlemen, There Is No Cause for Alarm"

After watching several Burroughs films, I was struck by the myriad of happy reflections and recollections about him, weighing against his writing persona that usually spoke the sour, cynical, and mercurial wand of drug-infested sorcery to many, if not most. Howard Brookner's 90-minute collage of Missouri screen stories and repeated interjections of his now-60ish cronies allowed for a greater modernist technique. Burroughs's hilarious outtakes and reflective minutiae stars historical narrations of the author's shadowy, criminal-derived social being, contrasting his visible torment and non-recognition with the happy, jubilant irreverence of his Beat friends 30 years after their works' publication. Audiences might add the more obvious reasoning when screening the Beats: their works had been received and distributed among scores of liberal dissidents, marking the success of their public and private being. Burroughs, Ginsberg, Carr and Huncke irreverently reflect on textual masterpieces that still somehow defied the journalist's simple inspection. Nonetheless, film technique must own up to censorship's evident shackles. For Burroughs, as with Ginsberg, addiction's fantastic-sounding reflections and castings are imperfectly and sporadically applied to augment the author's artistic and intellectual pretense. Despite the noteworthy exception of Eric Mottram, who wrote *The Algebra of Need* in 1978, critics had ignored relevant discussion of addictions and drug pharmacology that constituted part of Burroughs's more authentic development. Still, we should not dismiss the able, clever humor that details the absurdity of narcotic controls, nor ought we deter the seething ferment of modern, poststructuralist-friendly dislocations and vulgarizations of truth. Watching Burroughs in film adds subjective, introspective tones advancing cinematographic immersions that influence street-conscious re-writing. I believe that both instances of authorial reflection challenge Burroughs's classroom debut: without theory to guide us, we are led instead to carefully protected and preserved rock inclusions of one's "story." Because, too, I was given the opportunity to teach *Naked Lunch* once in 2008, I was always interested in Rob Johnson's efforts at the University of Texas that document biographical angles, which had been subtle and gained interactive ground because of Burroughs's biographical statements. I felt that instructional techniques benefit from a reading of the author's childhood and shaded memories of writing's interiority.

Internal shots of the writer's personal life, personality, and friendships are easygoing and limited criticism's analytic technique, enunciating the "larger than life" *métier* and so dislocating and ignoring key, substantial textual questions. One gathering found Burroughs, Ginsberg, and Carr on the Manhattan rooftops recalling their experiences and fame. The long exchange turns into a riotous laugh when Ginsberg recalled that Kerouac was a "foolish, ruddy-cheeked young American," as the godfather-like Burroughs reflected his gay composite pose so as to star Kerouac's limitations: "He was a nice boy, very nice boy."[29] Ginsberg, now in his late fifties, dredged up the crucial canonical shard: "I alone have this key to this savage parade which is tenderness."[30] The exchange pitted street energies against the illusion of fictional understanding: now men, they must sort out their private byways of imagination and memory, so extolling the author's happiness as a part of writing's success. Though it was unclear why Ginsberg opts for intellectualism's high ground, it is indeed brought on from Burroughs's drunken misreading of "Howl"—where he fails to remember the words, and a flustered Ginsberg admonishes him.[31] Perhaps a stab back at Ginsberg's rejection of Burroughs, the exchange also reveals their scholastic differences, yet gives us the tendril of civilization's redemption through creation once again, as though for a final time. Herbert Huncke compounds this divergence when he assaults Burroughs's marital tensions, saying that he had thought Bill and Joan "would make a great couple."[32] Gay synthesis did not, in short, re-write the Beat story's origins: instead, the writer's vehicle of adult reflections relaxed as it perused the documents and conflicts that spur on greatness. This was important because gay writers did not take advantage of biography's voluminous ethnic and historical moments of *differance*. Bowles's gay relationships were censored, and so his content resided safely within the modernist dictum, safe and sweetened so as to avoid any biological or physical interruption from writing's sexual *oeuvre*. "Gay Power" operated, then, distinct after-effects and operative forces in Bill Burroughs's movies, where it was hidden and beautified into romantic pretense in the Ginsberg films. Huncke gives a live demonstration of the "William Tell" act that killed Joan in 1951: he adds that Joan was suicidal, and had encouraged the act as a way to depart her responsibilities when out of favor with Burroughs's able, mobile cronies.[33] This recollection neatly intercepts literary momentum for raising the much-heralded liberal *ethos* that gave credence to the critical discussions of Eric Mottram, Oliver Harris, and Jennie Skerl. America's social paradigm that presented social and thematic *elan* to develop notions of genius reintroduces the transient social avenue to reverse key archival factors that hold together more masculine graphic and textual content that, as with Bowles, erased homosexuality's condemning cross when retelling the group's social development.

Comedic sketches of parts of *Naked Lunch*, *The Place of Dead Roads*, *The Exterminator*, and *The Wild Boys* were collapsed into an operating table scene with Burroughs as the doctor. The jokes sustain man's colonial and imperialist absurdity, much in the format of "Leif the Unlucky" and his super-material dislocation and disgorgement during his travels.[34] But the key minutes of the film's biographical episodes are found in the telling of Burroughs's childhood in St. Louis: this includes interviews with older residents who knew Burroughs as a child and instantly disowned his scandalous, obscene books, indifferently and inadvertently crowning the fiction's invention. Brookner's operative point was simple: Burroughs lived a distant, secluded life with private, internal terrors that scarred him, making his assemblage of narcotic writings more reticent and pointed. Burroughs wasn't accepted into wealthy social circles, and the isolation tormented him. Dropping out of school and encouraged by his father, Burroughs ascends the operating table: "Well, it isn't every corpse that can walk. Stench of a rank addict smell. Stay outta churches, son. All they gotta cater to is the shithouse."[35] If Burroughs could track his innocence and dreams from the view of his alter egos and predators, he could also assemble the unreality's comic depth amidst the sickness of mainstream institutions. Since Burroughs outtakes as early as 1961's *The Burroughs File* unveiled puerile disintegration and alienation, the contrast between confident and notorious narcotic progenitor, and the prosperity and Southern, genteel accenting of St. Louis neighbors, lawns, and studies, accentuate and surpass the modernist crux which inculcated tradition and culture. Megalomaniac tendencies were thus located in the child's internal struggles. Rather than define key molding moments in Burroughs's biography that pushed him into adulthood and onto today's modern avenues of thought and speculations, we tread the intellect's special and peculiar moments of terror and its gnawing lack of focus. The unique setting of St. Louis's suburban lawns and homes allowed Burroughs to crown his illusory semiotic quest for a more real understanding. Was Burroughs's vocational choice a luxury, or was it necessitated? We find that the question's fission, between obedience and messianic pretense, broadens our look at a man who had never been studied. Audiences will then note that Burroughs had not been given the biographical attention that could deepen our more-than-literary reading and its artificial microscope.

Burroughs's notoriety operated on a pendulum between aristocratic, privileged youth and his exilic genius that materialized lengthy and semantically rigorous expulsions from genteel life: when we render this contrast, the biographical film does attach normalcy and over-suggest the moment's controversy. It would behoove us to trace the development of an authorial Self against society's real, rather than imagined, expectations. In this manner, complications of originality and creation interrogate Burroughs as a creator, suggesting a broader inclusion in the mainstream that absorbed and scattered his persistent stream of rebellions. Class consciousness necessitated Brookner's form: when we understand the writer from either the Self's confessions or from its internal projection of cultural norms, we deepen the author's bold, materially satisfying stroke for rendering the individual's specially conceived moment of crisis and fear. Whether the mainstream path is passable or not, such unanswered pathways deepen the author's humanity. In strictly modernist terms, a more inclusive, rationally engaging life existed, and it is our choice to opt for vagrancy and peculiar, profane intellectual notoriety. The audience's freedom, then, is not essential, but is affirmatively and confidently its narrative recognition. The technique is comfortably applied through Burroughs's untouched childhood memories of elderly residents and citizens who condemn the Beat Generation and its spiritual sickness. Thus, postmodern generations absorbed the author's technique casually and with greater narrative mobility when brought to the crucial fault line of the idea's self-generation. More than the other biographical movies, *Burroughs: The Movie* posed both mankind's necessity and its absurdity, and cast doubt upon our learning of narcotic visions and resulting underground *pathos* that raised our timely, if relaxed, social indifference. The author's resulting indifference, and his static pose at a ripe old age, moves easily beyond the pale of once-firm illusions of class separateness and social rejection, causing us to choose fulfillment to be the key factor in social change.

Words of Advice, the Beats and Modernist Literary Redevelopment

The main facets of *difference* that recall Burroughs's biographical and narrative ambiguity, the modernist character's special role, and the text's ambiguities when shaping meaningful instances of the generation's counter-histories, were retold in the interviews and lectures found in Die Danske Filminstitut's 74-minute film, *Words of Advice*. The film features extensive footage of Burroughs's second coming and of his novels' renewed popularity during the 1970s and 80s, and include sympathetic critical overtures that are catalogued through Burroughs's primary biographers—music producer Hal Wilner, longtime partner James Grauerholz, and critic and School of Visual Arts professor Regina Weinreich. The greater air of American synthesis can be traced to modern man's fruition of directions, anxieties, and possibilities in a manner more closely graphic and modern than attentions given to his friend, Paul Bowles. Critics agreed that Bowles's novels operate from premises of post-atomic man's cultural and intellectual destruction when tangling with radical Otherness. Beyond Green's able rendition of the relationship between the two men, Bowles's fiction and commentaries suggest ample ground for re-examinations of his friend, who operated from a subjective, sublime attention to form that forwards liberal political discussions about man's spirit. A great deal of attention and hoopla, too, is added to the lecture circuit, one that began in New York in 1974 and carried Burroughs all over the world, and even to Saturday Night Live in 1981. Performances showcased Burroughs's tales of gore, graphic and moral insensitivity and waste, and anti-theistic redirection. Strong critical angles of the modern subject, too, gave rise to the interfacing of the Beat Generation with rock generations that shuffle and distend new consciousness's anarchist messages, pushing forth street-level defiance of The Word and the Story. But just as important was Burroughs's influence upon his compatriots. I will try to show how Burroughs's new, burgeoning career in his seventies rose from beneath the doormat of his friends' writing anxiety, with the chancy assemblage of modern and postmodern rays of insight that they did not resolve together. Graphic, visual, and textual anxiety and ambidexterity colored and poisoned his friends, restating modernism's failure: *Words of Advice* took special pains to confirm the strength of voice and thought in firming up the academic and cultural purposes of experimental change, forecasting the vehicle's resonant power that reaches the world stage a second time.

Burroughs accomplished the task of regenerating the Beat Generation's metric and vocal thrust, and indeed American Studies' ethnographic tinting that in turn revealed its antipathy and military-industrial constrictions of living, romantic spirit. In this inquiry, then, we extended his friends' prophecies. The gravelly-voiced, sneering, elderly man in a suit had garnered a considerable reception. Promoter John Giorno glowingly recalls that Burroughs's performances suited the rise of his new novels and drew large audiences. He noted the curious spontaneity and formal brilliance of the literary work's presentation, and the oddity, and even special anxieties, when presenting narrative forms in an increasingly media-controlled, politically correct world. Generations that responded to the rise of pop, and to the sustained political depression found in post-scientific paranoia, now surmised the ancient-looking queer with laughs and adulation while he read pages of depressive jokes, post-military hyperboles, scientific dystopias, and dirty vernacular transactions. Odd but strangely resilient, the reticent man with his fidgeting mouth and dragged enunciations of words would rebuild the Beat revolution's memory. He would also fuse his works' heritage with worlds of punk, disco, rock, R&B, and post-fashions that, in their heyday, craved exotic dystopia when forming the gamut of the mind's deranging leap into the Self's confusion and corporeal alienation.

John Giorno recalls the reading tour that began in New York in 1974, "[there were] several hundred people screaming"[36] and that he "knew what to do with his voice, and how to use his voice. How to use volume, pitch, and [...] William had developed into one of the great performers of the world."[37] Still, to conclude a rare mastery of the spoken form when telling fictional tales begets the crucial anxiety, and the mismatch against TV formats more common in the politically correct world of the 1980s. Giorno then interprets a Burroughs appearance on *Saturday Night Live*: though useful to the slapstick replays of the late night show, the host's dead calm and his tale of gore and sickness stood quietly in the historical past, a primer that might introduce the supposedly wilder, more live telling of political-familial-sexual oddities by comedians such as Eddie Murphy and Steve Martin.[38] I think it is worthwhile to state the precarious step of Burroughs's tour, or the uncertainty that messages of knowledge and critique would actually reach the audience's thoughts. Paul Bowles, who recorded his tales on tape as early as 1963, transposed his voice, pitch, and persona to state the timeless power of Arab-Berber storytelling.[39] I think that it is useful to recall Bowles's considerable influence upon El Hombre Invisible's live persona, and thus the intent of his graphic debacles and gory irreverence. But live readings gave Burroughs the chance to re-tread his spoken illusions and comedy, connecting them with his gravelly, Midwestern voice and prophetic-like, yet sardonic belittling of the intricacies of man's spirit and his social adaptations. Cold, cruel, and wittily anti-moral, yet targeting shards of Yankee imperialism and suburban decay, Burroughs wanders through the junked portrait this second time with much greater confidence that did not come from writing, from expatriate ambiguity, or from the annals of his own private alienation. Clearly, the punk youths and college students had come for something that Burroughs expertly delivered. Humorous pandemonium stood in stark contrast with more cleanly organized liberal political messages. From the doldrums of man's consciousness, we may presume Burroughs's spunky defiance of art as morality, or art as a social messenger relaying moral unilateralism.

Introductions concerning authorial anxiety and the visual-spoken angles of reflection and historicism are consistent with Bowles's audio mastery when telling tales of the occult, drugged agencies, and anti-corporate, drugged realism that opened and spread the liberal pandemic of ideas, issues, and underground solutions. In *Re-Creating Paul Bowles* I noted the fact that "continued literary emphasis on destruction complicates the picture, suggesting the rise of an alter-citizen who had many histories and teleological moments of focus."[40] Still, derivable generational points about Burroughs's life are often muted to star his occult tales of sickness, gore, and hilarity. When speaking his writing's form, Burroughs manifests his debut's emblem with seedy Moroccan tales and underground sicknesses, molding the spirit's special, brave journey to vindicate the Self's more essential truth. The first lecture gives narrative chances to Jack Kerouac, in a *haiku*-friendly unearthing of the details of modern man's poetic insouciance and indifference:

> [...] musical intelligence, information and directives/in and out through street sayers/musical broadcasts jukeboxes records/high school buds whistling boys/cabaret performers/singing waiters transistor radios/red scrolls in the sunset way out into the sea."[41]

This passage, taken from *Western Lands* and perhaps a "gay Western" that re-applies the perceptions and oddities of Burroughs's Western travels, accomplished through his gravelly, heavily Midwestern-accented crowing and sneering voice the aesthetic resonance of Kerouac's romanticist ramblings and the urban sphere's easy grasp of his more necessary geographies. It, too, cross-examines Kerouac's merry indolence as a traveler and writer. Accomplishing urban man's viability and health meant focusing attentions on the Self's more basic, everyday dialogues. Burroughs's archaeology, then, contradicts the thesis of man's destruction and does this easily, advancing the young generation's rich imagination that could contest or reject modern corporate-military dominance. Burroughs tied himself in this form to liberal modernist traditions. Yet we ought to ask, what was the usefulness of Burroughs's pathology, a subject of his considerable adulation and notoriety? Might Burroughs master the technique of depicting the gory shards that grew postmodern sickness and depression, without the rhetorical attachment to otherness that Bowles coveted and craved? Would inscribed tales, if they were spoken to an audience, garner the thoughtful *difference* to dislocate our readings of culture? After all, Bowles wrote from the outpouring wake of the Orient's distance, reading signs confirming the calculus of its moral oblivion: the patient, thoughtful voice takes over, and develops geography and action from beneath the Orient's special, remote historical domain. Burroughs did not, at least in his own estimations of his theory, accept his friend's rhetorical twists: he instead maintained an American dialect and a voice that pronounced the harshness and sickness of an American man's rhetorical distance from truth and romanticism. At a 1981 reading of his new novel, *Cities of the Red Night*, all of the biographical points of introspection became manifest. At one lecture, Burroughs gives a grave re-reading of the crucial geography of bodies and communities, of his laughing disparagement of conspiracy theory, of his science fiction-like treading of shadowy urban realism, and of his casual accenting and threading of stream-of-conscious meter:

> Virus B-23 now on the loose in our crowded cities [...] is an agent that produces biologic changes in those affected, fatal in many cases, and hereditary in those who survive and become carriers without stress [...] Which as a matter of survival, they will spread as far and fast as possible. To destroy enemies [...] Junkies however are only lightly affected and characteristically remain unaffected.[42]

In short, Burroughs' reading of the virus's crucial detail and the social characteristics of infestation transformed the aesthetic, romantic richness of Kerouac's readings. Summative comments about junkies restate comic, post-nuclear parables forecasted new dystopias in movies ranging from *Invasion of the Body Snatchers* to *Damnation Alley*, as they include dense graphic and societal detail that avoided conscious destructions that strengthen Bowles's more casually derived form in stories such as 1960's "He of the Assembly," 1950's "The Delicate Prey," and 1960's "The Wind at Beni Midar."[43] Burroughs, suited and fidgeting, appears to roll and extend syllables in a lecturer-like moment of ministerial truth. He then spells out his self-imparted doom's crucial enunciation to the audience without dropping the modernist subject's heavy baggage as he thought of elements beyond his immediate knowledge. The survival of junkies, too, is parlayed at the passage's end, an emphasis directly borrowed from *A Hundred Camels*: the drug user, and his specific and understood pathologies, processes and sustains global destruction with greater tenacity, spelling out the tale's extra-logical strength. But Burroughs tried to stretch beyond the annals of Bowles's novels and short stories that told civilization's destruction as it could be deciphered humanly, through modernist form and syntax. In these readings, Burroughs sketches the denouement of modern man's decline and suffering, confirming *Naked Lunch*'s apocalypse. As fiction by Thomas Pynchon, Don De Lillo, and T. Coraghessan Boyle made modernist pedagogical and semantic ideas appear to be irrelevant, Burroughs's task was to spell out the specific global sickness and the special tenacity of humanistic studies that started for him in Mexico three decades before when writing *The Yage Letters* in 1953. In truth, Bowles read and understood Morocco from its Arab-Berber interdependences, and then from the uniqueness of its community's graphic understanding of social context. Burroughs's meter, at times approaching postmodern rhetorical margins, imparts realistic shards of fiction, absorbing them into a summative statement of counterculture's newfound power, or the power to afflict society without a cultural medium. Classic, fulfilling readings, juxtaposed against modernist readings of Kerouac and Bowles, reached critical mass at a Copenhagen reading of 1981's *The Place of Dead Roads*:

> He meets a wide old assassin whose whispering cat's made aeol. He speaks in a dead dry whisper. City boy-yy, did you ever see a cat roll in dead carrion [...] Yes-sir, I was tempted to join him, sir. Ya ever see a black snake reach in to be a rattlesnake. Yes, sir, he cleaned himself up and dried his tail and ... brrp! Kes if you had your choice, would you rather be a poi-son-ous snake? Poisonous, sir, like a green spitting cobra. And that's your idea of heaven, feeling safer?[44]

Of course, Bowles's reading of *A Hundred Camels in the Courtyard*, and even his 1981 story "Allal," where a *kiffed* boy turns into a snake, developed from a much more sure ethnography and the historical certainty of folktales. Burroughs's invention and American-style comedy was more adventurous and unsure: the details of the subject's conscious investigation contrast with the haunting danger and the modern American youth's uncharacteristic paralysis. Live readings thus chronicle postmodern depression and isolation from true contexts that tell us adventure, travel, and intoxication. In short, the American boy's choice of language and agency was corrupted and unsure. The reading also projects haunting tales of death and beyond, tracing its unromantic, illogical pulse. Yet Burroughs opts for a paternal yet comic tone, as though to say that the wrong choice is actually the right one and thus useful for youth. Rites of passage exist in traditional cultures, but characterizing them as underground, radical syndicates tells us more of the wealth of discoveries beyond the mainstream's pale. In short, Burroughs succeeds at building a materiality and context that broadens the occult's formal discussion. He also confirms through *shtick* and pop-flavored comedy the instance of Burroughs's much greater popularity, and the broader range of artistic combinations away from his predecessor, who resigned himself to departure from America and Europe as a Moroccan recluse.

Weinreich, Grauerholz, and Skerl handle the collective task of teaching Burroughs's persona, crucial fictional anxieties, and political values. Collectively, they employ a simple technique, starring the depth of the writer's meditations and the substance of the internal suffering that caused them. The biographical sketch included Grauerholz's moving, warm recollections about Burroughs's home, his afterlife, and his instantly loveable charisma as a man, a gay lover, and a creature of spirit. At the film's end, Grauerholz holds back his tears and states that he "doesn't know where he is now," then states his hope that it is a universe that is sympathetic to his persona and ideas.[45] Weinreich adds a thoughtful motif of the Self's transference and mobility in the wake of sexual and social negation and the intensity of Burroughs's gay, junkie "question": "I think in his mind maybe up to that point [of leaving the United States] he was a citizen of the world and maybe not even that, but a citizen of time and place."[46] Professor Jennie Skerl states modernist imagination and cultural education aptly and thoughtfully: "hopefully his work is to break down generic boundaries and media boundaries and in many ways he is a multimedia artist working not only with words."[47] She states modernist form more aggressively: "[Burroughs] has influenced a lot of other artists and has really entered into popular culture. This persona, his image as a transgressive artist, has also been very influential."[48] Several scenes screen the commentary as a suited, hatted Burroughs walked the New York City streets and subways and loitered in its apartments, so as to trail more influential commentaries that lay beneath the technological-realist doldrums of today's society. This filming technique, or rather the ambivalence and diminution of urban landscapes in black-and-white films starring the protagonist, tracks a strong degree of isolation and ambivalence of place, and Burroughs's continuous narrative and mental navigations of existence. Film clips of Burroughs's New York City apartment, which Giorno notes was once a YMCA, turned to today's liberal epithets, slogans, and the slew of less famous Burroughs novels.[49] Biographically at least, we might have offered airs of continuity and celebration of liberal defiance of modern man's system of laws, principles and material-scientific estimations of the mind and body. Audiences could then accept the addict writer's peculiar and magic-like mobility across continents, cities, and histories: still, Weinreich stated Burroughs's writing power more interactively. She synopsizes Burroughs's presumed intellectual understandings of the outside world in ambitious, hyper-rational terms that loudly speak against literature's much argued-for air of public indifference:

> Burroughs seems to have these really crazy ideas. Ideas about a virus, for example, that existed centuries ago that could've been encased in a setting trapped in a sense, and then becomes unleashed at another time and space and this all came out in the early 1980s.[50]

Weinreich's comment favors re-readings and suggest science's incomplete dominance, or rather the incompleteness of the researched understanding of existence. In this light, Weinreich could be seen as favoring a biographical reading that could challenge modern man's objectivity when it comes to health and man's exterior world. But Weinreich assumes the contemporary point about pandemic, and in so doing posits the Beat Generation's narrative significance and relevance, as if to say that repressed archaeologies find the decisive instance of their studies' legitimacy. Weinreich notes that *Cities of the Red Night* appeared in 1981, the same year scientists told the American citizenry of the AIDS virus. She lengthens the writer's shadow, implying that the unheard tales professed future debacles from the suppression of the literary novel's archaeological and temporal recognition. The resultant chaos of ideas would then include instruments of a new, dislocating realism. She thus supposed mankind's symbolic and rhetorical dislocation where reigning questions about existence and civilization are relegated to a crazed irreverence and ignorance.[51] Still, Ann Douglas offers a trite, dense re-reading of the author as acolyte, even suggesting knowledge's fences and the special nature of drugged transferences from beyond: "he travelled outside the human condition imaginatively, or as far as a very human person could go, and reported back to us."[52] Douglass's point calmly re-iterates Norman Mailer's testimony before Congress about *Naked Lunch*, which he summarizes as an excursion to Hell. In this comment, man's pale cocoon of knowledge and its cultural organization are deftly exposed to be weak, cringing, and undemocratic. Burroughs performs, then, modern man's simple task of suggesting greater knowledge beyond society's realm, instead of viciously and parasitically within it. He therefore enacts man's deeply meditated struggle, and so the solid dimensions of his many-faceted transcendence of reality, suggesting that drugs and the occult beckon us to new, conscious frontiers, instead of to the author's residual, monolithic sickness.

In short, *Words of Advice* renders Burroughs's popularity and relevance thoughtfully, without the arabesque of complicated discussions of written form. It robustly cast the elder writer as an American, professing the astute meanings of his American history and maybe his fictional and material instances as an American character. I think, though, that key to this collage of interviews, film, and readings are the notes of rediscovery, in a manner that did not happen for the other Beats or Bowles until the 1990s. The anxiety and rhetorical ambiguity of a "has-been" author was patiently and lovingly explored, to suggest Burroughs's special talent. Other scenes explored the impact of rock and punk, with hordes of young cigarette-smoking European youths bringing their novels to be signed and laughing and enjoying the readings. It is at this point that multi-national and fictional notoriety meant to reach even the mainstream media, with Burroughs reading from "Benway, Inc." on *Saturday Night Live* in 1981. Yet audiences recognized the organized skill of post-liberal communities in the Reagan Era, and the relative agreement that sickness, the occult, and burlesque instances of the modern mind was good material when cross-examining what the "American Dream" hides or misrepresents in the general milieu.

The Commissioner of Sewers

Producer Klaus Maeck re-screened Burroughs against the haggard, sneering postmodern afterscript of the idea's persistent, subversive development of underground geographic context. When audiences project Burroughs's readings above the more intimate *salon* meetings, they are indoctrinated into the form of a greater, and less alien, synthesis. Reading from his works, Burroughs exclaimed his triumph to laughing and cheering multitudes, on the lecture circuit in support of 1981's *Cities of the Red Night* and *The Place of Dead Roads*, extolling man's departure from reason and sanity. When thoughtfully understood, the underground's encouragement turned *The Commissioner of Sewers* into rare and coveted minutes of street braggadocio. Far from *Naked Lunch's* obscenity trial and Burroughs's drug arrests, audiences were led into a communicative sphere that sounds the idea's vagrant transcendence, and the resonant, funny retelling of America's institutional demise.

Maeck's film introduced a central question: could the Beat Generation revive its message, twenty years into the future and against modern man's social, sexual, and graphic problems that it had not clearly understood? Can they shadow a more mature, resistant postmodern, who could easily withstand modernism's death because of its excessive self-evaluation and inflictions upon the Self? I will stress the affirmative: The West's moral and social codes had withered away, and so audiences, too, had made the elder writer less subversive. However, postmodern realism identified class-conscious readings as a recurrent obstacle to knowledge. Burroughs's lecturing moment misrepresents parables of knowledge and narrative elocution, giving way to free representation and the tenacious, promiscuous deciphering of the suffocating postmodern illness. My sense is that class-consciousness and anti-racial critique proliferated symbols and attitudes that were and are consistent with liberal joking that totally dismantled the wealthy patron's set of artistic pretensions. As with T.S. Eliot, the comic moment is the correct one, spurring on the military-capitalist phantom's disgorgement that could be read to demonstrate the materialist imagination's demise, letting loose a chain of symbols exuding neither authority nor rational simplicity.

Burroughs lectured at the Filmkunst Theater on May 9, 1986, delivering a reading of "The Commissioner of Sewers." The subject matter is that important: after reading the scrolls of *Naked Lunch*, the author inevitably turns to the most humorous, unreal moment of graphic and social exile. In all parts of the lecture, Burroughs's diction was effective and measured, and gave the sneering, haggard, and growling junkie greater vocal agency in the last years of his much-celebrated addiction. Clearly, Burroughs retains his prophetic attributes when sharing his words: the written text is thoroughly resonant and so is its rejection of mainstream American realism. As Burroughs read, the story would stand in the background: the camera moves to shots of a well-received author shaking hands with the event's organizers.[53] Clips of Burroughs shaking hands, putting his fix in his coat pocket, and admiring a cheetah, projected the writer's pedestrian underground membership: there were no pretenses to the author's life and exchanges with society that identified him as an underground person.[54] Burroughs flared out his extra-sensory dismay at history's eclipse, telling us how Egyptian tradition included the empty soul's demise:

> Immortality is a monopoly of the truly rich [...] So you got your mummy. However, your existence in the Western lands was contingent on the existence of the mummy. You shall not pass until you know my name [...] Sail through to the Western lands! Mummies rot in a sound condition. Transient hotels beyond the last checkpoint smell the churning house disposal of it—from their skimpy valves.[55]

The absurdity and dislocations of colonial travel operated from beneath Burroughs's knowing eye—he holds a meta-scriptural link that deranges us and rides us into ridiculing tradition's persistent aesthetic illusion. I repeat this point because the shady Midwesterner who is irreverent and irrelevant shadowed clear and cursory discussions of America's studies of the ancients and of the Orient. Characteristic forms of self-presentation limits the scholar's testaments to extra-normal greatness when building serious archaeologies of knowledge for the current academic world. Burroughs's second comment, "Mummies rot in a sound condition,"[56] records the tryst with materiality's over-necessity. Concerns of health and extra-corporeal integrity, or the soul's integrity, disfigure our Christian inheritance of the soul's responsibility. A reading of "The Commissioner of Sewers" is even more masterfully playful, if indolent: "My boyish dreams faded by this heady atmosphere and I'd better play ball or I'll put a sewer through his backyard."[57] Anti-materialist motions advance the vagrant citizen's nonliterary appraisal of his health and sanity: "I prefer a whiff of cold gas, the sewers rupture for miles around. I made a deal on the piping which has bought me a $30,000 home."[58] The narrative tension was deep: William Lee is an exterminator in *Naked Lunch* and voices his extra-sensory protest against the individual's grey, lifeless death because of the labyrinth of moral truths bearing the subject's economic and class determinations of democratic purpose. The narrator's gut feeling, that success is debatable and that poor citizens happily upheld useless forms of knowledge that made them rich, ends with the Commissioner "smoking the sheriff's reefer,"[59] in the shadows of his gloomy nudging that "drug orgies" are "the American way of life."[60] Product-subject relationships are enshrined in anti-class realism that perverted modernist stories. Burroughs's supreme cynicism and vulgar polemic destroys modern man's chain of moral associations, suiting his peculiar agency in a lifeless world.

The Jurgen Ploog interview was without gimmickry, and so Burroughs's spoken record was clear, clean and potent. Modernism's unabridged lessons restate man's imaginative, cerebral freedom to sustain what was true and inviolable. Although Burroughs disarmed biography's speculative moment, noting that writing sprung from his personal life,[61] his modernist imaginations are sure-footed and incisive. When pressed for a comment about Christianity, Burroughs's answer is nonchalant and guiding: "[The Egyptians] took to Christianity] like a vulture takes to carrion."[62] If Burroughs swore off collaboration, and did not encourage narcotic translations friendly to its form, his modernist simplicity was able and wide-reaching, welcoming new generations to form's derived meaning. It is important to realize that Burroughs's novels told of modernism's last imaginative epoch, and so its conclusive vision of the philosopher's joining of text and image with story, and thus with culture:

> My feeling about art is that it makes people aware of what they know and don't know [...] now no child would have any difficulty recognizing Cezanne. He shows people how objects look, seen from a certain angle, certain light. And literally people just thought he had thrown paint on canvas. Once the breakthrough is made, there is a permanent expansion of awareness. But there is always reaction of rage and outrage at the first breakthrough [...] Joyce [was the first one] accused of being unintelligible.[63]

Awareness was part of Burroughs's repeated conjecture—writing must, after all, convey what we do know, and narrates our geographic, verbal and cerebral knowledge. Burroughs tapped modernist tradition's breadth far from beneath its traditional looking glass—namely, from sentiments that the Beats operated a special, cryptically valid technique supported only among young dropouts and would-be criminals. Airs of social legitimacy were not consistent for the Beats—their reception at the hands of Kenneth Rexroth, Norman Podhoretz, and Norman Mailer pronounce their fatal ambivalence to nagging questions of story and theme. This reality forced them to start their own journals and closet interviews by the early 1960s, far from the publishing industry's main audience. Still, Burroughs cleverly synopsizes modernism's exact, classic didactic moment, saying that ideas and writing were endlessly projectable, and that audiences could understand them. Burroughs's references to Cezanne and Joyce spells out the writing's meaningful juncture with necessary social actions, pronouncing the Beat movement's opposition to the socialist realism that had guttered imaginative freedoms. From the instructional angle, Burroughs's commentaries are noteworthy, and suggest the canon's staying power and its intellectual synthesis consistent with and nurturing to man's private and personal domains. The casual link with biography was then explored: Burroughs's retort over Joan's death, "Writing isn't a conscious decision,"[64] collapses the distance between himself and his colleagues, so as to spell out a special, native understanding of intellectual and cultural freedom.

Beat biographies rethreaded this general minute: none of them had rejected freedom in their effort to publish their work. Locating writing in the adult agency's special, contrived situations, and maybe within one's talent for discovery, accentuated the thrust of non–Occidental departure. Whereas, too, Joyce isolates and alienates his characters while preserving their special, conscious dialogue of peril, Burroughs's comment enlivens the growing stress on freedom's optimistic gust that wrote decadence and re-conception. Our moment of self-estimation, too, exudes satisfaction and maturity, recording our growing comfort with the modern moment of truth.

Questions to stir ambivalence's central question—with the future ablaze with signs and realities that in turn stir modernist anti-reason and anti-institutional racisms—cause us to look for a decisive moment, one where public presentation could adopt most of the mainstream's rhetorical virtues. *The Commissioner of Sewers*, should it project that sort of rebirth, owes much to the bragging and building of liberal confidence in an increasingly conservative political world. With "The Word" as Burroughs's guide, and egged on by onlookers who knew a good time, American redrawings of the meeting of Spirit with capitalism projected a greater, more nuanced, writing grasp that could take on disparate social realities and retell them easily and without the acridity of text. Lighthearted readings and spontaneity-friendly performances aside, Burroughs offers the penitent reader the modern moment of achievement and fulfillment. The favored conscious shard, tearing down class sterilization with sincere confidence, absorbed its middle-class obsessions and self-denigrations. Anti-Reagan valor aside, we must remember that conservative Americans had nested a confident bunch of would-be philosophers and thinkers who knew that their grasp of everyday life was increasing and improving, and that drug subcultures had built their necessary circuit ahead of popular music and beyond the reaches of music's grass-roots power. Re-stating "idea" and "word" also builds Burroughs's collective achievement, though drug narrations such as 1991's *Drugstore Cowboy*[65] and 2000's *Trainspotting*[66] ensured the poetics of a complete disintegration that held neither symbol nor spirit. By tapping literary modernism and exceeding it, Burroughs confirms that liberal culture could proliferate its voices to new, novel situations, displaying the modern frame tale's flaws.

Dr. David Woodward's *The Dreammachine* and Renewed Intellectual Possibilities

Before we navigate the chancy relationship between Burroughs's writings and his re-historicization through films, and the semiotic rearrangement of facts and didactic forms in the visual setting, we turn to Erik Mortenson's tentative concept of Burroughs stating a pluralist, rhetorical beginning for modern mankind. Mortenson wrote: "The model of heterotopia that Burroughs proposes blends the need for heterogeneity and totality, for planning as well as objective, in such a way that a viable social alternative appears to emerge."[67] But if we adopt this position, we do so against the work of Eric Mottram in *The Algebra of Need*[68] and Oliver Harris in *The Secret of Fascination* (2004)[69] that supposed man's psychic ills, his modernist depression and sickness, and the failure of his democratic institutions to build rhetorical counterweights to idealism's tracing and sensing. Democracy and pluralism had operated from the sense of the human subject's invigoration, and from the strength of his guiding institutions. Burroughs not only dissolves this, but he also attaches modernist depression to the functioning of capitalist institutions that could advance presumed meanings from his utopian findings. The negotiation was common, where vagrant writers formed part of crime's multi-directional shadow spawning idealism and carrying forth its nebulous pretense to change Western societies. Still, I think that depression and isolation served as the main rhetorical foil, a stance that embalms modernism's special knowledge and its idealism underneath its dark, suspicious-looking canvas. David Woodward's *The Dreamachine* targets counter-history and cross-examinations of drugs in the contemporary scene: idealism, at least, would be tempered with the understanding that it was well within the grasp of man's commercial governance of the Spirit. I think that modern democracy in developed countries directly operates the principle of man's unaesthetic, depraved social and personal limitations, when joined to Burroughs's raw verse that scribbles post-industrial graphics and raw materials to again speak post-industrial tales of decadence. These limitations, in turn, restrict modern man's psychological and cultural estimations of Self when Burroughs redressed social and intellectual policy to be constructive components of experience. They either paraphrase the author's reticence or overstate his subversive *métier* when understanding his history and perspectives. More thoughtfully, the basic materiality of future narco-novels by Ken Kesey, Hunter Thompson, and Thomas Pynchon raised humor and dislocation to be emblematic of narcotic man's unreason and failure. From this light, we turn to Burroughs's emphasis on the mind's non-narcotic expansions, and his diminutive reasons for the street's psychic and semantic decline. If so, I think these developments provoke Burroughs's attempt to state idealism's constructive thrust.

David Woodward gives a sparing and basic yet very thoughtful retelling of the Flicker, a tall machine with portals of light that Gysin used to stimulate writing and painting in the 1950s. He recalls the machine's counter-imagism and counter-rationalism that broadened man's intellectual and perceptual rigor and easily interfaced with narcotic-colored literary and philosophical themes that indifferently shuffled drug humors and comic parapsychology. Shorn of purer moments of idealism found in Michelle Green's *The Dream at the End of the World*[70] or in *Conversations with William S. Burroughs*,[71] *The Dreamachine* aggressively posits the legend of the Flicker, and counter-histories that heralded it as a major philosophical achievement, and re-writings of subjective Man's attentions to media, technology and urbanism that figure in its questionable capitalist referents. Woodward adopted an ominous tone to be jocular and maybe indifferent, condensing the street license of the gangster-influenced Burroughs who ran with criminal mafias at his writing career's outset: "If you think you're perfect, try worshipping something that doesn't exist."[72] We will not realize man's practical necessity, nor any solutions to his special problems as could be found in psychology and science. Instead, Nostradamus's unheard-of archaeology signaled romantic visions of a greater, more inclusive aesthetic existence to diversify examples of reason, truth, and finally story. We are, then, broadening horizons *contra* Beat works that spread their very real, capitalist-funneled gangsterism to prescribe and limit man's perceptual grasping, and use of its *praxis*:

> Nostradamus would pass his hands, fingers outstretched, atop a tower in Florence in quick succession, intuitively and resolutely, translated by his optic nerve in a 12-pulse succession. [He] passed his closed eyes, allowing a neuro-cortical activity through his tissue, and leading him to a dream-state where he would verbally formulate his vision.[73]

Woodward's supersession of Immanuel Kant as rationalist and metaphysical thinker was not new: Eastern parapsychology stressed that man's specific perceptual powers included those linked to the brain and its psychic ordering of one's thoughts and conceptual development. This justified examples of cult ritual's specific, parenthetic rephrasing of primitive man's collective unconscious and conscious realism. In this sense, Woodward's excavation is cursory, an indie chance at new pathways to knowledge that could collapse Victorian social models through text-sign proliferations of an illusory multiplicity of vision, thought, and perceptions. It should be noted that Green's rendition was brief and summary: she attested to the proliferation of idea-concept relations anew, in a studied anticipation of future secular philosophies. But Woodward presses forward with his history and links the Flicker to Richard Wagner and Friedrich Nietzsche, both of whom surmised "an intoxicating sensual experience."[74] He descends upon Winnifred Wagner's donation of the machine to Adolf Hitler, who "proclaimed he had waited all his life to experiment with it."[75] I think that the mixing of modern man's post-structural *difference* with lingering romantic attentions to light and its sequencing, harbors much of Burroughs's collective archaeology. Ideas that mankind, too, alter the substance and logic of dreams and memories precede Green's tenuous commentary on the Tangier circle's psilocybin trips that, Green reported, extol the rearrangement of thoughts and idea-development. The legend of Burroughs as narcotics theorist, ontologist and therapist, too, could be given more theoretical weight. Woodward implies that Burroughs unearths an archaeological instance of intellection that idealizes man's renewed capacity to construct reality, and in doing so forced apocalyptic thinkers to puzzle the vicious emotional and psychic circles in penitent, suffering European societies. Woodward thus added one more air of legitimacy to Burroughs's broad and quizzical attempts at a counter-history, but carefully speaks his romantic attentions to thought, sense, and creation to a counter-creation in objective, concrete terms. The counter-thrust to Burroughs's picaresque revision of the Book of Genesis in "A.J.'s Annual Party" in *Naked Lunch*[76] is a valuable departure that led Burroughs away from the Beat movement's thematic singularity. If we were, then, to dismiss humor to be a non-constructive component of modern thought and subjectivity, we might tread man's impetus to social revolution to spawn liberal generations that continually sought counter-history as a vehicle for man's social change and indoctrination.

Woodward's account included an interview segment at Burroughs's home in Lawrence, Kansas, months before his death in 1997. Presenting a shadowy and reclusive Burroughs and airbrushed of any press or popular culture intrusions, the interview recalled Burroughs's able yet oft-forgotten critique of Drug War capitalism and the dying man's estimation of today's American moral scene. Haunting stories of the author's essential self-reflection of facts cannot be ignored: recorded in isolation, the interview features Burroughs's erratic intensities versus the lingering, post–Reagan tale of places that had underwent enough of the shock and spiked horror of drug tales that aggravate the lurking, penitent moralism which spurred endless speculation and preaching over the new scourges: crack, heroin, and methamphetamine. I still believe, though, that Burroughs's commentaries and reflections on the state of the War on Drugs relay a storied voice, or rather the collective of moral-sounding or prophecy-addled grit that surround drug-taking pretenses and "vicious circle" theories. I also will state that moral redevelopment of the Old World's narcotic truths, when they had first come from Burroughs, Ginsberg, and Huxley, challenges democracy's seriousness and its joining of histories and traditions in the multi-ethnic United States. Comments are summary, stating the author's verbal decline as a social messenger: "They're in jail, some sort of control. Possibly drug-related,"[77] and go on to read news articles where "1 oz. heroin, 1 oz. morphine"[78] had been found on the defendants. News clippings allowed Burroughs to doctor and crop the spoken content of words and concepts to assume a persistent, rather than generational or temporally limited, nexus of moral and personal repression.

Ploog's interview does not introduce Burroughs as a policy-friendly thinker, who spit out ballyhooed stabs at the current American policy and briefly postulated on the subject of anti-drug epithets, but avoids spurious examples of the gateway theory or other anti-drug analyses of addiction, or the guiding sentiment of today's laws that could make drug policy dynamic or epochal in its importance. The drug baron was at least reflective and broad in his stinging appraisal as a priest in 1991's *Drugstore Cowboy,* plainly attesting to the machinations of authority's conspiracy. By contrast, Woodward allowed Burroughs to sermonize from simple examples in the local newspaper in the projection of democracy's decay, making him attest to the decline of man's passive moral recognition of the now-residual problem that carries less cultural and cerebral context. Still, Burroughs favors his generation: "Is it possible to take drugs and still succeed in life?"[79] I think that this formal question hasn't been answered: studies and narrative confirm the overabundance of Victorian moral and societal controls today, in turn shadowing the literary great's sudden self-evaluation. In this light, I believe that *The Dreamachine* de-emphasizes aural and visual cues to highlight modern man's contemporary reflections, or indeed the weight of today's popular culture signifying authorial development of ideas that acquire external momentum. Between glasses of wine, the old man at his coffee table talks about modern man's basic problem without the savagery or spice of today's media-influenced social politic.

The Dreamachine did not take advantage of the richness of concerns of time and place: its visual and aural strategies take note of the author's resonant fame and occultism without considering the full weight of discovery's total impact. Early scenes that include the Flicker or "Dreamachine" operate the spinning machine's reflection of light against the crying, crashing intensity of Jajouka music, coinciding only with Ian Sommerville's discovery that was then relayed to Burroughs. We might add that the artistic and cultural ambitions of other philosophers and notables were not considered, nor is any attention given to the archaeological relevance of the Dreamachine to the history of art, media, and politics. Without exchanging crucial analogues of modern man's subjectivity, we are left instead with a New York café gathering where Burroughs and Ginsberg signed copies of their books with Leonardo di Caprio in tow, talking to the two men.[80] Fame's vague and distant application, in contrast to the Beat Generation's renegade pose as its undying social metaphor, neutralizes historiographical stirrings of truth. We might then believe that the two elderly men had forgotten the social negotiations of their ideas and public suppositions. There were no readings of the author's works, poetry, or private suppositions of truth: these were left out of the social picture of the underground's elderly *literati* shaking hands and holding newborn babies.[81] We do not exactly know why this gathering is clipped at the beginning to introduce Woodward's idea-shattering discoveries. The two men's nearing of death is the lone narrative thread, hence the suggestion of a literary transference that is incomplete and unadorned when detailing the author's biography and sayings. Perhaps death forced us to cough up the waiting, civilization-bending truths and dictums. Burroughs's avoidance of this angle had not been studied in this light, instead allowing us to peruse the fact that studies of drugs and Moroccan occultism were incomplete and had not been included in his films. The unclear relationship between public and cerebral Selves may force us to question form, too. Still, Woodward hangs special motifs of possibility, versus endless filmed examples that attenuate narcotic form. The classic idea—that authors can be studied during their lives, instead of when deceased and thus not cognizant of the idea's essential redevelopment—returned authorship to the author for a final time. From this beginning, we can apply the colors of Burroughs's moral and personal consistency, and the consistent thread of social recognition, to suggest a greater examination that engaged more signs of his considerable archaeology. In this last instance, *The Dreamachine* points to the unappealing template: recent films ignore large parts of Burroughs's studies of remote cultures, limiting our understandings of the man and his education and indoctrinations. We shall now turn to a newer example of Burroughs's partial translation of Orient meaning and self-conceptualization through the second example of a possible muse, Brion Gysin: *Destroy All Rational Thought*, which applied non-linear techniques and supposed mutual East-West universes in the modern imagination and setting, affects us when we traced ideation to its less stable, and therefore less academic, beginnings.

Destroy All Rational Thought

John Dover's review of the 48-minute collage of interviews, poetry readings, live Moroccan music, Burroughs's confessions, and art-indie mini-films in 2007's *Destroy All Rational Thought* includes the following verdict: "this strange film suffers from a complete lack of narrative focus, injudicious editing, and slapdash camera work. The big let down for the organizers, one suspects, is that their star attraction (Burroughs) was too ill/old to attend, instead sending his endorsement for the event via a brief video message."[82] Dover tore apart the unconvincing link between Burroughs's mind and the Moroccan occult arts, dismayed with the film's operations of Burroughs's biographical, artistic, and written content. He then summarizes his response to the event, hosted at the Here To Go Show in Dublin in 1991, saying that "what is depressingly absent throughout is any coherent explanation of what is going on and why."[83] The goings-on and conversational transparency of the theatergoers, Burroughs fans, and commentators associate Gysin with Burroughs's refreshed, vigilant imagination and perspectives as an author and thinker. Gysin is favorably compared with American expatriate writer-composer Paul Bowles, and the resulting synopsis of counter-cultural imaginings of the Orient notes Gysin's obscurity, his unrecognized co-authorship of Burroughs's short works including *The Exterminator*, his propensity to crime and to street relationships, and the unpublished errata during most of the 1950s. These themes contrast with the deeply literate, aggressively studious Bowles, who underwent a long career in music and fiction. They, in turn, attribute the instability of low-rent authorial engagements of Eastern philosophical works and their supposed mystical outlook. Themes that spoke to Gysin's repression, then, told us of the potentially greater, and historically much more irrational, humanist inheritance.

My sense of the film gathered the simplest instructional tone: Gysin transforms Burroughs's mind and in doing so opened new doors in underground visual and written text, yet also impeded straight translations of the occult with authenticity's façade. Occidental readings of drugs and their imaginative influences separate White-Other consciousness, place, and narrative, keeping separate domains that spawn sporadic breakthroughs of the mind and art as its subject. Pairing the two cultures accents Burroughs's private longing for Orient novelty and exoticism through Gysin, mismatching diffusions of thought and sensibility through drugs within domains of education, wealth and security in the West that, in turn, glorify Burroughs's authorship as the mark of his intellectual maturity. An aged Burroughs, seated in a garden filled with green plants, exclaims the sting of his loss, and of his generation's loss. These, in contrast to the hordes of young, clowning, and intoxicated patrons, restate form's ambivalence as it challenges our grounding of concepts and themes in their modern rhetorical and spiritual instance. Humanism is thus a more open concept, though legends and their remembrance mixed the archetypal reasoning of tradition with more inventive, postmodern effects reconciling the occult's mystery with reality, or even to overstate it when it comprised an engaging, continuous story. It is, then, possible to see at least some import of Gysin's role as a catalyst, even without much investigation into his life, times, and private imagination that greatly lengthens Burroughs's Orient pretense, even when far less schooled in Arab culture, history, or poetics than the studied, elite-sounding Bowles.

I think that Burroughs's confessions, plus the avant-garde film sequences that include short takes of Burroughs and Gysin, did more to accomplish Burroughs's private feeling of authorial and personal loss. They also stated his compassion for street figures and for their social life, rather than adorn or instruct us about the vocal, robust portrait of less-heard Moroccan celebrities who held undefined roles in cementing Beat works, community, and Euro-American underground ideations. Gysin's role in co-writing Burroughs works such as *The Exterminator* and *The Third Mind* was included: these, with the favorable discussion about how he held within him an indeterminate, yet engaging, consciousness that profoundly inspires Burroughs, are the subject of Burroughs's first interview. Critic and journalist Ira Cohen pays tribute to the tactile form of Gysin's private legend:

> Don't rage the seal of the sound of the word
> with water, don't touch the dimples of the beloved.
> Said the wild roach,
> Then the interior, the thing is outside you,
>
> Where the hand comes, yet make what you will,
> Throw fire in the wing of eternity—[84]

Ethnographer and scholar Peter Lamborn Wilson, who "met mystics of the Islamic world from Morocco to Java,"[85] reads a variation on his "Manifesto of Poetic Terrorism" to serve as the Beat ethical pretense:

> Don't be spontaneous, unless in poetic terrorism
> Dress up, give a false name, be legendary
> Best poetic terrorism has muted form, don't get caught
> Not in this time, nor in this life.[86]

Maintaining the criminal and heretic shadings of Eastern occult forms concentrated the dimensions of its active power, where textual references to *The Exterminator* complicated modernist attentions to the spirit's essential dynamic. Gysin's links to the Tangier underworld circuit, then, augment the literary movement's special message as it drew attention to Burroughs's persistent shadowing of Kerouac, sifting perceptions among underground readers instead of bearing prophetic testaments to timeless literary forms. More, these poems document the underground's rhetorical survival and the necessity of trans-symbolisms and the contra-canonical thesis to valorize motion, uncertainty, cleverness, and tact when conjecturing form's many-tongued expression. Burroughs, too, thoughtfully enunciates the artist's conundrum: Gysin was unrecognized as an artist, and was seldom part of the avid Tangerino social scene with Bowles. Green's narration of Gysin's engagement of social life in examples such as *The Thousand and One Nights* restaurant presumed his narrative isolation from Bowles. With this in mind, Burroughs's curt commentaries about him restated stinging, acrid and vehement criticisms of Bowles from Gysin, Alfred Chester, Mohammed Mrabet, and Mohammed Shukri, all of whom detested Bowles's indifference to their work and his skepticism about their own creative legitimacy. Contrastive shots of Burroughs, too, complicate art's symbolic message and co-authorship's deep uncertainty. *Destroy* includes private re-shootings of Burroughs standing alone in the shadows, privately meditating at times, his eyes shut, then open. These minutes are paired with the throngs of New York city street-goers amidst incandescent-lit advertisements for "Apollo, Finest Foreign Films," "Goldfinger," "Frank Sinatra," "The New Interns," and "Without The Beat."[87] The depressive hanging of images and reels spelling out Burroughs's loneliness and of his private, isolated self in his meditations are replayed over the glut of multiplicity, prosperity, and ubiquity in New York City's entertainment culture. Thus, the film's imagery and temporal motifs aggravate the author's deep personal guilt about being a herald of liberal virtue, relevance, and study. Culture's "force," then, operate Burroughs's private admission that Gysin held deep and meaningful sympathy with him. At one point, the silent Burroughs begins talking, and speaks silently without voice, "thank you for standing by me." Devoid of tears, Burroughs opines his necessary relationship to his lover, and counted his humanity against the signs and motions of the burgeoning capitalist world. Splitting Burroughs's face into halves and quarters, and into concave mirror images, could explain the depth of the cut-up's translation of authorial intent. Should we, then, view Burroughs's subjective sense of himself to be "cut," we would understand Gysin's gift to center on his compassion and friendship: he had an effect on Burroughs's life and writing, and his insouciant-looking artistic license and humor gave him a second chance at knowledge realization. Burroughs's internalization, then, pushed for meditations that told of his private spiritual and moral *pathos*.

Performances by the Joujouka were true to *jdab*'s syntactic form, and free of any interference or modification from the Dublin audience and staff: though the two worlds lie separate in this instance, many longhairs attended the event, and they occasionally mock the cameraman with fake grins and jokes aimed at the viewer. Alcohol and marijuana, though, are evident in many scenes, suggesting passive involvement in conscious transformations. The musicians render easily the complication of melody, harmony, and scale on small, wooden *rhaitas* (reeds): trance by the musicians, too, is easily rendered, and followed with an unrelated performance by the Baby Snakes who blare their noisy stage presence with songs about drugs. But if the film's administrative steps did not accomplish transcendence, at least the literary and artistic imagination had aggressively queried Gysin's persona during his thoughtful speculations. There are many comments about Gysin's work perusing its spiritual-leaning qualities, and also hint commentary underscoring Gysin's "problems with the area." We thus understood that he was unsure about Western understanding of the specific consciousness assembling sound and vision in forms of trance. An intoxicated and boisterous Hamri eggs on the players: here, too, the script included no examples of his painting, and so missed the chance that we could transpose visual instances of drug-induced trance or its specific impact upon community. Thus, Western ascriptions to Eastern mysticism and imaginations were pretense, far from mainstream development of the mind and actions resulting from it. There are no patrons who dance, with more of them simply observing: it must be said that exoticism's flavor, when contrasted with Burroughs's absence, forces us to recognize rhetorical and social difference anew, with no guiding metaphysics to assign meaning. But we also understand Burroughs as he recalls his visions' specific form, away from public life:

> A most important element was the vividness of [Gysin's] presence, perfectly clear, just as if he were there. He is present in many of my Land of the Dead dreams. If I look around in a dream and one person after another in the dream is dead, I know it's the Land of the Dead. Two young Samaritans helped me out of a wrecked BMW last Thursday, September 17th, that's one of my special dates. I even got the *New York Times* that day. They said, "Well, you're lucky you're not dead."[88]

Burroughs, then, opts out of the gathering because of his trauma and his self-imposed superstition: he, too, had examined emblems of his corporeal and conscious Selves in isolation, away from the magnet of public attention and notoriety. "Vividness," too, suggests a calculation favorable to the Tangier expatriate period and the cockiness of East-West transitions to favor the underground and its capacity to reify and render concrete its root logics that depended more on *shtick*. The offbeat relationship corrodes modernist art and pretends a nebulous, missing link that could only be understood with very careful studies of the underground's pretenses. Materialism's unsavory glut of images, plots, and heroes strode easily and densely past: the pathways of Burroughs's mind are, then, parallel to those of his eclipse and redundancy. Yet Dover was clear: what is the relationship between these disparate and seemingly unrelated shards of culture? Without a stronger penning of Gysin as the painter and thinker, audiences are limited to exoticism's more familiar pose. Even as an unheralded possibility, I believe that his claims are justified. It is certain that works by Michelle Green and, more recently, Barry Miles, documented much more artistically the deep narcotic immersion and the impromptu, hilarious conflagration of narcotic imaginations. When, for instance, Gysin stares at a mirror as he was plied with drugs and food items in a 36-hour "paranormal experiment" in Paris, Miles attests to the larger-than-life meditation on modern artistry and intellectual truth as it stood in the mind's pathways:

> He saw scientists in nineteenth-century labs, great battles, and chieftains of unknown races. After twenty-four hours the images disappeared and he wrote that "there seemed it was a limited area that one could see only a certain distance into, uh, where everything was covered with a gently palpitating cloud of smoke which would be about waist high [...] that was the end, there was nothing beyond that."[89]

Our answer appears certain: *Destroy All Rational Thought* did not excavate this peculiar hallucinogenic form with its lingering Freudian impulses to memory-derived truth as stimulating narrative and meaning, and misses the chance at sketching the wealth of his presumed accomplishment that memoirs and histories have targeted as the partial deconstruction of Burroughs's narcotic thesis favoring dislocations of the mind and its sense-perceptions and thoughts. The film does not convey much of the writing as information, instead featuring a few clips where Gysin hastily paints on the ground and wanders through the streets of Paris. In this tepid manner, an informative chance was missed: the absence of commentators and critics, too, meant that there were no formal characteristics to dreams and hallucinations when paired with the curious, uninformative tempo of Burroughs's deliberations about his friend.

Still, *Destroy All Rational Thought* ably performs visual and rhetorical technique. Politicizing and popularizing *jdab* as a de-intellective form showcases its partial survival in realms far from scripturalism, situating the coolness, mannerisms, and status-friendly separation of bodies, gestures, and attitudes against the warm, dynamic ritual. I think that, too, Burroughs includes a necessary bibliography of notables, all of whom infused popular art with new venom. Lastly, the well-attended event and the concrete criticisms and praises from long-haired youths cross-stroke Bowles's statement that Moroccan ritual arts exhibited purity and separation from the West's eyes: hippies are many in number, good-natured, and serious about their investigation into the man who invented cut-ups. The skill, too, for painting authorial isolation and depression was easily navigated, without textual examples. Thus, the author as literary icon and notable supplants fictional anxiety, and those of a younger man who published fiction in order to survive.

Author-catalyst relationships are also examined in the shorter plots, including one that portrays a suited Burroughs calling a fez-topped Gysin on the telephone and then catching the train.[90] Another includes Burroughs, behind a desk interviewing Gysin, who then accepts a loan to pay for his exhibitions.[91] These are retellings of the improvised framework for publication and the artist's representation: non-recognition, then, meant that the depth and breadth of the artist's message would not truly be understood, whereas Gysin would endure the street's temptations and instances of crime that favored Tangier's brawling, seedy underground that is first relayed to us in *The Dream at the End of the World*. It is unclear from *Destroy All Rational Thought* whether the mainstream or the Moroccan street scene, or both, had eclipsed Gysin. Still, it does seem that he operates tenable rhetorical links to the unknown, and in one poem was the first person to understand Hassan-i-Sabbah, Lee's nemesis in *Naked Lunch*.[92] Easily rendered examples of the Moroccan music's combinations of notes, chords and melodies all suggest the vindication of Bowles's thesis that *jdab* was *skhoun*, "the real hot jazz." Audiences derived, then, the stanzas' prescient fluidity, the dancers' increased motions, and pleasant enunciations of traditional body, spirit, and the sense that modernist verbal and thematic formulas revive the romantic, licentious spirit of derivable mind-body confusions favoring semantic growth and comic detections that destructed mankind's stereotypical *ethos*. From *A Hundred Camels in the Courtyard*, the appreciation of street subversions was clear: deep, challenging, and graphic challenges that distort or destroy human spirit and body were easily resolved and arranged thoughts, prose, and their sincerity from beneath the structure of not-so-complex brackets of notes that, as in jazz, inheres complex navigations of reality with a simple, movable idea-structure. American, European, and Moroccan conscious instances need not be profound to be understood, though links between crime and super-intellectual knowledge were and are a familiar testament to man's growing conscious powers as ascending, intensifying grand narrative rhetoric rose alongside 20th century industrial re-conceptualization and re-nationalization.

Silencing the living instance, or rather paintings and cut-ups that academically state Gysin's contributions to art, humanism, and counterculture affixes the negative for audiences. His link was secret, and a missing link to conscious understandings of drugs and the occult. Still, we rehearsed the obvious message: underground culture and community depended on non–Western cultures to trumpet the power of their embryonic, precarious message. Recalling that Gysin was a sometime criminal, too, concentrates the valor of his living realms and imagination. We are reminded that the general public must understand their peculiar, forbidden legends so that they will better understand themselves. Alongside Bowles, still alive in 1991, we may tend to the basic evocation of form: there is probably more to be understood from painting and literary manipulations about the drugged mind, so we must anoint its creator, not his formal criticism. This is true despite the fact Bowles discovered Moroccan folk music as early as 1933 and had studied it more comprehensively, with an academic voice. Gysin's link with rockers, then, projected the greater conversational moment against more dour arguments that speak of tradition's remoteness and narrative distance, painting greater cross-cultural agreement.

A Man Within and Rock and Roll's Invasive Attentions

A Man Within (2010) did more to excavate Burroughs's living moment and the constellations of friends and outtakes that nourished his underground mind and body. This film took noticeable advantage of Super 8 films, interviews with rock stars Patti Smith and Iggy Pop, and psychedelic visual and pornographic angles that elicit the sudden transformation of American visual aesthetics to turn into a deep and endlessly referential pandemic of the senses. We are shown a Burroughs that critics frequently limited or turned off in assessments of the writer's ideas and theoretical witticisms. Screening the sensitive, sympathetic instances of the writer's loves, pastimes, and obsessions did much to decenter the author's literary accomplishment. *A Man Within*, inasmuch as it augments Burroughs's biography, explains his life in accordance with his physical and psychic condition, and thus the man that rock vicariously earned its legitimacy through stirrings of the media-infused personality. Numerous outtakes, too, ensure a private, off-camera functioning of his morals and ideas and held many beguiling secrets that recover and rebuild his sexual and moral paranoia. It should be said that discoveries and inventions are inscribed in the cultural tale of *On the Road* to be part of a fantasy, or rather the fantasy for extra-normal transcendence, thus carrying no true material presence. The film's modernist form, when applied to basic angles of the individual's life, traces Burroughs's everyday to suit later viewings that attach sympathy and compassion to the writer's list of ills and legal scuffles. *A Man*

Within thus elicits the same consumption of Burroughs as rockumentaries might gather on MTV or PBS. Should we appreciate the author as a human being with private, delicate pathways of self-involvement and even *pathos*, we then showcase rock's true triumph of complete absorption of the elder generation's prophetic form.

Rock attentions to sex, psychedelic drugs and experiences, and idealism broaden the film's imaginative twist and so develop communitarian *ethos* friendly to Burroughs's written and public persona. We are led throughout the movie to rock descriptions of fairness, equity, and tolerance as meaningful descriptive themes that accentuate counterculture's tenacity at the fringe and the underscored depth of its meditations and history. It should be said, too, that visual technologies eschew the narrative and biographical mobility, building the tension and burden of authorship and identity. Black-and-white clips forecast the 1950s and its endless street multitudes, and speedily screened shots of Burroughs walking among men in hats from his factory, thus suggesting the author's possible role as progenitor.[93] The screened portrait also benefits from the shadowed biography given to Gysin, touted for his transcriptions of the Jajouka and his role in popularizing the "cut-up." Cuts featured Gysin walking and smoking in the Paris streets, and a barrage of graffiti-colored shots so as to simulate speculations about his unique and clever desiccation of consciousness.[94] Iggy Pop and Patti Smith give lighthearted excavations of Burroughs's gay romances, and the private instance of his sweet-sounding confession, diluting radical polemic's aggressive whims and urban super-rhetoric that tell us serious-sounding underground tales of power:

> Bobby Shafto's gone to sea,
> Silver buckles on his knee,
> One fine day he'll marry me,
> Pretty Bobby Shafto.[95]

As was true of Kerouac's biographies, every day or pedestrian reminiscences interrupt the critical looking glass that is theoretical and abstract. Smith's down-to-earth commentaries, when pointing decisively to Burroughs's gay tensions or over-suggesting her possible link and thus Burroughs's hetero-normativity, remind us of the author's human ends. Smith is clear to document the exchange of feelings, relaxation, and reticence that make Burroughs so beautiful to her. Recalling their nighttime sleeping ritual, her reticent warmth and unrealized love pacifies more acerbic readings of Burroughs as a man, which includes therapist Dr. Dennis M. Dailey's curt ejection, "I think Freud probably would think him deeply, deeply troubled, profoundly mentally ill."[96] The screen runs to a colored penis and the explosion of colored text-like squares emerging from Burroughs's brain.[97] Symbol-infused metaphors thus gauge or forecast Burroughs's countercultural and psychedelic transferences that were more suggestible to audiences, though they were erratic and irrationally drawn versus counterculture's possibly occultist origins. But filmmaker John Waters interjects the most durable thematic attention that raises and heralds the positive justice of Burroughs's archaeology and ethics: "in the 50s, anything opened up for good thinking. People talk about the 50s and see happy days. It was horrible, it was the most terrible time."[98] Raising homosexuality's guts in a heterosexual world—Kerouac had spun the foil of happiness, joy, and juicy sex that was "fun"—spins modernist ingenuity when arguing in favor of the author's special crisis. Idealism's solstitial, waning moment of relevance, its harrowing end, and its special techniques for building modern "life," trace Burroughs's lingering vagrancy and criminal pose among rockers who admired him. If we record, too, his pain and isolation, we augment modernist genius by tracing its novelty to the instance of a peculiar, guarded humanity that when exposed, is the human's basic, un-written, beauty and simplicity. These were, decidedly, not themes that made headlines in the general public's Burroughs, and it may be simpler to say he is pulsed for telling us that vicious street intensities are the "true" form. If we apply the simplest dictum from Hutcheon's analysis of historiography in film, "The camera, like the stage, is said to be all presence and immediacy,"[99] I think that Smith, Pop, the critics, and the filmmakers deserve credit for retelling their deep and productive sympathy that noticeably colors the rise of punk during the 70s and 80s. Burroughs's friends lovingly recall his pastimes and neurotic behaviors, and testified to his silence and reticence. Historiographically, the sustained, constant accent concentrates counterculture's power to change minds and attitudes through simple, plain didactic about a landmark figure who wasn't known and kept his gay "closet" hidden until well into the 1960s. There would be no verbal statement of genius in making "Beat"—Burroughs was gay, and Kerouac wasn't. Still, durable links between Burroughs's creativity and his message versus remain solid and intact, versus those which shoot the dying man's private reflections and subject status: these include Super 8 scenes of Burroughs's automobile travels and residence in Lawrence, Kansas weeks before his death in 1997.[100]

In truth, experiential foci in the making of *A Man Within* were narrowed and truncated to omit any kind of deepened homosexual belonging. Burroughs's gay friends, and rock musicians expostulating gay Burroughs's sometime affections for Joan Vollmer, left out the annals of pornography and drugged sickness that limited the writing's impact. Hence, modernist writing promotes imaginative revolutions owed to its examples of drugs, media, technologies, travel, democracy, capitalism, and so on. I think that, too, modern man's penitent realizations of personal and intellectual freedoms trace the image's appreciable landscape amidst the summation of many historical moments and signs of the artist's social power beneath the counterculture's umbrella pulling together many different semantic and national origins. The tendency to raise the hyper-rational collages of image, writing, thoughts and perceptions, in turn, calculate modernist intensity and its rock n roll navigation. These, it must be said, are construed in this film to be even more patient and fulfilling than the unfolding of Ginsberg's renewed idealism when meeting with Bob Dylan. The occasional examples of Super 8 film on the road, shooting at the Kansas home, and continuing on the American lecturer circuit established time and place, and the familiarity of settings that build thought and social perspectives in American Studies: the "American story" is detectable, formally consistent with today's issues-derived reading of underground short stories. This is counter-faced by an aggressive idea-building structure set off with decisive modernist dogma friendly to the Beat axis of creation. Memory's expansion, perhaps to World War I, also calculates political and revolutionary postures in the mid–20th century setting. *A Man Within*, inasmuch as it examined Burroughs from his obsessions, restated countercultural *pathos* as its legitimate triumph. It gave Burroughs what he and Ginsberg craved and adulated for so long—the tribes of rock and roll.

Adaptations of Burroughs's Novels and Post Rediscoveries of the Text

David Cronenberg's Epic Film *Naked Lunch*

Of William S. Burroughs, David Sterritt wrote about the cut-up's awesome semiotic and scriptural motions:

> Bodies of text created in such ways are acts of trompe l'oeil on the printed page, appearing as ordinary blocks of prose until reading reveals them as expansive networks of faux continuity, discontinuity, and paracontinuity that explode conventional ideals of linearity and coherence.[101]

Sterritt's immediate purpose was to examine Burroughs's rhetoric through audiology, so as to invite the collision of spoken instances to suggest modern catastrophe's re-reading. We are left guessing about the visual form in film, as character-splitting and conscious-splitting scenes and screenplay rhetorically dislocate or assemble modernist purposes in the questing adventure. When narrations were torn apart and re-formed, they reveal biographical scars consistent with the addict-adventurer's depressive pose, and that re-introduce his geographies of horror and addiction. In a classical reading, Sterritt's inflation of Burroughs's narrative variables can cause us to project anti-rational threads that escape and de-rationalize the sentient being that ensured narrative order. Nonetheless, audiences will inevitably add Oliver Harris's didactic premise: *Naked Lunch* presumed a specific, set biographical indoctrination of the Self, carrying with it necessary plots and subplots crucial to gothic retellings of drugged Orientalism.[102] My question has more to do with the narrative order, sitting in its formalist place with no greater pretensions, or had split into substrata that project Lee's necessary depression and isolation against his heroic pose. In either instance, David Cronenberg's *Naked Lunch* casually travels literary and narcotic worlds, with the stamp of Burroughs's carefully edited reflection as the partial guide to sickness and sorcery. If anything, the nucleus of major characters and side characters operate a separate synthesis, and one friendly to modernist writings about the story's timeless situation. Expansions of Lee's vocation and intellection sit beside the frame tale that ensured postmodern decay through "the exterminator," and are saddled with Burroughs's egoistic and practical unhappiness and unreason of being nobody. They also muse the intellect's greater realization in the maze of personal and extra-national journeys, and into unconscious evocations of love and humanity. Sterritt also references the projection of Lee as the main character—because of Lee's loss of Joan, Cronenberg's re-inscription of the muse's re-incarnation away from marriage and story dislocated Lee's essential, visible humanity and morality. Lee is, at best, a small group's ringleader negotiating intellectual rights with parasitic forces of self-indoctrination that strip the word of its necessary might. We might ask, then: "Was Cronenberg's film faithful to the modernist theme, or a corporate gothic that trounced all forms of intellection through sickness?" After all, *Naked Lunch* had been written within the Victorian insight of a staged battle between good and evil.

Criticism that covered the word's power and modernism's engaging, drugged debacles admitted to writing's privileged status and its postmodern attention to forms. Sterritt wrote of the audio technique of splitting or altering spoken voices in Burroughs's cut-up, noting intellectual and viewing sonic growth "when the text is chosen or written rather than when it is sound-recorded or edited."[103] When landscaping the story's background, *NL's* spoken screenplay operates on serious themes and materiality. The protagonist's diminished material surroundings, plus the dialogue's unstable format, force Cronenberg to noticeably alter the screenplay to suit perceptions of the protagonist (Peter Weller) to the novel's delectable humanity and visible virtue. Cronenberg greatly limited Weller's spoken portrayal: scenes such as Joan's impromptu "William Tell" are staged without words, and with a stoned Martin reading from *The Yage Letters*.[104] Meanwhile, literary fiction's presumed notoriety would appear more protected and real in its sensory minutes of viewing. When Martin offers to "put [him] in touch with the guy"[105] who publishes pornography, and laughingly disbars him from talking because he's an exterminator, it is part of a noisy dialogue about writing's originality.[106] Seated in the well-lit cafeteria interior, actors engaging "the Word" faced no peripheral obstacles or social or national polity that interrupted our viewing. Joan's death, by comparison, reached for marriage's futility, and even man's rhetorical absence of street determinations when the literary pretension activated Burroughs's surrogates. I think that Cronenberg's talent was to circumscribe his hero, instead opting for the classic, heroic American character who instilled legitimate archaeological purposes that, as with Peter Parker in *Spiderman*[107] and Christopher Reeves in *Superman*,[108] cross-examine the literary great versus the postmodern ruin of his health, his life, and his loves.

Jack Seargent wrote in his analysis of *NL*, "the narcotic fragmentation suggested in the metanarrative in and around *Naked Lunch*'s writing, becomes mirrored in the film's disregard for the division between reality/fantasy."[109] I think that limiting Lee's consciousness through drugs owed the details of his specific quest to the scrapping of whole sections of narcotics psychology and pathology, and the instruments of drugged states and rituals that brought drugs into the occult fray: this must be said against the weight of evidence that suggest the audience's traditional literary readings favoring drugged dreaming and its subversions of context. Michael Prince's reading of the film in *Adapting the Beat Poets* also favored metanarrative theory above specific drug cultures and their license to spoil and derange the American moral aesthetic. Drugs were barely a part of studies of the American social scene, and our speculations about them called for Lee's detailed accounts and for the subplots that arranged didactic engagements of Burroughs's pharmacology. Further, conspiracy theories might comprise a final stratagem to inflate the counterculture into a thematic force. Prince appropriately located Cronenberg's admission to the writing of a "more traditional narrative development,"[110] summarizing his admission that a faithful film narrative would lose money and incur censorship.[111] Yet I believe the time has come for a more genuine narration of context, and that cinematic and creative lust in filmmaking corresponds to a large number of films from the 1960s to the present that included deep social portraits that reached mightily for the substance, form, and facts of modern, urban existence in a changing, dynamic world. We would only have to reach for airy examples such as *Dr. Strangelove* and *It's A Wonderful Life* to call for comparisons of context that depended upon factual knowledge, post-nuclear investments of ideas and facts upon the body, mind and speech, and the irony of creation. Squeezing out the considerable subcultural data and occult archaeologies in *Naked Lunch* causes us to omit the chance for spelling out the mind's sensory and intellectual excursions, and the boiling pandemic that sought interactions and agency versus the West. We, then, draw upon drug and occult archaeologies, and cynical comedy forcing readers to accept the "Algebra of Need," to figure recurring and sublime Orient with the keys to pandemic and to alternative modes of self-expression. Prince's point about adaptations of Burroughs's text, namely that "adaptations are generally centered on plot,"[112] overstates the modernist attenuation of scenes and experiences: in short, Prince and Seargent gave high marks to Cronenberg and document the story's tenacious grasp in today's times, yet overlook Burroughs's more complex studies and wanderings that alter and challenge American viewpoints about drugs, the Orient, World War II, and so on. At the least, an amazing array of filming techniques could be used to dredge up Burroughs's drug archaeologies and characters: in this way, film aggressively transformed boundaries meant to keep America distinct, clean, separate, and unresponsive to the Orient's strange, beguiling *ethos* that held in itself parables or factual narratives that challenge the simplicity of America's figural domination of the world.

Succinctly, Cronenberg stripped *Naked Lunch* of its narcotic detail and crushed the impact of Lee's studies and excursions into the Third World slums and dens. He also totally silenced airs of extra-national discoveries through Orient drug cafes, rituals, and music performances. Thus, chances at true narcotics transcendences, Tangier's criminal savvy and its graphic presentations of the Self were all missed, instead favoring Lee's drugged dream that treats the central social operation of themes and experiences as nil. *Naked Lunch* was duly Westernized and sterilized, giving no agency or graphic power to the relentless mapping of Orient place and its crucial ethnographies that manifest into the waiting Orient phantom, Hassan-i-Sabbah. More consistent drug ethnographies did not censor its provocative content for an American-styled presentation. Besides erasing the drugged state's prism of comedy and introversion, audiences might easily favor opium and hashish excursions to favor greater narcotic self-creations, and even to advance the drug subculture's possible grass-roots political intonations. Just as important, the literary work was a weak link with narcotics phenomenology in all three major Beat writers due to colonial academic rhetoric denying the Orient its legitimacy. Humor and insincerity marked translations of drugged instances of conscious experience: this mark caused Beat criticism to devalue many of the writer's pretensions and ideals. It is paramount that we realize that academic studies states its ethical reality against the author's thoughtful, mercurial idealism that bore fruit in critical studies very late, with the 2006 publication of *The Beats in South Texas*. *Naked Lunch* stated the physical, communitarian, and epistemological power of Orient drug cultures, and these were consistent themes. It also jubilantly paraded through scenes of civilization's decay, sickness, and its willing inversion into parenthetic nothingness. Conversely, audiences learn much more from a patient, verbally diverse ethnography that pared Lee more equally with the Arab junkies and boys who breathed the intoxicant air of opium for more than a thousand years, and now sought their own narrative chances.

Drug narrations embalm the *pathos* and sickness into the guise of a pure, absorptive change into parasitic, gay literary organisms that vicariously live off the gist of intellection, thus perverting man's fragile sexuality. In context, audiences find that seamy sex scenes between Lee and Joan were augmented to vaunt a much braver, more widespread social history and made the two junkies to be more colorful, mainstream-looking appendages of down-and-out symbolisms. Lee and Joan are, of course fully sublimated in the depressions and isolation that their habits synthesized. Still, social models projected the same communitarian flavor and tactile bonds. Lee, and the members of his syndicate, breathe the air of ancient cultures and criminal gangs against colossal illusions about the Spirit's modern interchangeability. But what could we make of the complete denial, of drugs and drug cultures? My belief is that narcotic attenuation of the film's screenplay broadly restates the impact of drugs on both ethics and American studies. The film's cropped version of *NL*, given instance in the form of a gay typewriter-organism and zombie syndicates, appropriated the mass of drug absorptions that foment the idea that addiction and revolution were necessary, as functional ideas supporting their own community and deliberations. It is likely that audiences will debate this narrative move because its privileged agency in the film lionized the word's social geographies so as to invent them as being free, and requiring no anthropological referent. Characterizations are demeaning when recalling man's atrophied verbal and social skills through his overuse of mainstream American rhetoric-a gluttonous, gory sickness favoring the novel's organismic transformation. In turn, these moves denied man his occult transcendence. Art, occult, and religious models were neatly cropped so as to avoid indoctrination and performance: Lee operates on his own, within the spectrum of meditations that he has learned in his youth. It would be impossible to distort the protagonist's certain honesty, or his journey's ostensible purpose. Weller is meek, honest, and contemplative, hiding and protecting the valor and exercise of his story from outsiders. At this point we note that Burroughs's historiography exhibits and encourages the film's locus of control and engagement through Lee's dialogues with monsters, who extend literary parables and calls to presence in the shadow of their interrupting, negating force. Mortenson summarizes Harris deftly on the general point: "It must be noted here that these formulations are imaginary and reactive—mental creations whose sole function is to break free from the straitjacket of control."[113] Yet Cronenberg used the monster's gothic corporeality to interrupt the necessary narrative. Mortenson lays down Burroughs's theoretical ground, saying that: "Tape recordings, film splices, and hypertext now have the ability to alter surroundings, sundering the word-locks built into the nervous system that keep humans from achieving independence.[114]

Yet it is clear that Cronenberg interrupts Mortenson's methodology for achieving literary greatness and similitude with the modernist generation, and the enhanced cartoon is breathed life with familiar object-product relationships that divide and manage gay-straight interdependence. In short, we are brought into a more direct relationship with one's narrative adversity, and perhaps the attenuation of prophecy and dialogue with a "straight" receiver that exercises his sickness in silence and away from the public sphere to glorify America's underground multitude, possessed as it was of the kind of secrets that inhabit monster-beings whom have assimilated and acculturated the signs of drug addiction and its impoverished continuity. Teleological links conceived in *Naked Lunch* were effectively shattered in the film, with few characters said to have any special powers beyond the pale of reason. The shuffling of main characters to reside in all the social spaces meant to confirm the thrust of countercultural adventure. The film's total clipping of drug trips and hallucinations, however, invested Weller with a specific quest, one for which all the information conforms to sanity-sick and good-evil determinants allowing him to conform to the hero's necessary ethics. He, in short, is given his protagonist role because of his wife and friends: their continued presence versus Dr. Benway, the Mugwumps, and unnamed Arab characters who held the key to homosexual words, lessened multinational context's peripheral stimulation. When the typewriter instructs Lee to take homosexuality as the best of alibis, Lee shudders and for the remainder of the film laments his gay life with guilty stammering and shadowing.[115] Lee's depth as a character, to put it mildly, is not derived from hallucinogenic aesthetics or liberal world dominance and revolutionary power arming minority critiques. It is stated to be part of mainstream American pictures, and to the special attachment of Lee's lover and friends who anchor his specially nurtured conspiracy that is easily navigated and holds few interior portraits that could weaken our appreciation of him as a comic presence. No background characters bore weight: they are easily absorbed into the film's geography, and profess none of the explosive political or extra-natural intensity that is found from the pages of *Naked Lunch*. In other words, separating the revolutionary dissident from the moments of his private, shared revolution is easily accomplished through Cronenberg's meditations on the simple subjection of his American subject to postmodernity and crime. He is allowed to live within the cartoonish grandeur of private freedom and its special mobility. *Naked Lunch's* rendition of the battling of good and evil, too, was given greater depth away from the sickness and depression of drug cultures that lost their rational, reasoning stab at authority. Cronenberg stars the addicted root organism and so draws weight towards liberalism's essential and physical problems that could not be told narratively. Mankind's private perils mark the organism and provide his special, ingenious history that made addiction a cognitive subject. It is certainly possible that the absence of drug cultures cause us to appreciate intoxication and un-reason from more constructive internal dialogues: the root pretense is to find truth rather than archaeology's dictums, and without expostulations of the hero's personal valor and politic. Since Bowles operated from a greater humanistic vision, when compared to the limits of Burroughs's Eastern knowledge and sensitivity, I believe a fairer rendition might throw away the cracked, obtuse magnifying glass to discard real distortions that plague today's drug epistemology in favor of academic limitations that deny the modern subject's mobility and comic multi-dimensionality.

The typewriter's fuck of Lee, as Lee is either typing or having sex with Joan, sets up the narrating of *Naked Lunch* as extra-sensory academic transcendence: by extricating the writer's capitalist disintegration, or rather the excess and errors of his written and spoken symbols, establishes the basic form of pathetic indoctrination with gay sex to simulate motifs of creation and surrogate mismanagement of Lee's body, infested as it is with the symbols and metaphors of man's civilizational disease through drugs. Drug possession was not applied to Joan in the same manner as Lee: pathetic, sour and visibly flattened, Joan sadly hinges her literary pretenses on a "literary drug" in her silence and submission to Lee, the only active writer in the clique.[116] Fucking established the body's graphic terrors and the organization of Lee's peculiar sickness. Narcotic interrogations of physiology surfaced early in Burroughs's studies, as when he read James E. Lee's *The Underworld of the East*. Religious pathos was understood from the drug's effecting graphic pain, and from the Self's penitent distortion:

> [The cocaine addict] is in a constant state of exhilaration and stimulation and stimulation of the nervous system [...] He soon becomes like a living skeleton and although appearing to be full of life and energy to the last, but it is false energy; just the effort of the cocaine, using up his nervous energy at a greater rate than his system is making it.[117]

The free verse statement of man's clinical sickness, when applied to the rhetoric of the body and subject, then tears through the scaffolding of man's academic constitution as it derives itself from materialist critiques that limit or prescribe man's essential answers to ideation:

> [...] in a relationship of anxiety and desire to both the publishing industry, whose indebtedness to capital and the state shapes not only the university as a primary scene of subject formation but the organization of knowledge through which both epistemological and symbolic capital flow.[118]

In short, scene sequences in Cronenberg's film do much to direct the intellectual format of Lee's journey, and even more to the task of spelling out the valor and rightness of his quest to unearth occult and primitive findings in the wake of Dr. Benway's sterile thesis and his marriage to a Vollmer incarnation who carries the same history as Vollmer.[119] Casting religious or moral inferences aside, we must allow that gay sex and criminal liaisons formed a structural background, professing the technique's necessity. Lee's moral clarity when facing Tangier's studied labyrinths pursues the illusions surrounding Joan's biographical secret, that she is actually an Interzone spy trying to arrest Lee.[120] But we should prefer the obvious moment: the cartoon graphics and the overtness of Lee's fuck brought us closer to his epistemology, as if to say that serious archaeological inquiries betrayed a private history closer to one's total isolation and non-recognition, and a necessary confinement maintaining and comforting the writer's living Self. Scenes where Lee fucks Joan are performed with the typewriter as the required medium: gay reductions shadow the egoistic triumph of straight sex, or rather the expunging of narcotic paranoia through the link, to re-constitute the writer's essential, spoken purpose. It, too, laid the groundwork for necessary criminal controls of Lee as acolyte: indeed, the serious and secret journey inscribes its realism through the author's meditative seriousness to spare the kicks at his closet. Because the film includes no Eastern archaeology or historiography, it is worthwhile to know drug addiction's dialogues from its basic chain of symbols, which queer Burroughs and remove much of his masculine archaeology and its Yankee, jingoistic breath. All of Lee's male characteristics, save those related to writing and his grandiose international mission, are temporarily sacrificed and suppressed to save narration's typing of the basic object-subject and capital-creativity relationships. This move hoists a grand, artificial referentiality that appears privately, not publicly. It must be said that the suppression of basic narrative facts and mythologies about Morocco, Africa and Latin America erased much of *NL*'s intellectual notoriety: the substitution of a carefully airbrushed memory tempers the masculine form as it simplifies and streamlines the cues and signs of Lee's agency.

I believe that the most abiding testament to Cronenberg's mastery of the form of *Naked Lunch* is his studied effort to adopt the visual and spoken form to attribute American heroism once again through a deeply mimicked and programmatic history, not his engagement of symbols that could discolor or fragment the basic narration. A quite different cinematic episode could have resulted, but it's safe to say that the public's view of drugs in the 1990s inhered prejudices and misconceptions of the drugged state, and so preferred humor to reason when composing the drugged subject's language-ordered whims. Cleaning the unkempt and scandalous work called attention to the agent's basic symbolism, in turn the mirroring drug addiction with monstrosity and sickness. The typewriter, and Lee, become consumable: Lee's specific prophecy is to save the world and so needed few re-introductions of man's waiting cataclysm. Therefore, the highly captioned voice and agency of Lee counters the winds of archaeology that might blow anywhere, or totally off the map: drug addiction and crime are recognizable, well within the viewer's range of stereotypes, and so offer themselves to a familiar alien presence with no "true" moral conscience. In short, the protagonist and his written significance were to be carefully preserved and separated formally from the backdrop of exotic locales and ghetto ramblings that took mankind far away from his supposedly deep responsibility.

The attempts of the literary hero, too, would save the world and would be tempered by the film's wit, and one that patiently and repeatedly rebuilds anonymity and non-recognition as the primary tools to keep underground rebels in action. These strategies of rhetorical configuration are necessary tools in historical fiction film. To say the least, the literary word operates within the visual-heroic moment, as it would in comic strips. Cronenberg's stress directs Lee to the narrative form, not to the beguiling stanzas of Orient contemplation that made *Naked Lunch* so pornographically wild and explosive. Without treading the substance of Sterritt's more aggressive concept at the chapter's beginning, let us remember that film studies depended upon Hutcheon's identification of the audience's consumption of the film's content. Dropping heavy or deep analysis weakens rebellion's true substance, instead painting the Beats in noble, flattering terms away from the poetics of their debauchery. Lee is instead a normative subject entrusted with his community's collective stance of saving thought and humanism, and so is shorn of most of the degrading avenues. I believe that these, too, are suppressed if only to spell out and pronounce the greatness of saving the world from scientific-military crooks bent on neutralizing man's true psychic agency. Lee, in short, is purified, cleared of much of his real subversion of true contexts, as a countercultural acolyte: the scenes, then, operated discovery as much as they captured repressed or unheard social histories that, in operation, ought to be more confusing than they are *real*.

The films of William S. Burroughs developed from the author's acceptance in his later life: filled with intricate social histories and the archaeologies of notables and lay citizens alike, they represent a sustained challenge to academic puritans who intended to keep the ivory tower of higher education safe from drug-taking trolls who tore apart literature's mainstream ideas and struggles. Whether drunk and on the New York City rooftops, or getting high in Oklahoma as they talk about drug laws, the author, main characters, and friends were like dissidents anywhere in the world—they had envisioned a day where their ideas and collective would sit at the academic table, as equals where their findings would be recognized in the oft-rebellious modernist canon. I believe that here was an important instrument of film's consumption: without strongly political intentions to call up spirit, character, responsibility, ideation, the classroom would tend toward its Victorian tedium, favoring a dry, airbrushed similitude that, in its extreme distance, no longer evincing thought and reflection for today's writing classes. Burroughs's adaptation was and is cleverly formed to accompany his complete exhuming as a narcotics subject in his writing: the film, in its postmodern minute of comprehension, shadowed him with recognition of ideation's symbolic and practical values that intercept moral readings. I think that this technique has ensured future readings, but the didactic form is much more important.

I believe that, in all honesty, that films mixing modern and postmodern beginnings to understand the author's anxiety will produce a fairer understanding of the root context, one that many had said was useless and the work of dropouts with no true intellection. If we are to understand ideation and negotiation through drugs, we at least could point to the culture's tenacity and its rapid ascension into the publishing world. We might as easily unveil the drug addict to be a modern subject with strong agency who could communicate with modern social spheres promoting capitalist dominance. In short, the films are rich with interactive histories and the morphology of symbols, but in practice negate ideas of literary re-creation, instead surrounding paragraphs with postmodern visual atmosphere that isolates and strengthens prophetic visions. This technique, in favor of modernist reruns of film, deepens narcotic inquiry by stressing Burroughs's penitent isolation and the manifold, phantom-like confrontation with "the system" and the resultant engorgement at the hands its pundits. Modernist character and identity approached junk consciousness with a strong attention to form, and in doing so deliberately grew the network of thoughts, perceptions, and associations that eschewed a "modern" consciousness without God, reason, or nation as a partial guide to insanity. From Smith's pathos to Lee's gory adventures and findings, narrative technique gives most of its attention to story and its reconstruction, or rather conceptualizations of literature's past based on symbols, emotions, and story as they retell a contemporary humanism.

Four

Amiri Baraka, Lawrence Ferlinghetti, Carolyn Cassady and Gary Snyder

Films on the Relevance of the Lesser-Known Beats

There are a good number DVDs giving evidence of the less-known Beats' lives and their accomplishments. Chosen documentaries are useful, surpassing the scope of the main Beat nucleus that help to teach Beat literature and foster broader social, intellectual, and cultural discussions about the re-emerging *ethos* in the spirit of an enhanced, and thus expansive, Beat metanarrative history. Maria Beatty's *Gang of Souls* thoughtfully exposes the deep ethnographic and lyric influence of Ginsberg and Burroughs upon the current poetry scene, and activates the tendency to put poetry high in the realms of underclass development and personal expressions: this film includes poems, criticisms, and directions taken from followers who were inspired by the form and the mode of living. Anthony Harvey's *Dutchman* pulls together powerful modern expressions of race and the Beat tendency to use covert, sophisticated identities to conceal real barbarisms and historic racisms: these, when paired with the actions of one's violence, may cause us to doubt the scene's integrity, or even the common-sense paradigm for understanding Black-liberal relationships in New York. Lawrence Ferlinghetti pulls together key expressions of Beat philosophy from beneath deep liberal indoctrinations apparent in film, and from the many histories unveiling his European, American and Far Eastern roots: students can track the nicely interactive context's fruitions to spell out and suggest issue-derived ambitions that figure race, the environment, and history into class consciousness in our world. I think that this is needed in the college classroom because of the penitent escapism found in writings by Kerouac, Ginsberg, and Burroughs. The stain of critical renderings of mid–20th century liberal writers by James T. Jones and Greg Mullins notwithstanding, I believe it is time to pragmatically assess what "Beat" means in today's social dialogue, and what internal and written context we might then derive when writing our specific inquiries. I think that, too, documentary films detail the authors' beginnings and the exercise of their ideas: without these, crucial historiographies are unfocused and insincere.

Malin Kalekeaslo's 71-minute film of the life, marriage, and family of Carolyn Cassady in *Love Always, Carolyn*, was carefully ambitious and thoughtfully directed at the culture and imagination of Beat women, though dissonant when expressing feminine instead of feminist cultural themes that influence the American social setting. Students and professors alike can identify with the biographical logic: theory and criticism, life and communities, imaginations, and readings of the author's poems or fiction. Yet Carolyn's memoirs also compress her diminutive identity, fomenting her post–1950's dictation that Neal's possible fame and libations earned instead the destruction and subjection of her marriage and identity. Carolyn's foil gives way to her visible affectation for love's loss, and as she seeks her love's cherished emblems and moments: still, audiences may note the projection of American normalcy for women, and Carolyn's thoughtful pose as she recalled her husband's brilliant belonging to true Beat legend. Because the Beats' children bear the shadow of silence and comprise unheard-of remnants of the writer's traditions, the Cassady family's foibles and niches of personal expression complicate safe academic readings. But Carolyn's cross-examination of her love mixes emotional belonging with curt criticisms and historical attenuations of the arc of Cassady's greatness: her account etches contrasts between the celebrative, psychedelic-soaked Beat scene and struggling, neglected family members with straight moral characteristics. Archly cognizant of the bride's sudden ascent to statesmanship, Carolyn in *Love Always, Carolyn* complicates the Beat social picture and the collision of its ideas, etching female transcendences onto art's idiomatic forms, textual transferences, and legend-like superimpositions, onto her daily life.

John Healey's 52-minute film, *The Practice of the Wild*, did much to forecast greater social change as a result of Beat indoctrinations. Pulitzer Prize-winning Gary Snyder's career as a naturalist poet, when intermixed with the individual's technique to redraft modernist poetic forms, accents the development of modern mankind through his collective responsibility to Nature. The film, featuring interviews and readings of Snyder's community, is a conversation about the meaning of Snyder's studies and his specific environmental prophecies. Told in a simple, clear language, the resultant didactic strategy allows Snyder to document both the makings of his specific tutelage and his ability to surpass and re-conceptualize crucial Beat Generation themes driving millions of followers to the road and beyond. With guest appearances by Jack Shoemaker, Scott Slovic, and Jim Harrison, the film's tapestry of natural ruminations and conversations about Snyder's natural apprenticeship and self-realizations, and strophes of the curious idylls of knowledge, make us acknowledge the Beat form's dynamic redirection, away from apolitical ruminations on its naturalist truth.

Films about less-studied Beat writers marked an opening step to the authors' re-examination and so restated their specific consciousness and epistemologies: they also restate the much broader inclusion of the Beat philosophy in the modern world. Their primary content exposes new readings and sharp criticisms about the authors: from this new angle, audiences compare the individuated imagination with the scope of man's broader, communitarian values. They also reveal the searching voices of fans and scholars alike as they recall the word's dynamic moment in their lives. Lastly, new readings will build richer American history and scholarship. Because of the perspectives of aged Beats who held less critical attention and fewer traditional readings that noted their popularity and influence, we understand that Beat consciousness was much wider and built key academic influences into today's culture and institutions, displaying its modern tenacity and interactivity.

Gang of Souls

Maria Beatty's 57-minute axis of poetry spindling and interrogations in 1989's *Gang of Souls: A Generation of Beat Poets* does much more than documentary to situate poetic learning and vocal countercultural *praxis* than just trace the spoken granules of poetry: with appearances by the major Beat writers and their followers in fashion, rock, and publishing, this agglomeration of histories and voices attempts grandly, if sympathetically, to trace the human story's liberal roots through loud, defiant, and varying degrees of poetic engagements of the senses, syntax, and everyday life issues. Notwithstanding the very deep tribute to William Burroughs and Allen Ginsberg, the broadcast includes readings and Beat poetry analysis by John Giorno, Anne Waldman, Lydia Lynch, Henry Rollins, Jim Carroll, Ed Sanders, Diane Di Prima, and Richard Hall. It should be pointed out that liberal destructions of modern democracy and its numerous commodity and material fetishisms reveals the power of "the Word" and the deep sickness of "word viruses," but more succinctly that stand-alone graphic destructions of covenant and Spirit were part and parcel of moral critiques from all sides and could as easily been exposited from a conservative thread. Still, with volume and interruptions that speak proudly of liberal activism, *Gang of Souls* examines history and syllabic inspirations through the lens of liberal responsibility successfully, and patiently explain the brilliance of technique with Ginsberg and Burroughs. Because these poets were "queer" or at least lived the lifestyle for some of their lives, we may add the dint of indoctrination. Not only does this give us a refreshed critique of everyday reality and its numerous gothic and silent methods of deriving civilization, we may also understand depressively the realms and handles of greater excess perverts our legitimate social intentions, and the perplexing labyrinth of moral outcomes that cripple, and make comical, our democracy.

Gay "creation" is an antecedent to crippling and derogating the monolith of patriarchy, and indeed the false telling of legitimacy and continuity in our lives and daily mythology. Lynch's very able destruction of racist pretense borrows from an explosive, loud, intrusive derogation of the illusion of White idealism: it also coincides with strong conservative critiques and calls-to-action in the Reagan period, where protecting children and citizens meant identifying the sickened phantom. Anne Waldman's crying leaps and sudden targeting of the audience, too, allows for greater consumption of the poet's cry for meaning and interaction in a faceless, corporate society. Presence of being and voice all call testament to the counterculture's undying demand that their issues and private *hubris* be heard, funneling conservative responses that changes details for the social substrata and social governance that were the most questionable. *Gang of Souls*, then, exclaims the post–Reagan generation's frustrations and anger at not being heard, and more importantly not being recognized in realms of human interaction. By this time, Ginsberg had travelled to China and read poems at the Miami Book Fair, while Burroughs had gone on his historic European tours retelling his verses from *Interzone*. Crowning literary heroes meant explicating the poet's practical vocation, allowing for Burroughs's re-introduction as a poet and Beat figure whom Gregory Corso thoughtfully recasts as a poet. No attempt is made to situate the times, which stands in the backdrop as a lifeless, corrugating force that had dehumanized human instincts and processes.

Long-time writer and Beat colleague Jim Carroll ably puts the brakes on questions about influences and origins, stating baldly the isolation of his "trip" through poetry. At times slurring his words and his eyes wandering, Carroll betrays the tactic of intoxication, but thoughtfully and concretely nails community's absence to be the beginning fabric for being a poet:

> There was nobody in my family who wrote before me. I came from three generations of bartenders. I kinda started to write and it made me distance myself, not only from the people I was observing and my friends but also from myself.[1]

At a later part of the film, Carroll is allowed to share his poetry, which reveals both Ginsbergian romanticism, and the harrowing anxieties and material redundance, in sex:

> Black bra'd, bra'd beneath a dress which was so short that as I faced,
> Facing my sneakers on one knee, I could clearly see revealed the connection of
> Her black seamed stockings, and her red garters like two deadly circuit fused
> To activate the vice of total annihilation.[2]

At another point, red-haired, angry, and punctilious Lydia Lynch, a primary advocate of defying the system and a student of the Beat technique, rolls into rage at the conservative establishment's projection of terror in urban American society:

> I don't know about it. I don't know about anything about it, you know, don't tell me about it. I don't want to know about six-year old black girls getting raped by twelve pigs in KKK uniforms, throw her out in Staten Island like a sack of garbage in a plastic sheet! I don't want to know about prostitutes, six of them crossbowed by some white guy, because ass-murderers, are middle-aged white men with wife and kids and a nice, fat paycheck. Yeah, I don't want to know about it![3]

At times, anti-materialistic flavors of the pen growl and attempt to loudly voice themes of man's oppression, with Henry Rollins calling the working man a "rodent" and Lynch referring to poetry as a form of "infliction" against actions taken against her. Yet it is verbally and vocally clear that Ginsberg and Burroughs operate dynamic and didactic points of true inspiration: variations of the syllable, gusts of voice and shouting, and tight material-moral indications of the modern subject's suffering and inundation with racist and sexist suppressions of the mind, ethics, and the Self retell "Howl's" ambitious form for building anti-materialist critique. The paradox for borrowing from pre–Victorian poetry in the British Romanticist period, and the talent for slaughtering the Victorian devils of our everyday lives, calls upon Ginsberg as both messenger and social acolyte: the technique in the poems, too, allows us to judge favorably Ginsberg's "coming out" as a metaphor for Beat social change in mid–20th century America. Tied to this was the elder Ginsberg's very able sense of theory, when pointed to the task of explaining his purpose:

> The absoluteness of The Bomb being absolute power invoked an absoluteness of inquiry into the nature of consciousness. Because after all that year, '45 was the same year Albert Hoffman discovered LSD, maybe more important than the Bomb [...] it's the mind-bomb, the bomb that opens up the mind.[4]

Perhaps the most novel aspect of our learning is not "gay learning," but rather masculinity's false and dangerous construction as instrument of racism, destruction, and public and private sickness. It is not an unassailable point—millions of Americans offered support and self-indoctrination to be metaphors for growth and success in modern Eras. Further, it is only fair to say that, at least in published forms, LSD consciousness is only vaguely and imperfectly studied, and that songs and music from rock groups including Ed Sanders' The Fugs and The Grateful Dead explored cosmic and preternatural Hindu musical and philosophical roots with much greater success. Yet Ginsberg's testament reifies and pastoralizes the raging urban culture's dynamic minute, a point where knowledge and perspectives could be written and popularized to offset military-industrial deadness. This social metaphor may also problematize academic learning and ethnographies, both of which traditionally shy away from drug use's metaphor in a dynamic, modern society. Adherence to the form tells us what we are least likely to understand comfortably: gays studied man's forbidden treasures of knowledge, and praised criminal buildings of the moral Self as man's redemption. We ourselves may see Lynch, Rollins, Sanders, Carroll, and Waldman cavort and shout, but miss the fertile point of introduction: namely, that modernist poetic technique borrowed from both historic pasts and man's conditions during the post–Nuclear Age. Anxieties and anger raised from man's materialistic and journalistic undercurrents may propagate the myth of Biblical crisis and favor the underground's "cool" heroes, but must adhere the tormented, fragmentary point of origin: in this sense, *Gang of Souls* is excellent material for teaching poetic form. Without the trappings of place, or the richness of materialistic achievement, and instead the altering rancor of poet-warriors who contemplate and then explode, *Gang of Souls* calls up a collective testament that we are still reluctant to acknowledge, in our post-industrial tedium, as having been "meaningful," or even less the schizophrenic ramblings of disenchanted, middle-class generations.

Poet, filmmaker, and producer John Giorno adds succinctly: "these things arise in your mind and, you know, write them down and then, they're awful. What happens is figuring out a process in what you do, what works, and what doesn't work and so it's a tortured process of refining skills and finding a voice."[5] Poet Diane Di Prima, though looking haggard and burdened at times, points to the imaginative technique as a part of social necessity: "It's just a situation which, I think, has become quite easy, and I've never wound up with any vast sums coming from some university, say, job or bestseller, so there's always that edge and I don't mind it. I think it's good, I know it keeps things clear in some way."[6]

We may surmise the obvious paradigm: "slam poetry" and "open mic" are opportunities to rant and rave, and vocalize from a towering sensory and vocal register, and few poets are actually published and even fewer make money. From the perspective of teaching poetry, and understanding the private vault of emotions, feelings, and public pretenses to heralded, romantic power—the Beat Generation was and his highly influential, raising the standard of meter against the foil of poetry's pastoralist origins and rustic sureness. If it is true that mainstream poets such as Lord Tennyson and William Auden disdained the form, and lamented the lack of completeness in the human engine, it is even more true that they anticipated the form's changing and its populist re-invention to suit modern times, and even the grist of responsibility that colors the modern, post–Atomic mind. In these respects, *Gang of Souls* does ample work in both teaching liberal perspectives and underscoring poetry's new responsibility and even voiced hubris. Stripped of the arc of reasoning, we may then re-consider how man's public responsibility is inevitable and part of re-developing the Spirit and the Mind.

Dutchman and African-American Critiques of Beat Culture

Anthony Harvey directed the 54-minute film version of Amiri Baraka's play, *Dutchman* in 1966. The film stars Shirley Knight as a White tease in the character of Lula, and Al Freeman as an eccentric, thoughtful and racially sensitive young Black man in the character of Clay. The film replays the Beat Generation's Greenwich Village multitude and their violent, sardonic fracturing. The two meet on a subway train, reviving the classic Jim Crow tale of White woman-Black man engaged in a twisting, *id*-sensitive infighting and intrigue. Baraka's pivotal race drama also told of Greenwich Village's heralded degeneration and leftist notoriety, and its history and outlook, suggesting the Beat group's deteriorating, ironic developments through the actors' persona and private *métier*. I believe Baraka hints at his escape from Beat affiliations in *Dutchman*'s form, and that Clay's eventual ejections and Lula's violent return ushers in the chaos and uncertainty of countercultural generations after the Beat Generation's disbanding in 1964.

Baraka has not been considered in the light of the Beat Generation's critical influence: this relationship both encouraged his work, pushing him to seek pro–Black activism and revolution to contrast with the racist ills of his eight-year friendship with Kerouac and Ginsberg while editor at *Yugen*. Nonplussed by James Baldwin's dark socioeconomic renderings of "the scene," Baraka met Jack Kerouac and Allen Ginsberg, and published their poems during a period from 1957 to 1962. In the poem's contemporary expression, 2002's "Somebody Blew Up America" rethreads the social and moral geographies of "Howl," calling our attention to poetic form and ministerial *métier* to influence Black re-writings of essential truth. Baraka's call out to African-Americans to destroy White consciousness, his racist, "Crow

Jim" reversals of White intellectual and cultural control, and his demand for Black activism and self-ownership through "poems that kill" extol Beat poetic form. His body of work operates decisive counter-steps to Burroughs's crude, comic destructions of modern art. At length, the growing cultural antagonism unveils the strength of his imaginative and intellectual relationship with Ginsberg, a gay Jewish-American who had during the 1950s and 60s outlined the ascending forms of Baraka's angry retorts to Victorian neologisms and liberal copying alike. Baraka approves of and encouraged bop poetry as Black power's conscious grist: following the 1963 publication of *Blues People*, the first complete analysis of modern African-American music traditions, *Dutchman* was sociologically more pointed and less fantastic than his 1961 poem anthology, *Preface To A Twenty-Volume Suicide Note*. Harvey's film attests to visual immersion's historic richness: it also counted out the depths of racist intrigue and the two characters' sexy, if juvenile, ejections situating the uncertainty of urban, intellectual skills that mar pretense and outlook. My sense was that the visual form of *Dutchman* advanced the Beat Generation's New York axis to future renegade generations. Although repeating the play's conversational script, it narrates public exclamations to mar Black-White relationships and fringe perceptions that both looked back and raced far ahead into the social dimensions of racism's "new" criticisms. This was due to the lean, sparing attention to the spoken details of race's uncertainty in a less nebulous world of lingering, speculative isolation and moments of peculiar, overextended brilliance. These, in turn, display the subject's separation from today's social politic, as though to say that Blacks and Whites had mulled over racial criticism without clear understandings of one other.

Attentions to the body, to social circles and to unfound liberal destinies, are mixed with both traditional male and female stereotypes tracing the unkempt, anti-political destructions of conversational form. Knight's teasing, crossed with exclamations, ambivalent and aggressive sexual overtones, and the attentions of a perplexed and paranoid Black man, tease out Freeman's defiance of "the system." Though Clay refers to the jazz scene that was mostly gone from New York by 1964, the heralded *ethos* accomplishes the basic theme of total isolation, the brilliance of defiant re-writings of American history, and the hells of modern isolation that tore apart Beat inspirations that ruefully exhaled its romantic purity. It is Clay's anxiety, and Lula's ambivalent stress on racial conflict, which builds Baraka's rage about the literary group's persistent racism, one that separated the two races and kept the Black man's thoughts and circumspection isolated. Set in the sparing, moody moment of a subway train, and with no social engagement of colder, modern worlds, *Dutchman* tries to erase Kerouac's rich, myriad inquiries found *The Town and the City*.

Knight's garish clothes, bombshell-like novelty, loud teasing and writhing, and physical confrontation amplifies the play's more sparing conversational format: she also executes Mailer's attention to the harlot's erratic brilliance, as she seems irrational and her manner of speaking and teasing ranges far outside Jim Crow rhetoric. She may, in short, either use the racist form or ignore it, in a schizophrenic gyration of words and actions unseating Freeman's cool, matured pretension to wait out an unwelcome visitor. She also stood in contrast to the train's dim lights, the empty train, and the impassive silence of the tender, nondescript souls who sit in the seats. Her presentation of sex, too, took advantage of illusions of White female supremacy in the art of sex and courtship: her leering, shrieking, and bitching shadow her attraction to the suited, composed Clay. I believe that her challenge was novel and engaging: with a striped skirt, lipstick, and blonde hair, she is a far cry from more typical Beat women who eschew materialistic excess in fashion and sex. Producing an apple as an excuse to talk and cavort, she appears obnoxious and cuts apart a seemingly pleasant intimacy: Freeman's anxiety, then, supposes his uncertainty about associating with White literary groups. What is more important is that Knight purposefully misuses the Beat moment to aggravate its racial and vocational stereotype: there were few chances for Black writers to gain a career through White patronage and friendship, so Freeman's ground is apparently thinner. Freeman's true moment is much shorter: he refers to Charlie Parker's hatred of his patrons and the Black man's positive instinct for killing, exclaiming his disgust for "the White man's knowledge." Literature's ambivalence, then, was crucial: was Baraka looking back to a romantic pose, or suggesting the abolition of literary forms that project no clear direction? After all, Baraka was not a post-writer with truly "national" beginnings: this would develop later with a much greater immersion in more "pop" forms. It is important that Baraka retained his predecessor's elements: it is this that builds Clay's true isolation, the uncertainty of a new beginning that was not drawn from, nor bore comparison with, other Black writers who depend upon socioeconomic and sociopolitical writing. Freeman also dismantles Miles Davis's emphasis on "clean, mean sophistication"[7]: this, as it was a civilized pretense, had not considered the *Zeitgeist* that Baraka attested was to be the life-building *Ursprung* of the modern Black man. Still, I think it is much more relevant that Freeman takes down illusions of White sympathy and historic racial consideration: not allowed to write or speak, the Black subject in Greenwich Village was a racial anti-hero whom Baraka hated. Ascensions to glory and realization, then, accelerated the basic form of thoughts, ideas, and persona, producing the final moment when the "true" Charlie Parker is revealed, stripped of the White pretense for knowing otherness.

The drab, silent setting includes an advertisement featuring Dutchman cigars, and includes only passive, reluctant passengers who avert their eyes and involvement in Lula and Clay's quarrel. What is more thoughtful is the visual arrangement of the play's spoken form: Lula suggests she is poetess Lena Heidi and that her mother was a Communist, while Clay tells Lula that his mother was a Republican. The play's specific transferences bore Jim Crow's clear, racially noxious impact: when Lula suggests, "you tried to make it with your sister when you were ten,"[8] Clay simply fluffs her off, "did Warren tell you that,"[9] referring to a person at a party that does not exist. But the visual form accomplishes more necessary engagements of the play's erotic tension: as she writhes and cavorts in his lap and struggles with him, the key entanglement that kills Curley's wife in *Of Mice and Men*, and the fear that bridles *Invisible Man's* protagonist, who wakes to find himself fucking a white woman, is stated directly and openly: "you're gonna make me want you for real."[10] He also gives way to what Mailer referred to as "the flesh of the form," at one point suggesting that Lula is a "lady wrestler."[11] In the greater part of the film, Lula's overtures are met with Clay's toned down, cool rejections of what he sees as a childish, impish girl. Unaffected and confident, his ascension to race critique is slow and measured. When he finally ejects his true anger, it is out of context and reflects the Black man's intellectual isolation: Parker had been dead for twelve years, and the Jazz Era's notoriety was fading. Freeman's tirade, which includes the Black man's drive to kill and Parker's feeling that White people could "kiss [Parker's] ass," is isolated and fragmentary, a bygone moment in the building of Black political and cultural consciousness. There are no genuine referents to suggest the day's politics and activism that responds to modern social realities. Still, Clay's violent verbal thrusts and prophesied disparagement of White control are meaningful, laying bare the unknown, unspoken potency of real intellectual change: *Dutchman* appeared in the wake of Dr. Martin Luther King, Malcolm X, Frantz Fanon, and Aime Cesaire, all of whom used economic critiques rather than social and cultural fighting during modern truth's beginning stages. Space and isolation accomplish basic pretenses. Freeman is isolated, angry, scowling and rambling about his indoctrination, lost in a sea of New York City's non-recognition of human impulses that foretell a more essential Being. The mechanics of Knight's takedown, too, appraise modern impulses to control and dominate: at intermittent moments, she exclaims, "don't get smart with me, buster!"[12]; and, when Freeman quips that he was like Charles Baudelaire, "I bet you never once thought you were a black… nigger."[13] She then looks over the handsome, suited young man: "you know you could be a handsome man,"[14] then summarizing Freeman's collegiate pretensions: "colored college where everyone thought they were

April Harryman."¹⁵ Racist, Jim Crow phrasings of social and moral Being match the modern exercise of one's appearance and thoughts. Knight appraises the Black man's sexuality, his literary pretense, and the inequality of social transactions between Black and White people during the 1960s. In short, the crucial exorcism of Black intellectual and sexual pretense accomplishes the paring down of Black people to more instinctual, anti-racial, and "true" understandings of themselves. Knight's intrusive and abusive taunts are both Jim Crow and modern: she draws out the innocence of racial community, destabilizing what Jack Kerouac and Allen Ginsberg assured us was a safe relationship hovering around otherness's obscure, non-intellectual social spheres.

Dutchman, in short, revives the Beat attentions to the intellectual man's pain, isolation, and anxiety through an abstract format friendly with Beat novels and poetry that tested the poet's ascension to revolution through the young adult's insecurities when penned as a racial subject. Knight's stabbing of Freeman at the film's end is followed by the more obvious choice—she approaches another young, Black man whose casual appearance presume similar interrogations of his racial sensitivity. That, of course, signals Baraka's narrative and prophetic departure from Kerouac—by attaching violent conspiracies to counter-developments against Black moral consciousness. Faithful to the play's construction, the film took advantage of the 1960s screened ambivalence—was Baraka moving forward into the postindustrial world, or returning to Negritude discussions that called for unity and chances at fighting "the system" again? Solidly in place, however, is the call for mankind's human engagement versus the backdrop of a distant, unresponsive society that had shut out its social examination. Visual techniques are sparing, yet breathe the illusion of the changing face of society that Beat writers would attempt to understand for generations.

A Rebirth of Wonder

Lawrence Ferlinghetti's 79-minute film, *A Rebirth of Wonder*, appeared in 2010 and chronicled the intellectual, poetic, and anti-establishmentarian character of the Beat who, still living and 100 years old, holds the special attributes of a poet, soldier, revolutionary, and consummate and richly originated liberal political activist. At a glance, specific histories about him traversed our archaeological imaginations with the sense that a strong, underlying thread, grounded in the expatriate's mature moral and personal depth, guiding his far-ranging canvas of Beat history and its crucial nostalgia. They suggest that today's liberal scene develops in part from Ferlinghetti's broad, pluralistic values and from the veer of his easygoing, mobile wit that pokes fun at the intellectual man's dour sincerity. Ferlinghetti reads his poems, intoning his meditated prophecies to stroke the flair of artistic brilliance, yet *A Rebirth of Wonder* scored its highest marks by undertaking a century-long biography entrenching the American liberal tradition and democracy's far-reaching engagement of reality, politics, and the pains of modern man's crises. Statesmanship may be reassigned when favoring Ferlinghetti's accomplishments and experiences, but the most interesting theme answers the Beats' exile from the American literary canon. Stating the Beat society's possibilities today to be dynamic and to spell out the group's collective responsibility in posterity meant reintroducing the Left's convincing claims to mankind's democratic understanding of truth, a far cry from ecstatic words from Kerouac and Ginsberg telling us their isolation.

It is certainly worthwhile, too, to underscore liberalism as a consistent pragmatic force in the Beat tradition: audiences wary of the agonizing *tour de force* of one's specially located, neurotic genius will turn to this film to tether and sustain a durable writing and publishing tradition and its testament to man's fighting injustice, suffering, inequality, and racism. Ferlinghetti's career as City Lights Bookstore owner retold the Beat's living intellectual tradition, a biographical inference that filmmakers screening Kerouac, Ginsberg, and Burroughs avoid. But relevance is a nasty question for audiences: we are led to believe that the artist sat comfortably in his time period, free of inferential or comparative status. We are likely to deflate essential questions because of Kerouac's incoherence and cavalier wanderings of the mind at his moment of critical introduction. Faced with the coming onslaught of postmodern materialism, Kerouac relapsed, supposing faceless demons that scream, "lasi, lado."[16] Thoughtfully if maliciously, Ferlinghetti even denies his membership in the Beat circle—attesting to his crucial artistic development in France during World War II and afterwards, Dennis Hopper recalling his influence upon artist movements, communist activism, and immigrant worker rights to forecast a kaleidoscopic internationalism that drew legitimacy and interaction. Yet when we airbrush the writer's legacy of comparisons with today's fiction, we also sanctify its purity. *A Rebirth of Wonder* discarded this concept to favor the poet's continuing metric and imagistic beauty, tied to political and social discussions that advance the liberal rebel to be a persistent defender of human rights and an un-canonized messenger of liberalism's continuing force. I think, that fresh angles on the Beats, too, rephrased modernism's continuing relevance and interactions with today's social universe. It is more likely that today's adolescent is convinced of their complete cultural and social moment of precarious isolation, and gain intellectual strength and context when appreciating the validity of recurrent 20th century ideas. The cast includes Robert Scheer, David Amram, Barry Miles, Dennis Hopper, George Whitman, Sylvia Whitman, Dave Eggers, and Allen Ginsberg, Robert Meltzer, and Jack Hirschman. Their critical discussions mount the much greater dynamic intellectual and social movement of artists, writers, and citizens who imperfectly yet boldly express man's democratic impulses to freedom and non-national plurality, and thus the plurality of ideas and imaginations. *A Rebirth of Wonder* thus spelled out the movement's vision from its greatest band of social-intellectual width, bringing together different generations, political forms, nationalities, and historical eras to state neither the prevalence of any one historical moment nor the sealed non-transparency of Beat forms mitigating their fall from popularity.

The underlying thread of this film is Ferlinghetti's interdisciplinary *métier* and the surefootedness of his thoughtfully modernist poetry, which operates the relative difference between sense and modern sensibility, a key liberal critical angle from which to review contemporary poetry. I think that *A Rebirth of Wonder* accomplishes this by broadly staging Ferlinghetti's deep, novel, and imaginative intellectual history as a poet, soldier, activist, philanthropist, businessman, student, and thinker. The didactic technique is simple, reciting several of his best known poems: still, the slew of book titles that engraved City Lights Books' minutes of international repute and the racing glut of images, paintings, photographs and sweetened poetry readings where the elder statesman demonstrates his artful, high-voiced naturalist tenor to offset his daily testaments, curt philosophical ideas, and the commentator's adulation of him as a cultural figure: it is almost certain that *Rebirth's* narrative and visual techniques, then, confirm the positive redress of a depressive, shadowy literary circle giving way to its excesses.

Ferlinghetti is crisp, lighthearted and witty, and at times deliberately acerbic and erratic in stating liberal political necessity and the sting of left poetry that caused us to rethink our values and governing ideas. Because he poses a broad challenge to Kerouac's apolitical and highly artistically guarded universe, it is important that our instructional means for knowing him and the Beats' collective *oeuvre* narrate eras where he was fundamental in the development of perspectives, and the specific nexus of Left subcultures deemed relevant to cultural and political discussions. Ferlinghetti is not as crude as the polemic-infused Robert Coover, yet he is aphoristically light and thoughtful when handling modern existence. In this way, he unearths a more interactive, post-agrarian metaphor when writing about American democracy and its abstract intent after World War II. Tenacious relays of ideas and information topple Kerouac's supreme aestheticism, while marrying the artistic principle to the form of later Beats such as Ginsberg, Snyder, and McClure, all of whom painted liberal strophes of man's imagistic and sensual engagement of the world. My sense is that the literary technique favored creative re-invention, cross-examining arts and philosophies that the major Beats less actively pursued: these markings, and rich imaginations centered on America's political and entertainment cultures across the entire 20th century, navigate a greater didactic form which invites a much greater volume of teaching strategies, increases undergraduate writing choices, and sustains greater intellectual freedom among the students. After watching *A Rebirth of Wonder*, I understood that examples of Beat history and posterity might actually engender positive readings and supposition of one's own context in lights favorable to the literary impact. I believe that it is of note that Ferlinghetti examines the entire Beat period, adding motifs and imaginative techniques to build greater complexity: I think that, too, his commentaries envision a much greater development of American thought and *praxis* that appears more difficult for more studied Beat notables.

First off, let us say that Ferlinghetti's investigation of mid–20th century America explored its diversity, its comic derivations, and its political realism to extend liberal responsibility that influenced the Beats and counterculture. I think that, too, his dour, severe summarization of the years leading up to World War II offset the mitigating ambivalence of Ginsberg, Kerouac and Burroughs, all of whom supposed no historical impact and did not solemnize the carnage and destruction until later in their lives. Screened narrations and film examples of San Francisco streets, trains, and U.S. naval warships and their ports of call in France and Japan, along with oil paintings and Super 8 reels of the 1950s-era San Francisco streets, do not include spoken commentary and instead read Ferlinghetti's own reflections: they, in other words, suppose the aggressive chance to re-write America's history in terms of the individual subject's private, un-ideated investigations of time and place. Though Ferlinghetti infuses *A Rebirth of Wonder* with a deep, thoughtful literary history, his more severe comments are grounded in the exercise of historical truth. He relaxes at the Temple of the Zen Fool and later drives through the San Francisco streets, acridly calling upon writers to "put more mustard" on their writing while driving his car, but his biography of the Hiroshima and Nagasaki bombings is cutting and clear: he types them as an example of "a monstrous racism."[17] The point is valuable in the classroom: Kerouac, Ginsberg and Burroughs were Orientalists who lampoon swathes of Orient cultural and narrative content, yet remain morbidly cognizant of the ethnic/subcultural breadth of modern man's post-atomic challenges. But Ferlinghetti called our attention to the racial metaphor with sure sincerity, to say that our actions and experiences as White and non–White citizens grew from the history that penned our conscious racial actions. The reel shows Ferlinghetti's videos of D-Day in France, while recording the carnage and desolation on Hiroshima's streets. In short, Ferlinghetti tells us of artistic chances Kerouac was reluctant to pen.

Writer and friend Michael McClure is clear to document the ferment of liberal intellectual ideas through writing: "Radicals from Berkeley would meet to plan demonstrations. We'd all be reading at a bookshelf, get together and talk about things, think about what we could do and at the same time sit around in the chair and leaf through several fanzines while we were discussing the issues."[18]

But Ferlinghetti does not consider himself a Beat, and so we may ask more thoughtful questions about how poetry could build liberal culture and its intellectual propensity to challenge ideas and thought at mid-century. Ferlinghetti's poetry intermixes with commentaries and history: at times telling stories about the peculiar tedium and national-subcultural auras of San Francisco's liberal nexus, he also offers takes on reality and imagination and political interjections of truth and responsibility. Poetry engraves both the Beat Generation's immersion in greater literary form. More, the imagistic bend of ideas and thoughts mixed with the liberal community's peculiar tedium, as it wrote and gossiped about its introspective collages, destroying writing's form to snatch up the cultural rebellion's own trove of historic jewels in the mind and memory. A reading of "Poems des Pascoa" features Moroccan flute playing by David Amram, and re-introduces strange dispersions of the mind amidst the international street scene's lairs.[19]

Ferlinghetti also transposes national rhetoric and tale-telling to augment a poem about a baseball game in San Francisco, displaying the modernist form's positive lift from its anxiety in ways more clever and less emotional than with Kerouac's specific reading about playing football in *The Town and the City*. Here's an excerpt from "Baseball Canto":

> And everybody stands up for the National Anthem,
> and all facing east as if expecting some great white hope,
> For the Founding Fathers to appear on the horizon.
> But Willie Mays appears instead in the bottom of the 1st,
> and the roar goes up, he plows the 1st, one into the sun and takes off,
> And the ball is lost in the sun, and he keeps running through the
>
> Anglo-Saxon epic and Tito Puente's come up looking like a bullfighter
> in his tight pant and small pointed face, and the right field—
> Bleachers go mad! Sweet Tito, sock it to him![20]

Poignant American centrism intersects with internationalism and liberal political theory at so many points that we may suppose that Ferlinghetti's personal inquiry was sincere and that he built American authorship from a much greater epistemological moment that was both imaginative and erratic. His free verse also projects modernist themes of self-development. Stripping the imagination of place and re-assigning it to the American multitude, and to embryonic street cultures that hawk its international trinkets of wisdom, wit, and parables, heralds a more tenacious narrative voice and spunky defiance of American official culture: Ferlinghetti introduces children, dogs, and comic heroes as messengers of American freedom.

At several instances, Ferlinghetti spawns critical and artistic fruition that lay far outside the Beat circle: and at other instances, his commentaries about American popular culture shadowed and exceeded the romantic grist of Kerouac's own studies of film, television, and music that first began to appear in David Sterritt's 2004 book, *Screening the Beats*. Ferlinghetti's affection for silent motion picture actor Charlie Chaplin is strongly evocative and countered Kerouac's nutty expostulations about the Three Stooges.[21] Describing Chaplin as "an anarchist been sustained by definition,"[22] he recalls the comedian's happy, thoughtless impulse to experience life, citizenship, sports, and modern fashion, "it's as if [the little man's] state or modern civilization was out to destroy this objective in each of us,"[23] while a film clip finds the skinny yet boastful Chaplin training for a boxing fight with a much bigger competitor, in the end outlasting him.[24] I think it is important to relay the social *ethos* of modern man in the 20th century to herald man's masculine potential and invention, rather than dictums shoring up man's aristocratic-derived exclusion from society's mobile diversity.

Commentary from movie star Dennis Hopper is equally thoughtful and suggests the much greater proliferation of talent and perspectives. Hopper notes Ferlinghetti's influence on The Visual Movement in Los Angeles during the 50s and 60s. Of his impact on thought, Hopper says that "this stuff found its way down south and it was different in an enormous cultural way. [So] this commentary went back and forth between the poets and the visual artists."[25] The visual angle in *A Rebirth of Wonder*, too, was ambitious in accomplishing the centrality of Beat place and the ideation of forms from book titles, artwork, cartoon strips, protest placards, and rock stars. Still, Hopper's decisive point was that poetic techniques would be applied to film and photography, and in ways that diverged from the Beat Generation's own photography that was more linear and organized iconic presence. Radical poet and professor Jack Hirschman positively exclaims his friend's unique talent to supersede Beat poeticism and its crucial attentions to the social *métier*: "he superseded e.e. Cummings as the poet who probably inspired more young people of his generation. 1 million copies, Coney Island of the Mind. That's almost inconceivable!"[26]

Readings in black-and-white films accomplish the very broad and influential comic technique that has popularized poetry and political consciousness: indeed, the special flair of Ferlinghetti's pointed examples meant to dematerialize American democracy, showcasing the world's shuffling of context and thoughts to simulate easygoing deconstruction of the artifice. The example of Homan the Dog may offer us thematic dislocations that call our attention not to the artifice, but to piecemeal exclusions of it from the everyday man's robust, rambling sensibility that could escape the false political establishment and its incomplete racial dominance. Through Homan in "Dog," Ferlinghetti re-introduces San Francisco's jubilant disregard for democracy's ideas and purpose:

> Dog got totally bent and bent reality, and the things he sees are bigger than himself, And the things he sees are his reality dark in doorways, dig at old chickens in Chinatown windows, bareheads and walkways and the things he smelled, dog got in the streets, cats and babies, bundles and policemen. He doesn't need cops, he rarely has any use for them. He goes past them and past the dead cows hung up holes in front of the San Francisco Meat Market, he would rather eat a faded cow than a tough policeman, though either might make do, and he goes back past the Romeo Ravioli Factory, and past Point Tower and past Congressman Doyle of the Un-American Committee. He's afraid of Point Tower, but he's not afraid of Congressman Doyle although what he hears is very discouraging, very depressing, very ab-surd to a suffering dog like himself, a serious dog like himself. But—he has his own free world to live in, he live to eat, he shall not be muzzled but Congressman Doyle has put another fire hydrant to him. The dog got really in bet—that's a good dog![27]

Ferlinghetti's presentation invites political broadening of man's horizons: dogs are seen as public instances of community and so may oppose the government and can be emblems of the liberal community's spunky, working-class defiance of the American government's orders and laws. Broadening the community's *dramatis personae* carries with it our understanding of conscious existence, and the reality that citizens maintain the conduit of their own perspectives and necessary modern emblems. "The story's" diversities are therefore anti-modernist: they suppose the real world, and not one drawn from man's imagination. In short, where do we draw the line that ends modern man's achievement, so as to say it is no longer responsible or pragmatic to obey the dictates of man and his ideas? After all, *National Geographic* did not cover pollution and deforestation until the late 1960s.[28] Man's responsibility, then, calls upon him to reject the government, denying society's organizing themes and guiding perspective in favor of the Earth, which holds no given polity.

I think it is time, too, to re-assess Ferlinghetti's relationship with other Beat poets. It is clear that poetry's naturalist intent and strophes of perception, Nature, and emotions shadow both Kerouac and Snyder. If we may push for an answer to Ferlinghetti's unrepentant liberal activism, it is his poetry that reveals the crucial similitude. In one reading, for instance, Ferlinghetti states his principle: "time to change the world in such a way that there's no further need to be a dissident."[29] This theme operates very close to Kerouac's utopic nerve; still, it also states crucial logical anomalies of fact and historical principle that operate modern liberal thought and breaches in its democratic sincerity: Poetry as Insurgent Art [I am signaling you through the flames].[30]

I think that the learning technique is simple, and used fact and political agency to counter Kerouac's streaming, dislocating innocence that could be clever and erase man's stated purpose when it supposing Nature's ultimate powers. Ferlinghetti's call to arms builds a simple guiding principle: the world is not as it should be, and mankind must come together to address the environment's serious problems. But responsibility and activism were stated versus the modernist imaginative dictum. While visual examples of City Lights Books' intellectual production are explosive, suggesting a read of political injustice and genocide around the world, "babbled tongues" calmly reminds us of man's failure to know himself at the end of the 20th century. Ferlinghetti is careful not to avoid the imagistic and emotional testaments of his friend, Jack Kerouac. More, he recasts poetry's aesthetic qualities to revisit political, eco-centric evaluations. This call out to the world, to its inception of life-destroying conflicts and problems, synergizes the hippies' rallying cry to strike down America's gluttonous capitalism and racism. I think that, then, instructional techniques may document Ferlinghetti's meaningful, sensible involvement in today's global conflicts, and the concrete necessity of his restatement of the poet's social relevance.

A Rebirth of Wonder is, as a whole, a satisfying film that happily retells the author's story, life, times, and friendships. Through the endless tale of friends, writers, filmmakers, actors, poets, and booksellers, many imaginative shards that shouted of liberal political activism and community are revived in the eyes of a new generation possessed of its knowledge and civic responsibilities. The unique history also cross-examines those of Kerouac and Ginsberg: I believe, too, that the footage of cities, wartime ports-of-call, and *salons* demonstrated the Left's considerable visual angle, hence its biographical legitimacy of its studies. Depth is often denied to the Beats, who hated politics and were forever banished from its realm. Ferlinghetti's weaving of stories and thoughts, attractive to young people and heralding a timeless struggle with injustice, documents poetry's practical necessity, and serious Beat inquiries.

Love Always, Carolyn

Carolyn Cassady's meditations on the Beat circle's life, experiences, and humanity form an introductory part of *Love Always, Carolyn*: her memoirs, screened against films that feature the Cassady homes in England and Denver, photographs of the Beat circle, and introductions into the home's daily life, history, and archaeology of letters, books and rare items, are an enticing part of an American woman's cross-examination of the tryst with brilliance and discovery, and its social possibilities. With drugs no longer on the table and bills to be paid, Carolyn's private reminiscences form part of Beat historical experiences. Clearly, though, Kakeaslo's film took advantage of the Cassady family's casual interpretations of the movement's real significance, mounting Carolyn's artistic triumph against the cross of her neglect and uncertainty. Intermixing sharp diction and memory with more subtle and evocative internments of her steamy marriage to Neal and her prolonged affair with Jack, Carolyn exhibits the elder stateswoman's pose of responsibility and artistry, in a form eerily reminiscent of biographical films about Paul Bowles and William S. Burroughs. In this elucidation of the modernist form, its meaning moves and derives its expression from the modern setting, shadowing and lengthening the elder's reticence, peculiar and cherished memories, and stern defenses of Beat tradition. Carolyn, admitting the suppression of her identity, cherishes her love of Neal and Jack, and so revived the modernist balloon of facts, principles and aphoristic truths: this is versus very clear separations of social spheres, with Neal inviting the rapidity of his downfall through the excessive taste for life and its bohemian swagger. Not surprisingly, *Love Always, Carolyn* sharply limited modernist discussions: I will try to examine the specific meaning of her prophecies and memories, which sweeten the artistic picture to document a stronger, more interactive community that counted on recognition for holding up the Beat writers' cross of American intellectual and moral messianism.

Carolyn builds the positive *hubris*, and happy reminiscences about the years of Beat partying, writing, and travels, from the annals of her youth: in summary, family formed much of the movie's plot, and sequestered Carolyn's novel and jubilant talent for pleasures and discoveries against the tactile, conversational, and domestic registers of their daily lives, times, and specific criticisms of the Beat group's perceived genius and lyricism. Carolyn grounds the specific phrasing of childhood deprivation and confinement against the tale of her breaking out, if we may call it that. She records her isolation and depression, drawing the navel of artistry from the same meditative ground as that of Neal and Jack Kerouac to solemnize the movement's true, romanticist inquiries:

> So I was the youngest of five, therefore the least [loved]. Therefore at least, I was constantly reminded. And I had very solid Victorian parents, and my father's rule in life was that as long as everyone had a good home and education, that's all they needed. So, they were such strict Victorians. There was no touching or cuddling

after eating. That was a great ... loss. We had a household helper nanny I actually felt more warmth toward her than my mother. And also short of approval and most anything they did say, "well, that's alright but you can do better." Never were good enough, were quite good enough.[31]

Carolyn recalls her family's lack of bonding and emotional belonging, a biographical theme consistent with many Victorian, Romantic, and renegade fiction: we might say that the lack of parent-child relationship and bonding forces the writer to seek a new family, or at least a new cross of ethical involvement that justifies our sensory bonds and lifestyle appreciation. But Carolyn, like Bowles, curses her confinement and repression, and the specific trauma of not enjoying maternal and paternal tactility and feeling. It was not a fair comparison: Claude Bowles tried to kill Paul by leaving him outside the house in the snow. But as the story of Bowles, Ginsberg, Burroughs, and Cassady were told—Kerouac being the lone exception, as he was nurtured by the others and ultimately return to his familial, emotional bonds—anti–Victorian criticism often called our attention to family, to relationships, and to the import of political, philosophical, and cultural ideas that could liberate, directing us towards the ideal world: it also was a timeless guiding force for rock, pop, and punk generations.

Carolyn's comments about Neal and Jack, too, were more studied, and she reigns in the serious responsibility of her judgment against the waves of happiness and pleasure that she claimed for herself and was now the guardian of. She commented in a silly tone about Neal, "when he was good he was vetty vetty good and when he was bad ... he was horrid."[32]

But Carolyn spoke very simply and poignantly: Neal was the man that she wanted to spend her life with, and this is repeated several times. In fact, literary agonies play out against the turmoil that inscribed Neal's failure to write and publish in his lifetime, forcing the family to struggle with a much more bare-bones existence that swore off drugs, drinking and occult-like adventures into shamanism and Buddhism while on the road in Colorado, California and Mexico.

Carolyn's surmounting of the deep, messianic Beat threads that spoke to man's liberation and to his greatest moments of psychic and philosophical fulfillment are curt and cross-stroke the angle of the author's brilliance with the conscious statistics of their decline and self-derived suffering and loss during their adult years. I think that Carolyn's drug indoctrinations are fertile ground for both feminine and middle-class re-examinations of the role of drugs in American family and class relationships. Her prudish, dismissive curse of her husband's failure to sustain a writing career was a deep and difficult rendition that sharpens over the course of her life. In *Off the Road*, she recalls Neal's specific indoctrinations when she smoked marijuana for the first time:

Now, darling, listen to me. You must have no fear, hear me? It is completely harmless, I promise you. All those tales you've doubtless heard are entirely false, perpetrated by Anslinger to keep his narcotic squad boys employed. All this does is heighten your sensory perception and awaken you to your own true awareness and speed up your thought processes while giving the impression time has immeasurably slowed. You will see more and see better—colours, patterns—and music! You think you've heard music? You've never heard it until you hear it on tea; you'll hear every note and every instrument simultaneously as you never have before. Oh, ho, ho, ho—just you wait![33]

Of course, Carolyn's anticipation of Neal as narcotic messenger was innocent and real—Neal's testimony bore striking accuracy to written testaments of the drug's impact on the brain from Burroughs and Kerouac, and shadowed Carolyn's fears about the drug, a "devil weed." Conceived from Neal's true confession, Carolyn's use of drugs incur her more conservative assessment that drugs ruined Neal's chances of becoming a famous writer, pairing him with the tide of bitter complaints and family insecurities about living off the fame of drug-addicted figures whose content seems impossible in the real world.

Carolyn's internal criticisms of Neal are tart and thoughtfully displayed womanhood's coming of age: "you are nothing but a gutter snipe and I have feelings, too."[34] She also re-introduced the American cultural schism in revealing ways: as a topless Neal performs a Native American dance in the night, she remembers his family's stern dismissal: "he was a disgrace."[35] But not all of her criticisms of her husband and of Neal record the literary group's decline because of drugs and alcohol: at one point, she recalls her unheard advice to Neal, at the summit of the group's California parties and endless ramblings about life and humanity: "you're no better than you know, goodbye!"[36] Because Carolyn testifies to the literary group's drug-addicted tedium and the absence of responsible figures that could foster successful, inclusive relationships consistent with modern society's responsibilities, a cautionary comment restates the Beat movement's acceleration to truth with no street-sensible brakes to anchor the subject's basic probity about life's experiences. I think that, too, here was a time-honored theme of addiction therapy: seemingly miraculous findings and states of being were mixed with identity and mental health crises, distorting and ending what might have been the movement's possible tryst with the American scene.

Still, Carolyn is willing to share the sweet *jouissance* of her love affairs, and enjoyed this catchable sentiment, though now at the end of her life and burdened with the possibility of authorship that she had seldom thought about, as book collectors and agents appear at her house to congratulate her 2007 re-issue of her memoir, *Off The Road*. One recollection told of a botched sex act with Neal; in another, a sneering, ghostly-sounding Carolyn voices out the details of Neal's depression. It is not as though Carolyn is given enough opportunity to explore the deep and widespread ferment of Neal's ideas and experiences, and the truth of his imaginations. It seems more likely that, far from the stage of everyday recognition and irrelevant to the times, that she protects his quest's meaning while staining it with her regrets and vocal ownership of Neal's body, tongue, outlook, and spirit. Reticence accomplishes, then, the tactile composition of the idea's meaning in the literary group: she is able to raise the spectacle of Neal's memory without hiding the depth of his human sympathy and specific turmoil.

But Carolyn's specific memories of Neal, Jack, and Allen anoint the stateswoman's pose, and may even allow us a glimpse at a woman who finally had the capacity to reflect, understand and know the literary movement as a woman within her moral understanding of the literary scene. She repeatedly agonized about *On the Road's* publication, noting her own thoughts: "were you angry with Jack for reading so much of your private life?"[37] Neal's affair with Allen Ginsberg, where Neal takes Allen to San Francisco to fuck him, is framed against her emblem of marital innocence: "[Neal] was terribly good at giving me what he knew I could only accept, so I had no idea, like you know, that first road trip [...] Terrible shock! And yet he had all the bases covered and very responsibly and couldn't see any reason why he couldn't have a vacation. I thought of it as desertion, see?"[38] To state a woman's ethical understanding of the Beat story was crucial: women were far in the background of the Beat literary production, and girls did not enjoy any glib or garbled explication of social or intellectual facts. The directed criticisms, then, are straight society's criticism of genius: it was stealing ideas, and heterosexual poses were lies and treason. Gender stereotyping limit readings of Beat women throughout: just as true, the repeated stabbings of Beat prophecy re-introduce the Cassady family and their specific tide of practical agonies that separated discussions of the imagination and the spirit from social and personal objectives. The ambivalence of Beat form, and its subjugation to today's poetics and dialogues, project greater responsibility onto Carolyn. Still, examples of the Cassady treasure reveal Carolyn's happiness and insouciance about the whole journey: sporting $50 checks from Neal and Allen found in the old letters, and even locating a 1951 nighty used by Kerouac, amidst color photographs of her kids, she remembers the authors' everyday relationships and thus testaments to modern man's real communities, not legacies that rehash philosophy and ideas. Carolyn is, in short, very critical of Neal and Jack: she states the timeless judgment friendly with American normalcy, that an artist or entertainer might have been more successful if they weren't possessed with the artistic form that they wrote to. The Beats' deep intellectual ramble is offset with the family's rambling, incoherent bubble of practical responsibilities, re-introducing the anxieties for reconciling disparate cultural worlds at the moment of publication and recognition.

When Carolyn's daughter, Cathy, loudly shares the idea that she is going to sell wine using the Neal Cassady name and label, a dismayed Carolyn calls out at the dinner table, "what is this about?" When she finds that Cathy's idea is a serious one, she grumbles aloud, "we're ignorant."[39] But *Love Always, Carolyn* captures in full the family's middle-class stresses, and the children resurface as messengers of their father's unrecognized moment while criticizing his narrative basis and supposing mainstream life as a continuing ember. They try to protect the family's traditions but also bask in the light of the spacey, wild memory of syntactic craziness in the midst of their own depressed tedium that gave no constitutive answers to everyday issues. John Cassady's dour sympathies mount his plain criticisms of his parents and of their erratic tending to anticipations of success and fame: at Christmas, he admits the difficulties of paying for the house: he then presents the little Christmas tree to Carolyn, and they smile and accept its meaning lovingly.[40] John states his jealousy and regret: when asked about his mother, he adds, "she doesn't have that much to lose, to say for herself, but we have different friends, you know, it's a problem, we're just sitting by the rail."[41] At another point, John fails to convince Carolyn to go to the hospital, becoming emotional about her intransigence. But John, Jami and Cathy state happiness and depression about the family's fortunes, gathering at Christmas time but visibly unsure that they can pull together their differences. A rock musician during the 60s and sympathetic at first with the Beat form, John did not think much of his father's notoriety, and at least thought it would never affect him: he was a struggling artist who saw no tangible recognition or patronage because of his father, saying once in a Literary Kicks** interview, "there's always been the occasional letter or call."[42] But John triumphantly takes up his father's prophetic mantle, and that of the Beats in general, when *Off the Road* is published and ably performs his mother's key synopsis, that it was Neal, not Jack, who was the true genius and that Kerouac had successfully adopted his father's form. Family pride was hard earned: all of the children work, while Carolyn was successful as a seamstress from the 1940s onward. But the cross of modern responsibilities is in fact the key moment: Carolyn, in particular, underscores that Neal's 1958 arrest for marijuana possession was just plain irresponsible and that this made it much harder to keep the house and to pay bills. Middle-class depression and uncertainty appear to be a primary outcome, then, of the intellect's experimentalism, and the children repeat standard criticism that artists, selfish about their creation, lived unbalanced, shiftless lives that shadow their dependents, making their path to success less creative and imaginative. Of course, Carolyn and John field the Beat faithful and encourage their reading, and accept their congratulations: the abiding point was that the Cassady family, coming to terms with their own existence in the 21st century, relish in their memories but often complain of their diminished status in the everyday world. The cross of drugs, too, was avoided in the film's overview: Carolyn regrets her and her husband's use, certain that Neal might have been published and recognized had he and Carolyn not spent all their time "getting high."[43]

I believe that here is an operative conflict in literary and artistic production, and as many children of artists have disavowed drugs and alcohol because of their parents' addiction and sickness. Children, then, were less likely to confirm the interior mind's practical necessity, and found that their own artistic endeavors did not earn the kind of social change that they had hoped for. I believe that addiction, too, transfixes younger citizens' understandings of the times: not at all convinced of the wide possibilities of intoxication and rebellion, the children tend closely to the example of Christmas as the one get-together for the family, and their chance to share emotional and sensible bonds.

Prudish-looking, intermittently warm and oftentimes reserved and critical of her lover's acolyte status, Carolyn performs the task of owning the Beat legacy and summarized the movement's practical motions and necessity. I think, therefore, that *Love Always, Carolyn* cross-examined the basic idea of artistry and the artist's pose, in a manner consistent with movies, stories, and TV shows that explicate their addiction, depersonalization, and uncertainty in a changing capitalist world. Neal Cassady legend had been undiscovered and unvisited: we are, then, likely to ask why. Carolyn's epitaph, two years before her death, re-organizes the Beat story as a whole, and presumes its human responsibility to families and communities distant from the literary spectacle. Devoid of any visibly freakish play, *With Love, Carolyn* testifies to authorship's specific internal difficulties.

Gary Snyder's Naturalist Form in *The Practice of the Wild*

Poet, Eastern mystic, environmentalist, and University of California professor Gary Snyder appraised man's responsibility to Nature in his life, work, and self-expressions in *The Practice of the Wild*. It is likely that audiences will quickly grasp the potent and navigable *haiku* forms and their inspiring mediation of syntax: it is also clear that the film's choice of poetry

Four. Baraka, Ferlinghetti, Cassady and Snyder 191

and biographical examples favored modernist discussion of the true context of America and the Beat Generation movement in context. Without re-writing the essential Beat trade and histories that are more commonly accepted, Snyder sees the series of interviews and talks as a way of promoting environmentalism and the peculiar, dynamic aesthetic found in his poems: we also peruse film clips from the 1950s and 60s, and contemplate the very special and catalytic relationship between Snyder and the fathers of the Beat metric form. Mixing counterculture, wilderness travels, private biography, and critical discussions of the form, *The Practice of the Wild* examines the author's consistent development of environmental learning, reviving the ferment of Zen Buddhist teachings.

I think that temptations to read Snyder, who won the Pulitzer Prize in 1974 for his poem anthology *Turtle Island* and who was a committed environmental activist, far outside the Beat canon and partially negate Jack Kerouac's resilient fervor about his buddy's learned technique for transposing Buddhist ideas and principles onto the experiencing of Nature, and to the simplicity of novels such as *Dharma Bums*. Appearing in several interviews with American naturalist writer Jim Harrison, Snyder recalls both the decipherable intensity of Kerouac's legendary poetic form and the ascension to naturalist sympathies that could override Kerouac's simple, pious, innocent-feeling strophes that travel natural and industrial imageries of American civilization without hindrance or suspicion of modern man's true intentions. Notwithstanding the depth of Snyder's immersions in naturalist form, I think it is also apt to summarize Snyder's long Zen Buddhist apprenticeship and the impact of meditations and *koan* on his poetry: because Beat films ignore the group's considerable Eastern studies, *The Practice of the Wild* may allow us to restate the larger poetic tradition while at the same time puzzle a thoughtful introduction to modernism's growing minute of self-reflection in today's world. Environmentalism was not a stated political goal until Ginsberg and Snyder approached it in the 1970s: it must be said, too, that the concept of "wild" living and writing crosses theoretical boundaries, challenging the impact of Snyder's poems.

Snyder's discussion of his family origins documented the poet's doctrine of rebellion against their specific intellectual inheritance and thus accelerated Beat discussions of a possible authenticity. Snyder recalls his parent's aversion to Christianity, and indolently fluffs off his mother's determination to see culture and experience in terms of socialist dogma and collective responsibility.[44] For social necessity is bargained for and eclipsed the collective minute of social existence: this is why the Beats are imagined to be escapists, criminals, and anarchists adhering to no active political component in their understandings of "scene," nor in most of their writing. Kerouac was the most apolitical, writing amidst theorizations about utopic disarmament and voluntary supersession of the communitarian dynamic: when supposing the end of war, the triumph of love, the erasure of man's corporate sickness, he offered no plans nor any pragmatic momentum, and this was why the hippies repeatedly fell out of focus. Because of this, we might query Snyder's specific form and his communitarian perspectives and insights: were they organized, active, true to man's aesthetic and moral missions? Intermixing liberal and conservative forms of religious and cultural ideas may cause us to doubt Snyder's peculiar mission: they may also cause us to question the strength of specific meditations that revive tradition and signal it to work in any political direction. Because, too, environmentalism operates from strong determinations about the form of mankind's use of the Earth and compiles facts and political activism into complete representations of man's global responsibilities, Snyder's poems, and resulting actions, may doff serious analytical and moral discussions.

Counterpoint Press editor Jack Shoemaker comments ambitiously, "It was clear to a lot of us that the legitimate intellectual airs to the Transcendentalists were the new American poets. Snyder clearly came from Emerson, Thoreau, Rexroth, the lineage was very clear."[45] Literary form's widest ambition to spread an intellectual form of theology and philosophy adds considerable detail and self-reflection: Snyder had learned poetry from many American histories, and so had developed a unique metric imagination that thoughtfully and innocently mixed poetic forms. But University of Idaho professor Scott Slovic strictly and plainly states the poet's modern community and the calculated value of writing's political metaphors:

> Bioregionalism is a social movement that emerged in the American West, in the 1970s and basically describes a type of political orientation and that is local rather than global that is nearby rather than far away. And it's based on the promise that if people pay attention to where they are and think responsibly about their interactions with the local environment and with the local human community, they can do a better job.[46]

Slovic divides Snyder's career into several phases: his working-class childhood, his stint as a forest ranger in the Pacific Northwest, his period with the Beats and bohemians, his Zen apprenticeship in Japan during the 1960s, a re-inhabitation phase during the 1970s when he wrote *Turtle Island*, and his professorship at UC Davis.[47] The critical formulation is quite agile and thoughtful: Snyder developed his specific consciousness and message from indoctrination, work, and studies, building them into an environmentally-focused activism that challenged hippie generations to develop legitimate ethical perspectives that correspond to the modern world. Slovic thus divorces Snyder from the wheel of Beat written and cultural creations: the axis of his current persona situates the same graduation from Beat mentorship into wider critical avenues. Black-and-white film clips from the 1950s and 60s, too, feature a young Snyder, fresh from Japan and eager to justify his excursions, talking about the specific biographical origin of his much-repeated studies of Buddhism and Orient cultures in East Asia.[48] Still, he states the challenge of form internally, a conduit for his own meditations:

> What I'd like to do is, I got going on this when I was travelling and living in India. Okay, let's say reincarnation is the world we're in. Then, how am I different? It means that I have done everything already. Yeah, I've had every possible experience. I've had every possible form. I've been a woman, I've been a butterfly. I've been a mosquito, and so why be ready? Why be looking for new experiences? Let's settle in and see what we can really think about now. Put you in a different place.[49]

I would say that Snyder's ambitious self-assessment carried with it the modernist dictum to wield perceivable experience, and so transposed his specific consciousness and engagements of images, ideas, and perceptible moments onto form. His simple admissions color the fruit of imagination and meditation: they, too, easily spell out the special moment of stasis, where inaction spurs on naturalist inquiry and community as nurturing agents of "real" consciousness. The ambitious tone might supersede Kerouac's imaginative form and its satisfying, pastoral ambivalence in *Book of Haikus*: Snyder's poetry reveals many points of inspiration from his friends. Through his readings, Snyder applies the didactic form of words, ideas, and summarizations of modern context through Nature's instance. They, while acquiring political moss to gain greater active content, revive the active technique to create idealism. Simple, imagistic content builds necessary conflicts between Man and Nature, for instance, in "Oil":

> Soft rain squalls on the cells,
> Smooth of the Bonin Islands,
> Late at night, Light from the empty men-hall,
> Throws back bulky shadows of winch and forklift,
> Over the slating fantail where I stand.
>
> But, four men on watch, in the engine room,
> The man at the wheel, the lookout in the bow,
> The crew sleeps, in cots on deck
>
> Or narrow iron bunks down driving passageways below.
> The ship burns with a furnace heart,
>
> Stern veins and copper nerves,
> Quivers and slightly twists, and always goes,
> Easy roll of the hull and deep vibrations
>
> of the turbines underfoot, bearing
> What all of these, crazed, hooked
> Nation's need, steelplate and
>
> Long injections of pure oil.[50]

Snyder's environmental technique is more surefooted in "Oil," without the aggressive destruction of democratic emblems in poems that are found in *Turtle Island* and *Riprap*. I believe that the simple organismic metaphor for the machine, and the easy tactility which placed environmental sickness in comfortable, instantly recognizable feelings and intonations of the modern man's perceived universe, recalls both modernist acuity and Snyder's broad, relaxed recollections of industry's sweeping might and its coloration of his thoughts and inscribes themselves in his plainer meditations. "Oil" is, of course, devoid of *shtick* and any kind of verbal trickery: the simple, post–Duchamp treading of industrial realism accomplishes his idea's mobility. It is not to say that gory sickness and destruction built the collective *ethos* of man's true responsibility: man's education is cyclical, calling attention to the organism's growth and maturity away from the after-effects of mankind's technological-based ruin. It was not to say that Snyder aped Kerouac, whose easygoing *métier* recorded plain, simple points of sympathy between two disparate, fighting worlds. More aptly, imagistic forms and the elongated poem spur on the film's private, special dialogues and thought-process favoring Nature over industry, technology, and masculine confinement. Snyder records his particular biographical moment with no anger or aggression: more, countercultural generations have endlessly recorded their travels and experiences as part of a doctrine of maturity, growth, and fulfillment. Questions, then, about "what we learn" are couched in our perceptible and simple reflections that weld our emotions and thoughts into action. Lastly, it is without a doubt that as an elder poet Snyder had argued for the point of his writing's continuing relevance, as he moves farther from the point of romantic wisdom that inspires Kerouac's hitchhiking revolution in 1958's *The Dharma Bums*. It was not without a peculiar anxiety that this minute was reached: Snyder had struggled with political realism to produce guiding themes and slogans of environmental and Eastern empowerment in the American counterculture. Cross-examining the specific inspiration re-mounts the unrealized depth of Snyder's predecessors, Kerouac and Ginsberg. I found that Snyder's readings of his poems, now older and more professorial in tone, enliven our contextual understanding of the weight of his journeys and studies.

The film includes several interview segments with Western novelist Jim Harrison, and noticeably catalogues the latter's amazement at Snyder's memory and his specific use of poetic technique. Harrison's eager prompting met with Snyder's diffidence and innocence, at one point causing Snyder to state, "You know I got interested in Asia for the wrong reasons."[51] Harrison, for his part, coughs up the unkempt realization gained from reading and studying Snyder: "I thought in my nickelante satoris I call 'em, they're often, it was from no effort. You know it's a realization."[52] Yet Snyder's ambitions are deliberate and sweeping: the force of his prophecies demanded change, and against the tide of politically correct aphorisms for global change. At a dinner party with Harrison with wine and food, Snyder dismisses politics, stating the obvious totality of our debt to the environment and, perhaps, his sanguinary choice of Nature over culture:

> What would be a normal planet would have lots fewer people and lots more animals. And what we have now is an irregular, abnormal and dangerous community. There's too many human animals, and the habitat and the existence of too many other creatures is endangered and we all need each other to be together with sanity. It's a matter of planetary sanity.[53]

The verbal statement was obviously controversial and overreaches man's practical functioning: Snyder demanded that Man change his habits and even surrender the Earth to animals and vegetation, recording his deep imaginative immersion and his clear departure from modern man's ethical *topoi*. It was not new: as I mentioned, Kerouac and Ginsberg were hardly pragmatists and affixed man's romantic rebirth against necessary political, social, and academic actions to implement more gradual, piecemeal change. He, too, drops the air of human aesthetic responsibility to tradition and to Man's historic engagements of Nature, its processes, and its wand of the imagination that colors man's emotions, thoughts and actions. Yet Snyder is clear to document his sense of environmental ruin and effacements of true humanity, observing the following:

> This is something you can't ever talk about anymore in Europe and Asia. Because Europe and Asia are too humanized. Their populations are too large, too urbanized, too agrarianized. There's not enough habitat, there's not enough wildlife, there's not enough people left that are engaged with interacting with other creatures in those parts of the world.[54]

Against Snyder's specific memories of Asia which included memories of his Zen apprenticeship and efforts to learn Chinese language, arts and music, the practical stain of reflection appears sour and cynical: with the continent now polluted, filled with urban mega-cities, and with numerous examples of serious environmental ruin, Snyder traces the Old World's sickness to the parameters of their human over-ideation, so as to make mankind responsible to man's thoughts and studies as they produced ethical governance of man, his environment, and his legacy. To state humanity's crisis is to register the plain tone of his conceptual excess: Snyder ably points out that man had ruined the Earth through his quest for self-understanding. This was without instances of total ruin that are a serious problem for most Asians: without touching pollution, deforestation, and global warming—all of which could kill life in Asia in the current century—Snyder touches on the effects of man's quest to order and govern the Earth according to his ideas and specific goals for humanity. To say that the future of the Earth is not human, but for the other creatures of the Earth, is an able transference away from Orwellian dystopia, but Snyder's technique and vivid emotions are very simple, recalling without boast our tryst with moral governance. In short, Snyder made able use of his career as a poet, if only to broaden discussions away from the making of laws and practices that, of course, favor humans over the Earth.

In fact, *The Practice of the Wild* accentuated liberal strategies for global change through the specially conceived ideation found in modern American poetry, calling our eyes and ears to its history and pushing even further to state the Spirit's greater movement against mankind's collective ambition to subjugate Nature, which had given mankind its life and purpose. Statements of the movement's forceful demands weigh against the opportunity to read his verses and stain the elder poet's gradual transformation of living context into a still romantic voice that breathed life into idealism once again. It was not an easy task: most of the arguments for environmental security developed from political analysis and grass-roots activism depending on facts and research, not upon one's free engagement of the natural world holding no trace of social Being. Alternation between strophic and analytic engagements were common in Snyder's poetry, and from the tactic for studying man's specific ideation as it moved from culture to actions, synopsized his fruitful development and the width of his penitent wisdom, while mixing in his very real contemplation of Kerouac's aesthetic realism that reflects many points of development that could tackle man's emotional causes. Students too, will appreciate the professor's agile didactic thrusting that mixes the professor's contemplative pose with his positive affirmations of the inspiring powers of Zen and Nature. Without a doubt, Shoemaker's identification of Transcendentalism repeats a deep anxiety that was greater than the Beat moment: Snyder's theoretical nexus, then, informs new readings that may then re-appoint the Beat metaphor, whether among humans or on behalf of the Earth's lesser creatures. Without touching the forms of feminism and postmodernism to trumpet activism at the 21st century's inception, Snyder romantically reconceives his later eco-criticisms, while intuiting a strong, unyielding purpose that came from his studies and personal life. I think that, in today's classroom, it was and is able commentary that documents the student's personal struggles with planetary issues that they try to understand.

Conclusion

Sixty-Five Years Later, and What Did We Learn?

I think of numerous reasons why I am unhappy with the state of contemporary scholarship when I read the Beats. The main reason is that scholars, for whatever reason, are reluctant to derive anything from the authors other than the published literature, in teaching the literature classroom. Though scholars such as David Sterritt and Erik Mortenson have conducted cinema-friendly explications of the written work, few actually confront film due to criticism's aversion. Few scholars pursued the possibilities for teaching the Beats as narcotic and sexual literatures to American students who had no familiarity with the Orient and instead feigned passive sympathy for the oft-disregarded 1960s counterculture. This is based on the assumption that Left writers had written and outlined anti-normative escapes from man's material and moral conditions, clouding their relevance in today's ethical and cultural discussions of writing and context. After all, we understand rebellion through "word of mouth," the "underground," and our positive rebellion militates itself against teachers and authority figures. So before we alienate the student into thinking that his/her thoughts inhere no reason or context, it is high time that we gave credibility to both topic and methodology. The latter point is also sincere: thinking in terms of the rhetoric and descriptive angles of the film accentuates and builds attachment, whereas literature, frozen in its specific moment—or rather the specificity of its notoriety and thus its peculiar artistic location—forces us to miss the mark if we are ever to afford pluralistic education in the United States. I also believe it is the film's cultural, conversational, and imaginative force that forces open the door to ideation and its memory: we are wrongly led to believe that man's passions and romanticism were resolved in authority's favor twenty years before college undergraduates took their seat in a class. I believe that we depend on this, as it is Richard

Nixon's essential and final dictum: the system would have power, and we could no longer oppose it or put into terms what was morally or semiotically "wrong" with its power. Lengthening rebellion's shadow professes the work's relevance to students and lay citizens, many of whom have not shared their ideas in public.

Censorship of the Beat Generation's writings and histories form a convincing tablet that builds our interest in both author and literary work. The added grab—namely, that these authors were controversial and had done bad things—extends the memoir's memory, and evinces from us the plebeian standard of shared literary community. In context, I also believe that the maintenance of a literature-only estimation will do nothing to add knowledge—the authors remained a bygone past, and were basically crazies who never added up to anything. If at all, this last idea *must be advanced* if we are ever to use literature in the development of student ideas. The contribution to ethnography, archaeology and history speak in invaluable terms across America—indeed, there is much ferment within the good-natured literary hero who nurses his private terrors and explodes into happiness and subversion when his ideas acquire voice and meaning. In this regard, I think the films did much to force Americans to recognize that history's controversy and its alternate pathways. Audiences and students will, then, project new referents and cosmologies that will, in their turn, "grow" American self-knowledge against the *tableaux* of cultural lies and syllogisms that extruded from *bourgeois* materialism and cynicism that interrupted youthful thinking and its post-expressions.

Because post-structuralism and postmodernism are such pervasive, guiding, pathological forces in today's culture, let me say that it becomes necessary to teach the American literature classroom from the sole moment of defiance: it is these authors who attempted to reconcile modern thought with modernist narration and character. Popular culture's appreciable "force" then must mediate from the strength and power of its literary immersion: it is equipped to fight postmodernity from the perceptual and poetic angles of this force. To this end, excavations of the authors' personal lives paid attention to the force of biography from childhood: these interrupt consumption that depends upon the visual instance and the screened cues of environment and people. The author's humanity, his choices, his meditations, contrast with the much briefer minute of recognition in the film. Because the Beats engaged and wrote about complex philosophies, it is necessary to devise the social sphere and the realism of literary man's social transactions, so as to mold him into a believable subject without pure abstraction. I do earnestly believe that the film offers a grand array of poststructuralist navigations of idea and meaning, but these are only valuable when connected to the memoir's romantic, aesthetic themes. I am not saying that these films might be read in separation from the literary work, but add the guiding sense that history will become familiar, easy, enjoyable, just as the sitcoms and serials from the time period elicit a dull and wordless nostalgia from post–Reagan citizenry.

Beat Generation film should not become the sole province of White students who profess interest in counterculture's peculiar act of making legends: I know and believe that student critique of liberal writing is constructive when it advances an alternative appraisal of the American experience. Decentering this experience meant showing films that escaped America's crass materialism: *Big Sur* competed with *Freedom Writers*, a much more criminally landscaped urban tale that confirmed writing's absence and the irrelevance of the written form in today's classroom. Students, by contrast, appreciated the legend and easygoing notoriety of *Sur*'s main characters: there would be, at last, a gradient by which students could learn outside the curriculum that greatly limited their ideation. The adolescent parable is then derivable, and with it the sense that the outside world includes much knowledge that cannot be stereotyped or discarded because of our postmodern similitude. I believe that ideas operate in the open, along with the uncertainty and awkwardness of unwanted and unheeded contact with the outside world. Although we privilege the form and its practical necessity in today's culture, as a comfortable part of the literary work's American ownership and an instance of its chosen, everyday subject, responsibility tells us today that we cannot hide our ideation and projection from foreign students, and those who are capable of using the ideas and cultural variables to suit his/her own world. This means that film criticism made Beat literature more competitive, or at least signals crucial archaeologies that found them to be legitimate answers to modernism's dogmatic illusion of loss and de-nationalization. Philosophically, a student will contrast the Beats with their own writers and citizens: clearly, much of the student's growth is away from the classroom, so we should cease to view knowledge exclusively through the Victorian looking-glass that processes students into degree-earning citizens.

The wide range of films associated with the Beat Generation grandly reflects a re-opening of the historical period, and one friendly with our more positive or affirmative perception about it. Without nostalgia, the recorded interviews and sojourns profess history's ambiguity. Without contradicting our teachers, it is my responsibility to further the objective debate, that students at many instances disown the patriarchal, Victorian organization of knowledge into society's repressed context and livelihood. I always knew the Beats were instruments of symbolic and personal growth, and that their works will be endlessly circulated and admired because of their paving of a new road, and one we travelled on but never recognized as a pathway to anything. A strong affirmative chart appears that many drug cultures and their heroes had obviously failed to find. "Beatitude," too, causes us to covet the Beat's peculiar history, romantic and unswervingly pious and free: they are a constellation that has never been studied seriously with a view to learning. Like other history-based films, Beat film makes the writing more accurate and active, as another collage of stories that intersect America's normative order, and thus are the advancing of questions and ideas that had not been fully dredged up. Knowledge, after all, can grow most when its context and study is rich and complex: there exists, in the classroom of today, no apparent reason why the Beats escape study and exist purely in the unwritten imagination.

APPENDIX

Audiobooks and Recordings
New Beat Consciousness and Teaching the Beats

Inevitably, Beat works would be read aloud by patrons, critics, and fellow Beat writers and their friends. It is, of course, an afterthought: WDNA aired Kerouac's recordings and introductions to jazz tunes about 20 years ago, and thereby offered much greater chances for understanding Beat attunements to music and society. Audiobooks constitute a major part of the current literary humanities, with examples ranging from Leonard Nimoy reading Jewish short stories, to readings of African-American, Latino, and Asian authors on NPR, and a very broad range of both literary works and commentary on audio that go as far back as Shakespeare's plays, the ground for creating Beat analogs was always fertile and could count upon a vast, repressed imagination. Controversial Beat works, or rather the controversy of their legitimacy and place, would invite the chance to hear texts as spoken consciousness, consistent with the undying inspiration.

In this section, I examine four Beat works. A key question always has to do with the re-invention of literature's story and truth: is there any additional value to reading the printed word? Yet a special nexus exists with all Beat writers—*they were, and are, meant to be read aloud*. Attentions to jazz, media, and protest all figure bravely, yet there is the added motion to authors who depended on orality, both because of the erasure of syntax in form and because of the added theoretical and intellectual impulses uncovered in the new science and philosophy. This fracture challenges the Beat reader to express a crucial sincerity of ownership: there is meaning to the tale, and spoken words eschew writing's narrow consciousness to paint a broader, more complete picture. Reflexively, some of Kerouac's works were less ably written: my job is not to re-introduce these, but examine biography as a tool for future readings.

Doctor Sax and the Great World Snake

James Sampas's production of the 2 hour, 12-minute audio CD, *Doctor Sax and the Great World Snake*, first appeared in 2003 and featured Lawrence Ferlinghetti. The audiobook, flavored with variations of voice and pitch that favor Kerouac's Lowell neighborhoods and childhood personalities anchors the fictional persona of Jack Duluoz in his nightmares and dreams, and the CD's positive favoring of street characters and woebegone myths gives a glimpse of the fantasy for seeking organic links between Duluoz's many adventures and a childish point of origin, an attempt to synthesize the outside world from the depths of a child's imagination and his unkempt, wandering memories connected firmly to place and French-Catholic identity. We might view this work, as it puts together excerpts of Kerouac's 1959 masterpiece, *Dr. Sax* and contrasts Robert Creeley as an omniscient, elderly narrator with sketchy, sumptuous voices in the dark and the rambling glitter of Jim as a youngish, beatnik-meandering voice pulling together cool, hip, backcountry, and Black intonations of spirit and meaning, as a thoughtful effort reconciling the so-called Vanity of Duluoz, his multi-language adventures, and philosophic ramblings with the ecstasy and horrors of a child's wanderings of the unknown. If we remember the obvious—*The Town and the City* remains the primary document of Lowell's biography, firmly written prose and not at all diaphanous when telling the everyday tale of modest origins—we may then suppose a much greater modernist inclusion, surpassing adolescent identities that mask the real development of culture and persona in works by William Faulkner, F. Scott Fitzgerald, and Ernest Hemingway. Childhood and adolescence, without the daily prescriptions of urban-institutional necessity, unveil a greater moment of pre-rational truth that changes our estimation of the Beat legend to one friendly with its ethnic and regional variations. We might also allow that *Doctor Sax* blends White and Black tongues to suggest translation's ambivalence, and hence the purity of inquiries. Besides adding to the detail of existing documentaries that use Kerouac's readings and rich, hushed voice adding texture and intonations of the peculiar, proud hearth, this reading brings us closer to film techniques starring the adaptation of history, places, images, and so on. I believe that audio readings precede and favor film, and so star the timeless journeys of children with few rational anchors limiting the depth of their expulsions of feeling.

Featuring Robert Creeley as the omniscient narrator, *Doctor Sax* plays as a dramatic reading, with the narrator and several other readers who comprise the *dramatis personae*. This development situates the teen comedy and its counterculture-flavored search of spirits, tales, and the daily hearth as the beginning for a young boy's quests into the unknown wilderness outside. The arrangement itself projects our viewing glass, and the conduit of our meditations on the darkness and home. Colored with occasional jazz saxophone playing and noises to simulate the terror, *Doctor Sax* plays up to the middle-class youth's ethnic uncertainties and realms beyond the grasp of a small manufacturing town. "Duluoz" is featured in a binary simulation, at times the adolescent boy who roams the streets and trains of New York, and at other times a groovy, idea-befriended Jim Carroll, with a diction and stretched uncertainty like a young hippie meandering the town streets. Hippie flavoring accents the special minute of discovery, while beatnik neighborhood-gathering grows the insecure Duluoz into a journeying teen on the walk for life and its mysteries. Voice, and the accenting of diction and syllables, projects the power of one's feelings and the special moment of human engagement of language and its foreign-sounding aura. It should be noted that *Doctor Sax* is not faithful to the novel, instead borrowing excerpts of the novel that favor spoken exchanges over description. Key to the talent for showing fiction readings are accentuations of spoken text, which may then anchor metaphors in the descriptive text. Clearly, however, this CD means to please children, reviving the tactic for storytelling that may gather author anxieties as they may express themselves in a dream about the unknown. *Doctor Sax* takes a chance in replacing Kerouac with Creeley, yet speaks to our wish to be given sensory enunciations of voice and thoughtful evocations of place that are emotionally broader than in film. I think this is what builds our interest in audio readings: it may create a greater audition and involvement in the action of a literary work, free of the endless visual patterns that usurp the story's telling.

Narrator Robert Creeley's deep, hushed and crackling voice projects the multitude of silence and isolation complicit with unearthing the treasures of multi-ethnic rambling found in a child's mind: the expansion of dialects among Duluoz and the other actors pairs the closeness of dialects across the United States. Given that the disparity between Southern or black enunciations of the "a," "e" and "o" vowels to twang the syllable, and Northern or Irish, Italian, and street dialects that raise or collapse them, we might add that the fantasy for experiencing ethnic otherness, White, Ethnic, or Black, suggests the exchange of common-dialect witticisms and the totality of Being in the Beat context. Creeley's authoritarian full stop, too, accents the isolation of place and the special, nuanced moment of childish pain and possibility. Kerouac fondly recalls his childhood, parents, and special communities that he seems to have the sole key to. Deanna Stefanyshyn notes criticism of television/film instances in the classroom: "they were too complicated, [and] teachers would become robotic, or that commercialization would take over."[1] Stefanyshyn points out the obvious point of idealism: radio brought people together. Sampas's welcoming of past and present diction and auditions, including jazz, Great Mahogany Radio, and private recollections of phantoms, TV and film stars, and a brown Virgin Mary (translated in his letters into a "black Christ cunt"),[2] make Kerouac's community and visions audible and comprehensible, a special moment. Still, the practice of teaching through audio presentation allows us the myth of ethnic diversity that can take the mind and its perceptions in any direction.

But what can be known from visions? If we believe key characters like Creeley and Kerouac's mother, who repeat the present's authority, and the auditory coerciveness of authority and domesticity, would far-fetched visions and dreams tell us much about Lowell itself, or Kerouac's idea-creation? What we have, as an answer, is the true richness of audition that tells the deep sensual involvement in the American Dream, or "dreams" that suppose adventure, pain, and personal struggle. When transposed onto the myths themselves, they easily suggest the timelessness of American Being and cool modulations of authorial purpose. Kerouac is beholden to his dreams, and tries to understand them—these figured into his adolescent/young adult possibilities. Cross-examining the tortured genius of Burroughs is aided as well: Kerouac's specific torments and anti-rational rambling suggest modern man's common anxiety, and hence the width of Beat Generation excursions and studies that state modernity's powerful ambivalence in both fiction and theory.

Prose is varied, with the standard determination of the soul's wandering mind and organized purpose. They may range from Duluoz's naturalistic ramble, noting with everyday terms and ejections the power of Nature:

> Even for my fa-ther's home, I could hear (the river) rise for the rocks, ul-ulating with the water, sp-losh! Ma! Zoom! All night low-ing, the river says Zoom! The stars affixed in rooftops like ink. Merrimac River, oft names sported dark valleys. My Lowell had the great trees in the antiquity of the Great Nawth. Moving onward in cal-varies, barging, eu-platis, electronics, King gray, looped and curly like artist work with clay souls, snow curlicue, Mr. Tobas in the fore-front, I had a ter-ror of these waves [...].[3]

To more ambitious tear-downs of syntax and syllabic wholeness, as with the storyteller who sells magazines to the children:

> Well, part-nahs! Are you goin' to ben in the arms of tha old treeman! But yew rememba me tee farm! Me kid, Tee John! Me kid, come in! That's at night, the man will howl! And when he hears that, path-nas, close ya windows![4]

Lesser cues, destabilizing syntax and confirming Beat alterations of syntax, are traditional enough: they include Creeley's dropping of the definite article to express the immediate strength of place and diction, and the use of a White reader to impersonate Dr. Sax's haunting call-out to the kids, "Mwee hee hee hah hah!"[5] It is clear that Kerouac intended Dr. Sax to present a Black or Latino superhero akin to jazz, and the chapter that includes "Transcendenta" unveils the minority subject's power, mystery, and erratic synthesis of street anxiety. These, when paired with syntax favoring the diction of works like *Visions of Cody* and *Tristessa*, mean to hoist the reader's voice to suggest what printed words could not: the haunting mobility of one's mind, and the many pathways and corners through character and place. Further, not only does *Doctor Sax* record childhood terror, but also possibility—it clearly situates Duluoz's questing and private certainty with the massive re-development of the urban world, and the true sincerity of a youth's purpose against the shadow of insecurity and obscurity, common traits in middle-class America. Breathed into life is an imaginative production of many trips, and many exchanges that are privately surmised in the form of Duluoz's love of nature, the city, the scene, and the irrational gainsay of what lay far beyond and only came to him in hints and dark, shadowy moments of redundant isolation.[6] The selling of magazines that include both Westerns and those of the jazz spirit, too, announce the coming of the American frontiers, telling us that a forbidden world sought our emotions and tactile belonging from the beginning of life. Because Kerouac didn't paraphrase Mark Twain, John Muir, or James Fenimore Cooper, we might add that the ambivalence and irrational full stops in the haunted portraits of night meant to suppose cartoonish anti-reason that brought forth a new, garbled modern legend bearing no true mythology.

The success of audiobooks does not merely inhere our ambiguity in returning to the author's time period—it, too, depends upon sensory and auditory involvement in the literary text, and resuscitations of the text that bequeath our special inculcation of one's memory. Sampas's recording of *Doctor Sax* took examples from Kerouac's childhood, and the surprising strength of his memories. Because most modernist authors moved far from their early years and grew from academic or vocational inspirations, we must conclude that the Beat Generation, and the counterculture that rose from it, spurred on the misfit's re-exertion of living purpose and without the benefit of institutions other than those found at home or on the street. At the same time, Lowell is nicely preserved and intact as the adventuresome whole's beginning.

Allen Ginsberg's Reading of *Dharma Bums*

Allen Ginsberg's reading of the 2 hour, 42 minute *Dharma Bums* accomplished both the errata of spoken translation and the bonds of love and charity for his beloved friend, Jack Kerouac. More importantly, Ginsberg's reading enunciates the humors and poetic inflections guaranteed by success and notoriety—the young poet's insecurities and bluster are

206 APPENDIX

replaced with the charming, happy recollection of the rising hippiedom and its semantic and syntactic freedoms. Light, airy and funny steps of inspiration and self-presentation augment the happiness of Kerouac's natural parable: plus, the Buddhist meter is accented repeatedly, as to invoke breath and geography with its spontaneous and free direction. I intend to read the *Dharma Bums's* audiobook from the tactic for spoken rehearsal and its supersession of the written word: *Dharma Bums* was not Kerouac's best book, and the modernist acuity and symbolism had already begun to decline after the 1957 publication of *On the Road*.

Ginsberg's reading began with the story's restatement of the tales of hoboes with unique, directed witticisms and personal endeavors that appear to complicate mendicancy and hoboed travel, with a flair for Buddhist-pop symbolism. Ginsberg's reading took advantage of his own private humors, and even a humorous reflection of his elder: he laughs when he introduces Kerouac's desire for hoboed travel, and passes over the words with a lightly amused voice:

> Since then I've become hypocritical about my lip service tired—and cynical because now I've grown so old and natural—but then I already realized in the reality of charity—and kindness and humility and natural tranquility to ecstasy.[7]

Of course, humor and sarcasm was common enough for Ginsberg when reading, interrupting his polite tone during his 50s and 60s. It also replayed his innocence at reading a work Kerouac would have enunciated more seriously and prophetically, as a testament to his meditations and ideas. Lighthearted readings set the emotional and declarative tone of mendicancy, and Kerouac's otherwise statement of All-Soul:

> I had not met Japhy Ryder yet. I was about to next week or heard anything about Dharma Bums, though at this time there was a perfect dharma bum—myself and often considered myself a religious wanderer. The little bin in the gondola solidified my warming up to the wine and finally whipping out a tiny slip of paper which contained a paper by Nate Theresa and something that after her death that she will return to the Earth by powering it with roses for heaven for all living creatures.[8]

Humor-laced reading, or rather the happy, insouciant and peering re-introduction to Kerouac, accomplished the Buddhist parable of living within the Earth's elemental and syllabic development of health and mendicancy. It also repeats rucksack symbolism, as a drunken Kerouac finds his self-prophecy and imagines his friends' self-prophecies telling about one's redemption. I think it is fair to say that Ginsberg's later readings were more polite and scholarly—inspiration and satisfaction about the Buddhist tale, then, replaces the stinging voice possessed of his own weaknesses, as a young Ginsberg would not have successfully retold of his elder's quests. In short, the complete improbability of the protégé's translation is replaced with the invention and approval of a friend who could now reflect, and surmise the greatness of the tale's inheritances. It would, of course, be asked as to who would read the Beat works, and who could carry out the effectiveness of a reading—Ginsberg had accompanied Kerouac on many travels, and enjoys repainting his friend's persistent imagination.

Ginsberg pushes a reflective, easy tone and voice when spelling out metered reflections without syntax, placing them in a statement of elemental coolness and self-satisfaction:

> But the little bum had much patience than I had and lay there most of the time chasing his cud forlorn and bitter-lipped my teeth were chattering my lips blue my dark with sun in relief with the familiar mouths of Santa Barbara taking shape and soon we'd be stopped and and we were in the worms' night—by the tracks.[9]

It is here, of course, that Kerouac's poorly adorned meter and complete syntactic ownership might be revisited most successfully by Ginsberg—it is, of course, an outright point that any lay reading of Kerouac will respond to his authorship's authority and legacy-and maybe, what we even thought of *him*. Because Kerouac's scholarship and written dilly-dallying is questioned and criticized from all angles of criticism—and crucially, because James T. Jones attributed Ray and Japhy's trek to symbolize the failure of man and families, that Ginsberg's reading accomplish the spoken happiness and mobility of the non-syntactic form, so as to lend legitimacy and community to the spoken representations of hoboed self-reflections. It is said without a doubt that man's meditations on Nature and poverty are seldom accomplished without irrational or un-historic pretense, and Ginsberg tends to this reading point with some care. Authority of place, ideation, and sensibility repeat those of Kerouac, whose nature—and solitude—meditations were sensitive and easily misunderstood from the society at large.

Strictly speaking, it must be said that "free verse" had never been accomplished in prose fiction, with the exception of works such as *Ulysses* and *The Sound and The Fury*. Many scholars attribute the confusion of forms and the tangled mess of memory, meaning, and history—they are enough to unravel the main characters, calling the modernist body of experience a whimsical and torpid delusion that weakens the spirit's discursivity. Ginsberg and Kerouac were not masters of the form, nor knew any true master *per se*—translations of text, then, could not be indifferent, and it should be said that readings accomplished the tactility of place and idea. *Dharma Bums*, then, complements existing readings of today's fiction, and joins the many readings of Kerouac that spell out a positive vivification of peculiar Beat aesthetics.

A Contemporary Reading of *Tristessa*

Folk singer William Fitzsimmons's reading of Jack Kerouac's 1960 novel, *Tristessa*, is an attempt to imagine and resurface a younger generation's admiration for Beat form and story. It takes risks: without the softened tone of Beat notables, or the archetype of writer/legend perusing scenery and diction, the high-voiced, contemporary model may easily sweep away sympathies and connections with the characters. As a criticism, I believe it is important to recognize that many will state calmly a generation's ownership of context, and that persons from previous eras would find events and people to appear misplaced. Still, it is just as likely that stories will find their way to students, as they always have done: Fitzsimmons, at many points, chooses points of description over love, accomplishing the active distance of time: sparing, hushed readings, too, accomplish the remoteness of place and identity, suggesting again the Beat mystique and possible whirlwinds of discovery when traveling the outside world.

I think that acceleration of diction and voice accomplish the spoken momentum, and maybe even the possible triumph of understanding Third World domains. Fitzsimmons slows his voice and maintains a tone of pain and isolation when introducing Mexico City:

> Here I am in Mexico City rainy Saturday night, mystery old dream side streets. The little street where I walked into crowds of hobo Indians wrapped in Yaqui shawls enough to make you cry you thought you saw leaves flashing in the Fall.[10]

Should we sustain the impressionist theme, where sojourns into society framed distance, pathos and the author's abstract purpose, Fitzsimmons' stressed pauses and careful attention to words may suit Kerouac's sojourns by framing his self-perceived isolation. Fitzsimmons speeds up his reading, building momentum to the waiting free verse that opens the story of place:

> Outside is a brakeman by of light lumbering in the sad, vast mist trembling life. But now, on that vegetable plateau Mexico. The moon of silaful of nights earlier humble too on the sleepy roof on the way to the trippy stone on toilet. Tristessa's high, beautiful as ever goin' home gaily to be in bed and enjoy morphine. Night before, I've had a great hassle in the rain would darkly, early bread and soup and drinking at every inch.[11]

I think it's important to count stresses of emphasis in fiction readings, and ask ourselves whether or not they carry any able pretense to tell either story or meaning. In truth, readings in historical film are dismal and in many ways completely offensive, ignoring customs, persons, and history. It behooves us, of course, *not* to sound prophetic—who might we be to declare history as "our" moment of discovery at all, and since the world would not reveal itself as I would today. Pretense did not accomplish romantic reading for Kerouac, either—without shouting, sneering, or any kind of pointed energy meant to uncover sickness, inequity, horror or the like—Fitzsimmons's pale yet loquacious voice again accomplishes what Creeley may be credited for in the reading of *Doctor Sax*. I believe, of course, the positive error of today's "slam reading" may be its false, prophet-contrived obsession with loudness. As the Beats were vilified for their loud presentations in prose, geography and history may get a nod from us when we exercise our dispassion, so as to negatively star the existence of life and happiness against our stereotypes and prejudices.

Fitzsimmons's tone of approval becomes warmer and lighter as he continues to describe Tristessa's house. While not measured through Kerouac's *paean* to pious expression, he continues:

> Allowing little drizzles to fizzle in the kitchen with the chicken garbage in the dry corner where mi-ra-cu-lous-ly now, the little pink eat taking pile of the vulgar chicken feed. The inside bed is littered by mad-men with torn newspapers and the chickens pecking and the rice sandwiches on the flower on the bed by Tristessa's sister, sick, wrapped in pink coverlet its as tragic at night Eddie was shot at the....[12]

Fitzsimmons's tone does slow down as Kerouac approaches the bed, recalling Tristessa's pain and the family's suffering, but the important thing is to document her home and neighborhood with the same tactile and sense-object approval found in any modern society, including ours—the house's disheveled mess, plus Tristessa's visible happiness at being high, consecrate the slum house and its inhabitants. It isn't actually possible to say whether Kerouac was "idealistic" about Mexico City: clearly, though, sense-geographies are refreshing for him and constitute his external portrait of his girlfriend and the effects of morphine. Matt Dillon remarks wistfully in the film *Drugstore Cowboy*, "everything in life was beautiful," as his girlfriend races through the streets of an impoverished Portland neighborhood at sunset. Many films do not carry forth the sweetness of drug transcendences, nor the happiness at living among poor people. Fitzsimmons's ascent and circumspection interrupts and solemnizes poverty's experience and addiction's positive, angelic pretense in neo-aesthetic terms, and may redress what poetry collections such as *Mexico City Blues* may only do imperfectly. This may not alter the imperfectness of Kerouac's translation, but attests to the vigor of discovery that he had imagined.

Fitzsimmons pairs Kerouac's isolation and alcoholic dependence with a sour, depressive tone upon arriving in Mexico City: "my Mexican whiskey has soft cover cap that I keep worrying will slip off and be all my bag bedrowned perf whiskey through the crazy Saturday night drizzle street."[13]

Completely dropping Kerouac's emotional overtones and positive diction, to spell out his isolation and Orientalization of Mexico City as place, accomplishes the pretense of Yankee traveler and writer: it, too, may shelter Kerouac's imagination and self, which are praised for adopting poor life and the ambivalence of purpose in a poor country. Keeping in mind that letters to Neal Cassady took advantage of the saleability of poor Mexico's economy, restating the positives of discovery:

> And we came out in the whore street district, get off behind the fruity fruit stands and tortilla beans and taco shacks, with fixed wood benches. It's the poor district of Rome, I pay the cab $3.33 and the cabbie 10 pesos and seis for change with count.[14]

One would probably count Kerouac's voice in—it accomplishes the race and thirst of adolescent discovery, consistent with any kind of Orient travel that backpackers would enjoin today. But Fitzsimmons's dry, haunting voice positively accomplishes Kerouac's distance from his experiences, and translation's raw necessity. Frequent criticism of "typing" may complicate future Kerouac studies, but authorship is fragile and asks for a new generation's less enthusiastic appraisal. By creating gaps in the narration, and gusts of more happy, infused tale-telling, Fitzsimmons's reading is sympathetic with Kerouac's own anxieties.

The Yage Letters Redux

Andrew Garman and Luis Moreno's re-reading of Burroughs's exhaustive and controversial study of ritual drug cultures in Colombia and Peru in the 4 hour, 45-minute *The Yage Letters Redux* may or may not rehearse or confirm the author's goals in narrating hallucinogenic experience. The simple, plain diminution of drug concoctions taken by drink such as *yage, ayahuasca, and cumbiamba* may force us to admit the neutralization of contexts, histories, and any kind of real significance: by the time Michael Harrington published *The Vast Majority* in 1976, it was pretty clear that backpackers and tourists were only interested in mainstream "street drugs." This appears grandly in Oliver Harris's splitting of intention: "it reads at times like a Yaqui way of knowledge by Carlos Castaneda,"[15] purely devoid of the operating guidance of one shaman, and then: "at other times like Che Guevara's *Motorcycle Diaries* reporting on the same region junta a year before Burroughs's travels and what of the specific object of its quest,"[16] despite the obvious documentation of Burroughs's disgust for any kind of Communism or socialism, and in tune with the persistent mythology that communism was patently against drug-taking. Yage's specific properties, and the impact of them upon Burroughs's imagination, are the mark of Harris's book, *The Secret of Fascination*: my effort, by contrast, will question re-reading's sincere appraisal of the author's pretensions and his specific goals in seeking mysticism through drugs.

Burroughs's April 15, 1953, letter to Allen Ginsberg appears to accomplish the customary appropriations of legend, conspiracy and co-conspirators, and the adventure's ambitions:

> Back in Bogota. I have a crate of yage I've taken it, and know more or less. By the way, you may see my picture in exposure. I see a reporter going in as I was going out. Queer, to be sure, but about as appetizing as a hamper of dirty laundry. Not even after two months in the brush, my dear. This character is shaking down the South American continent for free food around transpor and dissents with everything he buys, as we got two kinds of publicity, favorable and unfavorable which do you want, routine. What a shameless mooch. But who am I to talk.
> Flashback, retraced my journey. Popaya and Pasto to Mukaya. I was interested to note what Mukaya dragged Schindler and the two Englishmen as much as it did me.[17]

Garman's hardened voice, with full stops, may engender what Burroughs's own sneering, dried voice could not—the dislocation of the Beat author's visible Yankee jingoism and contempt for his surrounding environs. "Appetizing as a hamper of dirty laundry" repeats, in queer terms, the same sincerity as that of Kerouac or Cassady, while "shameless mooch" returned in his impromptu bowdlerization, "Willie The Moocher," while in Tangier.

Garman's exterior presence appears to also accomplish what Burroughs cannot as an "international criminal": his positive reception and the makings of practical agency in a capitalist world, repeating spheres of legitimacy and modernity first excavated in Rob Johnson's *The Beats In South Texas*. It is evident that, at many points, the voice of Burroughs ought to be replaced because of the results of addiction and old age:

> This trip, I was treated like visiting royalty, under the misapprehension. I was a representative of the Texas Oil Company travelling incognito. Free boatrides, free plane, but everyone in the Putumayo the Texas company will return like the second coming of Christ. The governor told me the Texas company takes 2 samples of oil, 80 miles apart and it was the same oil. There was a pool of the stuff 80 miles across under Mocoa.[18]

It should be admitted that future Burroughs narratives would operate many facets of his voice and the visible projection of addiction and sickness—straightening this voice and giving it to younger men might reinstate memory's authority, and the intactness of both conspiracies against society and even the seriousness of academic and professional purpose. It isn't an easy task, and many critics will point out that multi-geographic adventures may disfigure or erase the integrity of any kind of true purpose, culminating in the violent destructions of body and Self through "Leif The

Unlucky" and "Dr. Benway" in *Naked Lunch*. Burroughs's grandfather had invented the adding machine, and he was a Harvard graduate. Still, we attribute his weakness and insincerity to his voice's passive languor, maybe only once again granting credit for his inquiries when he ruminates on a hotel bed in *Drugstore Cowboy*. Still, Garman spikes his voice, admitting incredulity at quitting drugs, re-establishing the younger generation's tone of defiance and granting power to drug interactions:

> I was getting off junk, and he nagging me why I was kidding myself. Once a Junkie, always a junkie. If I quit junk, I would become a sloppy lush or go crazy through cocaine.[19]

Adopting a more preternatural, prophetic tone, he continues to describe his addiction's details:

> One night I got lushed paregoric and he kept saying over and over I knew you'd come home with paregoric. I knew it! You'll be junkie all the rest of your life. And look at me with his little eat smile, junk is a case with him. I checked into the hospital junk sick and spent four days there. They would only give me three shots of morphine and I couldn't sleep, [....] desperation besides which there was a Panamanian hernia case in the same room with me. And his friends came and stayed all day and half the night. One of them did in fact stay until midnight. Recall walking by some American women in the corridor looked like officer's wives. One of them was saying, "I don't know why, but I can't eat sweets." "You got diabetes, lady."[20]

Given the labyrinthine attention in Burroughs's novels for the word "junk," and his obvious affection for the types of drugs administered in the hospital or penitentiary, one might wonder why the gift of Burroughs's voice, so as to document and refresh the voice of addiction itself, is missing. Pausing stresses on "junk" and "paregoric," or the incredulity of Burroughs's first admission, refreshes the hospital's depressive labyrinth, and sets up the last cowl-splitting joke meant to reclaim the addict's domain as theirs, and agency as pointed and real. Burroughs enthusiasts may not believe that is fair, instead heralding the dry, gravelling, yet relaxed voice that climbs to his self-realizations in the prose. A chance is taken—still, it is a game one, and one where addiction's experience is stilted to project its reality and necessity in a society that includes addicts, hence their desire to live a life colored by addiction. Addicts, users, and advocates have frequently noted the obscenity of being forced to give up their habits: meanwhile, Burroughs's study of the Lexington prison where "the cure" is given, document its absolute failure and the junky's pitiful, subnormal state. In this case, of course, *pathos* would be replaced with junked possibilities by stating the incredulity of institutions and the junkie's compassionate rendering, where voice and agency are activated instead of repeatedly pathologized.

It is obvious that Burroughs's younger followers—and, as Giorno and

Harris document, there were many—expected to take up their elder's mantle at some point—possessed as they might be by activism concerning drugs, gays, and hospital patients. The deteriorating ladder that moves from pretense to status to subjection and redemption, naturally replicates Burroughs's own spiritual quest for identity. Still, it should be clear that Garman took advantage of "new" situations and voicings for drug addicts, building strength, force, and possibility into experiences that Burroughs, and the elocution of his voice, clearly saw no idealism from within.

Chapter Notes

Preface

1. Robert Stam, *Film Theory: An Introduction*.
2. Alan S., Marcus, et al., *Teaching History With Film*, 19.
3. *Ibid.*, 111.
4. *Ibid.*, 115.
5. Oliver Stone, director, *The Doors* (Oliver Stone Productions, 1991).
6. *Ibid.*
7. Kiran Rao, director, *Dhobi Ghat* (UTV Movie Productions, 2010).

Introduction

1. Jack Kerouac, *The Unknown Kerouac*, 107, 153.
2. *Ibid.*, 161.

Chapter One

1. Linda Hutcheon, *A Theory of Adaptation*, 31.
2. Jacques Derrida, *Grammatology*.
3. "Tales of the Mad Bop Night," c. 1950. Box 3, Folder 10, *The Jack Kerouac Archive*, Berg Collection, New York Public Library.
4. *Ibid.*
5. "Benzedrine Vision," from *The Jack Kerouac Archive*, Series 2, 40.1.
6. Sigmund Freud, *The Interpretation of Dreams*, 474.
7. Norman, Mailer, *Advertisements for Myself*, 373.
8. John Byrum, dir., *Heart Beat*, Orion Pictures, 1980.
9. *Ibid.*
10. *Ibid.*
11. *Ibid.*
12. *Ibid.*
13. *Ibid.*
14. *Ibid.*
15. *Ibid.*
16. *Ibid.*
17. *Ibid.*
18. *Ibid.*
19. *Ibid.*
20. *Ibid.*
21. *Ibid.*
22. *Ibid.*
23. *Ibid.*
24. *Ibid.*
25. John Singleton, dir., *Boyz n the Hood*, Columbia Pictures, 1991.
26. Neal Cassady, *Collected Letters, 1944–1967*, 245.
27. Jack Kerouac, *Visions of Cody*.
28. Stephen Kay, dir., *The Last Time I Committed Suicide*, Multicom Entertainment Group, 1997.
29. *Ibid.*
30. James Joyce, *Ulysses*.
31. James Thurber, "The Secret Life of Walter Mitty."
32. Ella Fitzgerald, "A Tisket, a Tasket."
33. Tex Avery, "Magical Maestro."
34. Miles Davis, *The Birth of the Cool*.
35. Kay, dir *The Last Time I Committed Suicide*.
36. *Ibid.*
37. *Ibid.*
38. Marcus, et al., *Teaching History With Film*, 187.
39. Jack Kerouac, *Journals, 1948–1949*,
40. Jack Kerouac, "Journal, 1951," in *The Unknown Kerouac*, 167.
41. Northrop Frye, "The Archetypes of Literature," 505.

215

42. Richard Lerner, *What Happened To Kerouac?*
43. *Ibid.*
44. *Ibid.*
45. *Ibid.*
46. *Ibid.*
47. *Ibid.*
48. *Ibid.*
49. *Ibid.*
50. *Ibid.*
51. Hutcheon, *A Theory of Adaptation*, 8.
52. *Ibid.*
53. Lerner, *What Happened to Kerouac?*
54. Catherine Morley, *The Quest for Epic in Contemporary American Fiction*.
55. Lerner, *What Happened to Kerouac?*
56. John Dos Passos, *U.S.A.*
57. William Faulkner, *The Sound and the Fury*.
58. Mailer, *Advertisements for Myself*, 374.
59. Lerner, *What Happened to Kerouac?*
60. *Ibid.*
61. Kerouac, *The Unknown Kerouac*, 161.
62. Lerner, *What Happened to Kerouac?*
63. Allen Ginsberg, *Indian Journals*.
64. Lerner, *What Happened to Kerouac?*
65. *Ibid.*
66. *Ibid.*
67. *Ibid.*
68. *Ibid.*
69. *Ibid.*
70. Michael J. Lennon, *A Double Life*, 2.
71. John Antonelli, prod., *Jack Kerouac: King of the Beats*, Kultur, 2012.
72. *Ibid.*
73. *Ibid.*
74. *Ibid.*
75. *Ibid.*
76. *Ibid.*
77. *Ibid.*
78. Jack Kerouac, and Ann Charters, *Selected Letters, 1940–1956*, 213.
79. *Ibid.*, 213–4.
80. *Ibid.*, 248.
81. Ranald MacDougall, dir., *The Subterraneans*, MGM, 1960.
82. *Ibid.*
83. *Ibid.*
84. *Ibid.*
85. *Ibid.*
86. Vidhu Vinod Chopra, *Lage Raho Munna Bhai*, 2006.
87. Frank Tabbita, dir., *Beat Angel*, Beat Angel Productions, 2006.
88. *Ibid.*
89. *Ibid.*
90. *Ibid.*
91. *Ibid.*
92. *Ibid.*
93. *Ibid.*
94. *Ibid.*
95. Jack Kerouac, *On the Road*, 198.
96. Tabbita, dir., *Beat Angel*.
97. *Ibid.*
98. *Ibid.*
99. *Ibid.*
100. Sigmund Freud, *The Ego and the Id*, 2.
101. Tabbita, dir., *Beat Angel*.
102. *Ibid.*
103. *Ibid.*
104. Jack Kerouac, "Journal 1951," from *The Unknown Kerouac*, 135.
105. Lerner, *The Unknown Kerouac*, 161.
106. *Hollywood Reporter*, "Review of *On the Road*."
107. Walter Salles, dir. *On the Road*. IFC Films, 2012.
108. Kerouac, *On the Road*.
109. *Ibid.* 113.
110. Salles, dir. *On the Road*.
111. *Ibid.*
112. *Ibid.*
113. Jacques Derrida, *Grammatology*, 134.
114. *Ibid.*, 135.
115. Salles, dir. *On the Road*.
116. *Ibid.*
117. *Ibid.*
118. *Ibid.*
119. *Ibid.*
120. John Madden, dir., *Ethan Frome*, Miramax Films, 1993.
121. Gerrold Freeman, dir., *Native Son*, Cinecom Pictures, 1986.
122. Steven Spielberg, dir., *The Color Purple*, Warner Bros., 1985.
123. Joe Wright, dir., *Anna Karenina*, Focus Features, 2012.
124. Roland Joffe, dir., *The Scarlet Letter*, Buena Vista Pictures, 1995.
125. Salles, dir., *On the Road*.
126. Kerouac, *On the Road*, 143.
127. Kerouac, *Tristessa*.
128. Kerouac, *Desolation Angels*.
129. Allen Ginsberg, "Review of Jack Kerouac's *Big Sur*," October 10, 1991.
130. Jack Kerouac, *Big Sur*.
131. *Ibid.*
132. *Ibid.*

133. Raj Chandarlapaty, *Re-Creating Paul Bowles, the Other, and the Imagination*, 98.
134. Jack Kerouac, *Book of Haikus*, 11.
135. *Ibid.*, 10.
136. *Ibid.*
137. Michael Polish, dir., *Big Sur*, Arc Entertainment, 2014.
138. *Ibid.*
139. *Ibid.*
140. *Ibid.*
141. *Ibid.*
142. *Ibid.*
143. *Ibid.*
144. *Ibid.*
145. *Ibid.*
146. *Ibid.*
147. *Ibid.*

Chapter Two

1. The Beatles, "Revolution."
2. Wikipedia, "Kill Your Darlings."
3. Wikipedia, "Kill Your Darlings."
4. Barry Miles, *Call Me Burroughs*, 113.
5. Bob Ezrin and RogerWaters, *The Wall*.
6. Peter Weir, dir., *Dead Poets Society*, Buena Vista Pictures, 1989.
7. John Krodikas, dir., *Kill Your Darling*, Sony Pictures, 2013.
8. Joe Wright, dir., *Anna Karenina*. Focus Features, 2012.
9. John Steinbeck, *Of Mice and Men*, 99.
10. Krodikas, dir., *Kill Your Darlings*.
11. Miles, *Call Me Burroughs*, 104.
12. Krodikas, dir., *Kill Your Darlings*.
13. Weir, dir., *Dead Poets Society*.
14. George Orwell, *1984*.
15. Mario van Peebles, dir., *Panther*, Gramercy Pictures, 1995.
16. Allen Ginsberg, "Howl."
17. Hutcheon, *A Theory of Adaptation*, 106–7.
18. *Ibid.*, 107.
19. Robert Epstein and Jeffery Friedman, dirs. *Howl*. Werc Werk Works, 2010.
20. Mary Harron, dir., *I Shot Andy Warhol*, BBC Arena, 1996.
21. Stone, dir., *The Doors*.
22. Richard Attenborough, dir., *Gandhi*, Goldcrest Films, 1982.
23. Epstein and Frideman, dirs., *Howl*.
24. "Luncheon With Aldous Huxley, March 31, 1961," from *The Aldous Huxley Collection*, UCLA.
25. Epstein and Frideman, dirs., *Howl*.
26. *Ibid.*
27. "Private Philologies," from *The Unknown Kerouac*, 41.
28. *Ibid.*
29. *Ibid.*, 42.
30. Epstein and Frideman, dirs., *Howl*.
31. *Ibid.*
32. *Ibid.*
33. *Ibid.*
34. *Ibid.*
35. *Ibid.*
36. Ginsberg, "Howl."
37. Morgan, Bill, *Howl on Trial*, 52.
38. Allen Ginsberg, *Indian Journals*, 161.
39. Epstein and Friedman, dirs., *Howl*.
40. *Ibid.*
41. Taylor Hackford, dir., *Ray*, Baldwin Entertainment Group, 2004.
42. Deborah Baker, *A Blue Hand*.
43. Jerry Aronson, dir., *The Life and Times of Allen Ginsberg*, Docurama, 2013.
44. *Ibid.*
45. *Ibid.*
46. *Ibid.*
47. *Ibid.*
48. *Ibid.*
49. Owsley Brown, dir., *Night Waltz: The Music of Paul Bowles*, Owsley Brown Presents, 1999.
50. Aronson, dir., *The Life and Times of Allen Ginsberg*.
51. Catherine Warnow, and Regina Weinrich, dirs., *Paul Bowles: The Complete Outsider*, First Run Features, 1994.
52. Jack Kerouac, *Desolation Angels*, 69.
53. Jack Kerouac, "Man, Am I the Granddaddy o' the Hippies?"
54. Aronson, dir., *The Life and Times of Allen Ginsberg*.
55. *Ibid.*
56. *Ibid.*
57. Raj Chandarlapaty, "Through The Lens of the Beatniks: Norman Mailer," *The Mailer Review*, Volume 7, 231–47
58. Aronson, dir., *The Life and Times of Allen Ginsberg*.
59. *Ibid.*
60. *Ibid.*
61. Excerpt from "Kaddish" by Allen Ginsberg, currently collected in Collected Poems 1947–1997. Copyright © 1961, 2006 Allen Ginsberg LLC, used by permission of The Wylie Agency.

Chapter Three

1. "Over the Hills and Far Away," c. 1961, New York Public Library, Berg Collection, Box 3, Folder 10.
2. *Ibid.*
3. Alan Govenar, dir., *The Beat Hotel*, First Run Features, 2011.
4. *Ibid.*
5. *Ibid.*
6. *Ibid.*
7. *Ibid.*
8. Wikipedia, "French Drug Laws."
9. Sarah Bakewell, *At the Existentialist Café: Freedom, Being and Apricot Cocktails.*
10. Miles, *Call Me Burroughs*, 355.
11. Chandarlapaty, *Re-Creating Paul Bowles, the Other, and the Imagination*, 96.
12. Leo Braudy, ed. *Film Theory and Criticism* 138.
13. *Ibid.*, 137.
14. Govenar, dir., *The Beat Hotel.*
15. *Ibid.*
16. *Ibid.*
17. *Ibid.*
18. *Ibid.*
19. *Ibid.*
20. Allen Ginsberg, *Collected Poems.*
21. Govenar, dir., *The Beat Hotel.*
22. *Ibid.*
23. Michelle Green, *The Dream at the End of the World.*
24. Govenar, dir., *The Beat Hotel.*
25. Francis Ford, Coppola, dir., *The Junky's Christmas*, Koch Vision, 1993.
26. *Ibid.*
27. *Ibid.*
28. *Ibid.*
29. Howard Brookner, dir. *Burroughs: The Movie.*
30. *Ibid.*
31. *Ibid.*
32. *Ibid.*
33. *Ibid.*
34. *Ibid.*
35. *Ibid.*
36. Lars Movin and Steven Moller Rasmussen, dirs. *Words of Advice: William S. Burroughs On The Road.*
37. *Ibid.*
38. *Saturday Night Live*, November 7, 1981.
39. Paul Bowles, *Paul Bowles Reads.*
40. Raj Chandarlapaty, *Re-Creating Paul Bowles, the Other, and the Imagination.*
41. *Words of Advice.*
42. *Ibid.*
43. Paul Bowles, *Collected Stories.*
44. *Words of Advice.*
45. *Ibid.*
46. *Ibid.*
47. *Ibid.*
48. *Ibid.*
49. *Ibid.*
50. *Ibid.*
51. *Ibid.*
52. *Ibid.*
53. Klaus Maeck, *The Commissioner of Sewers.*
54. *Ibid.*
55. *Ibid.*
56. *Ibid.*
57. *Ibid.*
58. *Ibid.*
59. *Ibid.*
60. *Ibid.*
61. *Ibid.*
62. *Ibid.*
63. *Ibid.*
64. *Ibid.*
65. Gus Van Sant, *Drugstore Cowboy.*
66. Danny Boyle, *Trainspotting.*
67. Erik Mortenson, *Capturing The Beat Movement.*
68. Eric Mottram, *The Algebra of Need.*
69. Oliver Harris, *William S. Burroughs and the Secret of Fascination.*
70. Michelle Green, *The Dream at the End of the World.*
71. Allen Hibbard, *Conversations with William S. Burroughs.*
72. David Woodward, *The Dreamachine.*
73. *Ibid.*
74. *Ibid.*
75. *Ibid.*
76. William S. Burroughs, *Naked Lunch.*
77. David Woodward, *The Dreamachine.*
78. *Ibid.*
79. *Ibid.*
80. *Ibid.*
81. Pop Matters, "Destroy All Rational Thought."
82. *Ibid.*
83. John Ambrose and Frank Rynne, *Destroy All Rational Thought.*
84. *Ibid.*
85. *Ibid.*
86. *Ibid.*

87. *Ibid.*
88. *Ibid.*
89. Barry Miles, *Call Me Burroughs*, 344.
90. Ambrose and Rynne, *Destroy All Rational Thought.*
91. *Ibid.*
92. *Ibid.*
93. Yony Lesser. *A Man Within.*
94. *Ibid.*
95. *Ibid.*
96. *Ibid.*
97. *Ibid.*
98. *Ibid.*
99. *Ibid.*
100. *Ibid.*
101. David Sterritt, *Screening the Beats*, 79.
102. Oliver Harris, *The Secret of Fascination.*
103. Sterritt, 98.
104. David Cronenberg, dir. *Naked Lunch.*
105. *Ibid.*
106. *Ibid.*
107. *Spiderman.*
108. *Superman.*
109. Jack Seargent, *Naked Lens.*
110. Michael Prince, *Adapting The Beat Poets.*
111. *Ibid.*
112. *Ibid.*
113. *Ibid.*, 25.
114. Mortenson, *Capturing the Beat Moment*, 162.
115. *Ibid.*, 162.
116. Cronenberg, dir., *Naked Lunch.*
117. James E. Lee, *Underworld of the East*, 36.
118. Robyn Wiegman, *The Future of New American Studies*, 275.
119. Cronenberg, dir., *Naked Lunch.*
120. *Ibid.*

Chapter Four

1. Maria Beatty, dir., *Gang of Souls: The Generation of Beat Poets*, MVD Entertainment Group, 1989.
2. *Ibid.*
3. *Ibid.*
4. *Ibid.*
5. *Ibid.*
6. *Ibid.*
7. Quincy Troupe, *Miles: The Autobiography*, 198.
8. Anthony Harvey, dir., *Dutchman*, Eugene Persson, 1966.
9. *Ibid.*
10. *Ibid.*
11. *Ibid.*
12. *Ibid.*
13. *Ibid.*
14. *Ibid.*
15. *Ibid.*
16. Jack Kerouac, *Desolation Angels.*
17. Christopher Felver, dir., *Ferlinghetti: A Rebirth of Wonder*, First Run Features, 2010.
18. *Ibid.*
19. *Ibid.*
20. "Baseball Canto" By Lawrence Ferlinghetti, from THESE ARE MY RIVERS, copyright ©1993 by Lawrence Ferlinghetti. Reprinted by permission of New Directions Publishing Corp.
21. David Sterritt, *Screening The Beats.*
22. *Ferlinghetti: A Rebirth of Wonder.*
23. *Ibid.*
24. *Ibid.*
25. *Ibid.*
26. *Ibid.*
27. "Dog" By Lawrence Ferlinghetti, from A CONEY ISLAND OF THE MIND, copyright ©1958 by Lawrence Ferlinghetti. Reprinted by permission of New Directions Publishing Corp.
28. *Ibid.*
29. *Ibid.*
30. *Ibid.*
31. Malin Korkeaslo, dir. *Love Always, Carolyn*, WG Film, 2011.
32. *Ibid.*
33. Carolyn Cassady, *Off The Road*, 40.
34. *Love Always, Carolyn.*
35. *Ibid.*
36. *Ibid.*
37. *Ibid.*
38. *Ibid.*
39. *Ibid.*
40. *Ibid.*
41. *Ibid.*
42. "The John Cassady Interview," *Literary Kicks.*
43. *Love Always, Carolyn.*
44. John J. Healy, dir., *The Practice of the Wild: A Conversation with Gary Snyder and Jim Harrison*, Whole Earth Productions, 2010.
45. *Ibid.*
46. *Ibid.*

47. *Ibid.*
48. *Ibid.*
49. *Ibid.*
50. "Oil" by Gary Snyder. Credit: Copyright © 1957, 1958, 1959, 1960, 1961, 1962, 1963, 1964, 1965, 1965, 1966, 1967, by Gary Snyder, from *The Back Country.* Reprinted by permission of Counterpoint Press.
51. *The Practice of the Wild.*
52. *Ibid.*
53. *Ibid.*
54. *Ibid.*

Appendix

1. Deanna Stefanyshyn, "The Influence of Television and Radio on Culture, Literacy, and Education," October 2012..
2. *Jack Kerouac: Selected Letters 1940–1956.*
3. Creeley, Robert, narrator. *Doctor Sax and the Great World Snake.* Gallery Six, 2003.
4. *Ibid.*
5. *Ibid.*
6. *Ibid.*
7. Jack Kerouac, and Allen Ginsberg, *The Dharma Bums,* Audio Literature, 1991.
8. *Ibid.*
9. *Ibid.*
10. *Jack Kerouac's Tristessa: Abridged Reading by William Fitzsimmons,* Reimagine, 2013.
11. *Ibid.*
12. *Ibid.*
13. *Ibid.*
14. *Ibid.*
15. Harris, *William S. Burroughs and the Secret of Fascination.*
16. *Ibid.*
17. *William S. Burroughs and Allen Ginsberg. The Yage Letters Redux.* Recorded Books, 2013.
18. *Ibid.*
19. *Ibid.*
20. *Ibid.*

Works Cited

Ambrose, John and Frank Rynne, dir. *Destroy All Rational Thought: Celebrating William Burroughs and Brion Gysin in Ireland.* Screen Edge, 2006.

Antonelli, John, prod. *Jack Kerouac: King of the Beats.* Kultur, 2012.

Antonioni, Michelangelo, dir. *Zabriskie Point.* MGM, 1970.

Aronson, Jerry, dir. *The Life and Times of Allen Ginsberg.* Docurama, 2013.

Attenborough, Richard, dir. *Gandhi.* Goldcrest Films, 1982.

Avery, Tex. "Magical Maestro." Produced by Fred Quimby. 1952, MGM.

Baker, Deborah. *A Blue Hand: The Beats in India.* Penguin, 2008.

Bakewell, Sarah. *At the Existentialist Café: Freedom, Being and Apricot Cocktails.* Other Press, 2016.

Baldwin, James. *Going to Meet the Man.* Dial, 1965.

Baraka, Amiri. *Blues People.* William Morrow, 1963.

_____. *Dutchman.* Dial, 1964.

_____. *Preface to a Twenty-Volume Suicide Note.* Grove Press, 1961.

_____. *Yugen.* Poetry periodical co-edited with Allen Ginsberg, 1958–62.

Barnes, Djuna. *Nightwood.* Faber & Faber, 1936.

Beatty, Maria, dir. *Gang of Souls: The Generation of Beat Poets.* MVD Entertainment Group, 1989.

Bowles, Paul. *Collected Stories.* With an introduction by Robert Stone. Ecco, 2001.

_____. *Paul Bowles Reads A Hundred Camels in the Courtyard.* Cadmus, 2008.

_____. *The Sheltering Sky.* New Directions, 1949.

_____. *The Spider's House.* Random House, 1955.

Boyle, Danny, dir. *Trainspotting.* PolyGram, 1996.

Braudy, Leo, ed. *Film Theory and Criticism*, 7th Edition. Oxford University Press, 2009.

Brookner, Howard, dir. *Burroughs: The Movie.* Criterion Collection, 1986.

Brown, Owsley, dir. *Night Waltz: The Music of Paul Bowles.* Owsley Brown Presents, 1999.

Burroughs, William S. *Naked Lunch.* Olympia, 1959.

_____. "Over the Hills and Far Away." From *The William S. Burroughs Papers,* Berg Collection, New York Public Library, Box 3, Folder10.

_____. *The Yage Letters.* City Lights, 1963.

_____, and Allen Ginsberg. *The Yage Letters Redux.* Recorded Books, 2013.

Burton, Tim, dir. *Sleepy Hollow.* Mandalay Pictures, 1999.

Byrum, John, dir. *Heart Beat.* Orion Pictures, 1980.

Carver, Raymond. *Cathedral.* Knopf, 1983.

Cassady, Carolyn. *Off the Road: Twenty Years with Cassady, Kerouac and Ginsberg.* Black Spring Press, 2007.

Cassady, John. "Interview, July 24, 1994," *Literary Kicks Magazine.*

Cassady, Neal. *The First Third.* City Lights Books, 2001. Penguin Books, 2005.

Chandarlapaty, Raj. *Re-Creating Paul Bowles, the Other, and the Imagination: Music, Film and Photography.* Lexington Books, 2014.

_____. "Through the Lens of the Beatniks: Norman Mailer. *The Mailer Review,* Volume 7, no. 1 (2011), 231–47.

Chopra, Vidhu Vinod. *Lage Raho Munna Bhai*. Vinod Chopra Productions, 2006.
Coppola, Francis Ford, dir. *The Junky's Christmas*. Koch Vision, 1993.
Creeley, Robert, narrator. *Doctor Sax and the Great World Snake*. Gallery Six, 2003.
Cronenberg, David, dir. *Naked Lunch*. 20th Century Fox, 1991.
Davis, Miles. *The Birth of the Cool*. Capitol, 1949.
De Bont, Jan. *Speed*. Mark Gordon Productions, 1994.
Derrida, Jacques. *Of Grammatology*. Translated by Gayatri Chakravorty Spivak. Les Editions de Minuit, 1967.
Donner, Richard, dir. *Superman*. Dovemead Films, 1978.
The Doors. "When The Music's Over." From *Strange Days*, 1967, Elektra.
Dos Passos, John. *U.S.A. Trilogy*. Houghton Mifflin, 1946.
Dylan, Bob. "Like A Rolling Stone." From *Bob Dylan's Greatest Hits*.
Emerson, Ralph Waldo. "Nature." James Munroe & Co., 1836.
Epstein, Robert, and Jeffery Friedman, dirs. *Howl*. Werc Werk Works, 2010.
Faulkner, William. *The Sound and the Fury*. Jonathan Cape, 1928.
Felver, Christopher, dir. *Ferlinghetti: A Rebirth of Wonder*. First Run Features, 2010.
Fitzgerald, Ella. "A Tisket, a Tasket." Al Feldman, 1938.
Freeman, Gerrold, dir. *Native Son*. Cinecom Pictures, 1986.
Freud, Sigmund. *The Ego and the Id*. Pacific Publishing Studio, 2010.
———. *The Interpretation of Dreams*. Translated by James Strachey, 1955.
Frye, Northrop. "The Archetype of Literature." In *An Anatomy of Criticism: Four Essays*. Princeton University Press, 2013.
Ginsberg, Allen. *Collected Poems 1947–1980*. Harper & Row, 1984.
———. *Indian Journals*. Penguin, 1970.
———. *Reality Sandwiches*. City Lights, 1963.
———. "Review of Jack Kerouac's *Big Sur*," October 10, 1991.
Govenar, Alan, dir. *The Beat Hotel*. First Run Features, 2011.
Green, Michelle. *The Dream at the End of the World: Literary Renegades in Tangier*. HarperCollins, 1991.
Hackford, Taylor, dir., *Ray*. Baldwin Entertainment Group, 2004.
Harris, Oliver. *William S. Burroughs and the Secret of Fascination*. Southern Illinois University Press, 2004.
Harron, Mary, dir. *I Shot Andy Warhol*. BBC Arena, 1996.
Harvey, Anthony, dir. *Dutchman*. Eugene Persson, 1966.
Healy, John J., dir. *The Practice of the Wild: A Conversation with Gary Snyder and Jim Harrison*. Whole Earth Productions, 2010.
Hendrix, Jimi. "Purple Haze." *Are You Experienced?*, Rhino, 1967.
Hibbard, Allen, ed. *Conversations with William S. Burroughs*. University of Mississippi Press, 2000.
Hollywood Reporter, "Review of *On the Road*."
Hoover Institute. *Firing Line, William F. Buckley, Jr., September 3, 1968: The Hippies*. Leland Stanford Junior University, 2008.
Hurston, Zora Neale. *Their Eyes Were Watching God*. J.B. Lippincott, 1937.
Hutcheon, Linda. *A Theory of Adaptation*. Routledge, 2012.
Huxley, Aldous. "Luncheon with Aldous Huxley, Toronto, March 31, 1961." From *The Aldous Huxley Papers*, UCLA Special Collections.
Ibsen, Hendrik. *Hedda Gabler*. Republished in Penguin, 1951.
Ives, David. "Sure Thing." *All in the Timing: Six One Act Comedies*, Dramatists Play Service, Inc., 1994.
Jameson, Frederic. *Postmodernism: Or, The Cultural Logic of Late Capitalism*. Duke University Press, 1991.
Joffe, Roland, dir. *The Scarlet Letter*. Buena Vista Pictures, 1995.
Joyce, James. *Ulysses*. Sylvia Beach, 1922.
Kay, Stephen, dir. *The Last Time I Committed Suicide*. Multicom Entertainment Group, 1997.
Kerouac, Jack. "Benzedrine Vision—Mexico City, 1952." The Berg Collection, New York Public Library, Series 2, Folder 40.1.
———. *Big Sur*. Farrar, Strauss, & Giroux, 1962.
———. *Book of Haikus*. Penguin, 2003.

———. *Desolation Angels*. Random House, 1965.
———. *Dharma Bums*. Penguin, 1958.
———. "Journals, 1948–1949." From *The Jack Kerouac Collection*, Harry Ransom Center, Austin, TX.
———. *Maggie Cassidy*. Avon, 1959.
———. "Man, Am I the Granddaddy o' the Hippies?" Blaketimes, 2, 1981.
———. *On the Road*. Viking, 1959.
———. "The Beginnings of Bop." From *The Jack Kerouac Papers*, Berg Collection, New York Public Library, 1952.
———. *The Town and the City*. Penguin, 1950.
———. *Tristessa*. San Francisco: City Lights, 1962.
———. *The Unknown Kerouac*. Edited by Todd Tietchen. Penguin, 2016.
———. *Visions of Cody*. New York: Penguin, 1972.
———, and Allen Ginsberg. *The Dharma Bums*. Audio Literature, 1991.
Kerouac, Jack, and Ann Charters. *Selected Letters, 1940–1956*. Penguin, 1996.
Korkeaslo, Malin, dir. *Love Always, Carolyn*. WG Film, 2011.
Krodikas, John, dir. *Kill Your Darlings*. Sony Pictures, 2013.
Kroopf, Scott, dir. *Bill and Ted's Excellent Adventure*. Interscope, 1998.
Lagrevenese, Richard, dir. *Freedom Writers*. Paramount Pictures, 2007.
Lardas, John. *The Bop Apocalypse*. University of Illinois Press, 2001.
Lee, James E. *The Underworld of the East*. Originally published in 1935. Green Magic, 2000.
Lee, Stan, dir. *Spider-Man*. Grantray-Lawerence Animation, 1967.
Lennon, J. Michael. *A Double Life*. Random House, 2013.
Lerner, Richard. *What Happened to Kerouac?* Nathaniel Dorsky, 2012.
Leyser, Yony, dir. *A Man Within*. Oscilloscope Productions, 2010.
Luhrmann, Baz, dir. *The Great Gatsby*. Village Roadshow Pictures, 2013.
Madden, John, dir. *Ethan Frome*. Miramax Films, 1993.
MacDougall, Ranald, dir. *The Subterraneans*, MGM, 1960.
Maeck, Klaus. *The Commissioner of Sewers*. Klaus Maeck, 2003.
Mailer, Norman. *Advertisements for Myself*. Harvard University Press, 1959.
Marcus, Alan S., Scott Alan Metzger, Richard J. Paxton, et al. *Teaching History with Film*. Routledge, 2010.
Miles, Barry. *Call Me Burroughs: A Life*. Twelve, 2013.
Miller, Arthur. *The Death of a Salesman*. Viking Press, 1949.
Morgan, Bill. *Howl on Trial*. City Lights Publishers, 2006.
Morley, Catherine. *The Quest for Epic in Contemporary American Fiction*. Routledge, 2010.
Mortenson, Erik. *Capturing the Beat Moment*. Southern Illinois University Press, 2011.
Mottram, Eric. *William Burroughs: The Algebra of Need*. Marion Boyars, 1977.
Movin, Lars, and Steen Møller Rasmussen, dirs. *Words of Advice: William S. Burroughs on the Road*. Plagiat Films, 2007.
Naylor, Gloria. *Bailey's Café*. Vintage Books, 1992.
Oates, Joyce Carol. "Where Are You Going, Where Have You Been?" Originally published in *Epoch Magazine*, 1966.
Orwell, George. *1984*. Secker & Warburg, 1949.
Parker, Alan, dir. *Pink Floyd: The Wall*. Metro Goldwyn-Mayer, 1982.
Pease, Donald S., and Robyn Wiegman, eds. *The Future of New American Studies*. Duke Univeristy Press, 2002.
Peebles, Mario van, dir. *Panther*. Gramercy Pictures, 1995.
Polish, Michael, dir. *Big Sur*. Arc Entertainment, 2014.
"Pollution: Threat to Man's Only Home." *National Geographic*, 1970.
Pop Matters, February 4, 2007. Review, "Destroy All Rational Thought."
Prince, Michael. *Adapting the Beat Poets*. Rowman & Littlefield, 2016.
Rao, Kiran, dir. *Dhobi Ghat*. UTV Movie Productions, 2010.
Richardson, Robert. *Emerson: The Mind on Fire*. University of California Press, 1996.
Roszak, Theodore. *The Making of a Counterculture*. University of California Press, 1969.
Salles, Walter, dir. *On the Road*. IFC Films, 2012.

Scorsese, Martin, dir. *The Godfather, Part III*. Paramount Pictures, 1990.
Seargent, Jack. *Naked Lens: Beat Cinema*. Creation Books, 2001.
Silver, Joel, dir. *The Matrix*. Warner Bros., 1999.
Singleton, John, dir. *Boyz n the Hood*. Columbia Pictures, 1991.
Smight, Jac, dir. *Damnation Alley*. 20th Century Fox, 1977.
Spielberg, Steven, dir. *The Color Purple*. Warner Bros., 1985.
Stam, Robert. *Film Theory: An Introduction*. Blackwell, 2000.
Steinbeck, John. *Of Mice and Men*. Covici Friede, 1937.
Sterritt, David. *Mad to Be Saved*. SIU Press, 1998.
_____. *Screening the Beats: Beat Culture and the Media Sensibility*. SIU Press, 2004.
Stone, Oliver, dir. *The Doors*. Oliver Stone Productions, 1991.
Tabbita, Frank, dir. *Beat Angel*. Beat Angel Productions, 2006.
Thurber, James. "The Secret Life of Walter Mitty." Published in *The New Yorker*, 1942.
Troupe, Quincy. *Miles: The Autobiography*. Brittania, 1990.
Tzu, Chuang. *The Way of Chuang Tzu*, 2nd Edition. New Directions, 2010.
Van Sant, Gus, dir. *Drugstore Cowboy*. International Video Entertainment, 1989.
Wanger, Walter, dir. *Invasion of the Body Snatchers*. Allied Artists, 1956.
Warnow, Catherine, and Regina Weinrich, dirs. *Paul Bowles: The Complete Outsider*. First Run Features, 1994.
Weir, Peter, dir. *Dead Poets Society*. Buena Vista Pictures, 1989.
Woodward, David. *The Dreamachine*. National Film Board of Canada, 2008.
Wright, Joe, dir. *Anna Karenina*. Focus Features, 2012.
Wright, Richard. *Uncle Tom's Children*. Harper, 1938.

Index

Aaronson, Jerry: *The Life and Times of Allen Ginsberg* 91
AIDS (Acquired Immunodeficiency Syndrome) 137
Alfred, Randy: *Beat Angel* 61–5
"Allal" 35
Allen, Steve (talk show host) 45–47
American University of Afghanistan 1, 7–8, 79, 87; terrorist attack 7
Amram, David (poet, musician) 181
Anderson, Sherwood (writer) 11
Anna Karenina (2012) 76, 94

The Baby Snakes 150
Baez, Joan (folk singer) 105
Baker, Deborah (literary critic) 42
Baldwin, James (writer; d. 1987) 12
Balestri, Vincent (actor) 63–70
Baraka, Imamu Amiri (playwright, essayist, activist; 1934–2014) 9, 45, 105, 109–110, 167, 173, 177
Barr, Jean Marc (actor) 84–7
Barthes, Roland (philosopher) 116, 119
Baudelaire, Charles 176
Beat Angel 61–5
"The Beginning of Bop" 26
"Benzedrine Vision" 8
Big Sur (2013) 81–83, 87, 199
Bill and Ted's Excellent Adventure (film, 1988) 36
Birth of the Cool (1948) 140
Book of Haikus (poem anthology, 1961) 84, 193
Bowles, Paul (writer; 1910–1999) 22, 28, 83, 108, 147–9, 152–3, 186; "Allal" 135; *A Hundred Camels in the Courtyard* (short story collection, 1962) 135, 152
Boyle, T. Coraghessan 135
Brookner, Harold (film director): *Burroughs: The Movie* (1986) 20, 131
Buckley, William F. (talk show host): Ginsberg and 107; Kerouac and 45
Bunn, John (film director) 93; *Kill Your Darlings* 91–2
Burroughs, William Seward (writer, actor, anthropologist; 1914–1997): cut-up method and 22, 116, 121, 149, 152–4, 156–7; drugs and 114–5, 126–7, 145; Freud and 154; homosexuality of 117–9, 123, 132, 154; literary progeny and 119–20; *Naked Lunch* (novel, 1959) 5, 20, 34, 114–7, 119, 123, 125, 128–9, 135, 137–140, 144, 152, 157–62, 164, 212; *The Place of Dead Roads* (novel) 129, 138; *Queer* (novel) 123; "Red Scare" and 124; Reich Orgone Accumulator 114; *Saturday Night Live* 138; surrealism and 116; use of Claymation 126
Burroughs: The Movie (1986) 20, 127, 131

Carroll, Jim (writer, actor, audiobook reader) 169–72, 203
Carver, Raymond (writer; 1938–1988) 12
Cassady, John (writer, musician; 1971–) 189
Cassady, Neal (writer; 1922–1968) 9, 16, 18, 27, 30–41, 49, 55, 57, 60, 72, 85–6, 106, 189–90, 210–1; *The First Third* 31; on marijuana 187
Cesaire, Aime (philosopher; 1913–2008) 176
Cezanne, Paul (painter; 1839–1906) 141
Chapman, Harold (British photographer; 1927–) 116, 119–22
Chester, Alfred (writer; 1928–1971) 149
Cixous, Helene (feminist literary critic; 1937–) 33
Cohen, Ira (literary critic, poet; 1935–2011) 148
Cooper, James Fenimore (American writer; 1789–1851) 205

225

Coover, Robert (writer; 1932–) 179
Coppola, Francis Ford (film producer and director; 1939–) 126
Corso, Gregory (poet; 1930–2001) 44, 91, 115, 117, 119, 121–2
Cronenberg, David (film director; 1943–) 157–9, 161–4
Naked Lunch (1993) 157–65; pornography and 158
Cummings, E. E (poet; 1894–1962) 182

D-Day (American invasion of France, 1944) 181
Damnation Alley (film, 1977) 134
Die Danske Filminstitut: *Words of Advice* (2010) 131–2
Davis, Miles (1926–1991) 26, 40, 74, 175, 192; *Birth of the Cool* (1948) 140
Dead Poets Society 93
Death of a Salesman (play, 1949) 60
Densmore, John (rock drummer; 1944–) 7
Derrida, Jacques (cultural and literary theorist; 1930–2004) 26, 74
Desolation Angels (novel, 1965) 26, 79, 108
Dharma Bums (novel, 1958) 194, 206
Dhobi Ghat (Hindi film, 2011) 7, 9
Di Caprio, Leonardo (film actor, 1974–) 79, 146
Dillon, Matt (actor; 1964–) 109
Do the Right Thing (film, 1989) 35
Dr. Sax (novel, 1959) 174, 181, 202
Donkin, Nick (Claymation director) 126; *The Junky's Christmas* 20, 125–6, 149
The Doors (rock band; 1965–1971): "When the Music's Over" (song, 1967) 7
Dos Passos, John (writer; 1896–1970) 47
Dostoyevsky, Fyodor (Russian writer; 1821–1881): Kerouac and 43; *Notes from Underground* 36
Dover, John 147
Drugstore Cowboy (film, 1991) 88, 142, 145, 209
Dylan, Bob (Robert Zimmermann, rock singer; 1941–) 111, 156

Eggers, Dave 179
Eliot, Thomas Stearnes (poet and essayist; 1899–1965) 139
Ellington, Duke (jazz pianist, composer; 1899–1974) 54
Ellison, Ralph (writer; 1914–1994) 26, 74
Emerson, Ralph Waldo (American philosopher; 1813–1882) 82, 85, 87

Epstein, Robert (film producer): *Howl* (2010) 95–97, 99
The Exterminator (1980) 129, 149

Fanon, Frantz (political theorist; 1925–1961) 176
Faulkner, William (author; 1897–1962) 47, 202, 207
feminism 196
The First Third 31
Fitzsimmons, William (audiobook reader) 208–10
Forrest Gump (film, 1994) 63
Freedom Writers (film, 2010) 199
Freeman, Al (1934–2012) 173–77
Freud, Sigmund (neurologist; 1856–1939) 69, 154; drugs and 69
Frisell, Bill (jazz guitarist; 1951–) 86
Frye, Northrop (literary critic; 1912–1991) 43

Gillespie, Dizzy (jazz trumpeter and composer; 1917–1993) 27
Ginsberg, Allen (poet; 1926–1997) 1, 5, 9, 13, 17, 19–20, 28, 32–3, 39, 49–53, 58, 80, 83, 88, 90, 92–102, 105–111, 124, 128, 145–6, 156, 170–2, 174, 177–80, 184, 186, 205–7; drugs and 88, 109; Hinduism and 52, 90; "Howl" 5–6; on literary theory 100; pornography and 100; *Reality Sandwiches* 97; re-invention 90; relationship with Neal Cassady 188; "Wales Visitation" 50, 107
Giorno, John (producer; 1936–) 9, 172, 212–3
Glickenhaus, James (film director; 1950–): *The Exterminator* (1980) 129, 149
Grauerholz, James (biographer; 1953–) 9, 131, 136
Green, Michelle (literary critic) 120, 131, 143–4, 149, 151
Guevara, Che (activist, revolutionary) 209
Gysin, Brion (writer, filmmaker businessman; d. 1986) 22, 118, 120–1, 124, 143, 147–53

Hamri 150
Harris, Oliver (literary critic; 1978–) 117, 120, 123, 129, 142, 157, 161
Harrison, Jim (writer; 1937–2016) 194–5
Harry Ransom Center 6
Hawthorne, Nathaniel (writer; 1804–1864) 13
Heard, John (actor; 1946–2017) 32–3
Hedda Gabler 35

Index

Hedlund, Garrett (actor; 1984–) 71
Hendrix, James Marshall (rock guitarist; 1942–1970) 32; "Purple Haze" (1967) 32
Hesse, Herman (1877–1962) 85; *Steppenwolf* 85
The Hippie Trail 2
Hirschman, Jack (1933–) 179, 182
Hitler, Adolf (German dictator; 1889–1945) 144
Hoffman, Abbie (activist, poet, politician; 1946–1989) 19, 49–52, 111
Holmes, John Clellon (writer; 1926–1988) 54, 91
Hopper, Dennis (actor; 1936–2010) 87, 178–9, 182
"Howl" 6
Howl (2010) 95–97, 99
Huncke, Herbert (poet; 1915–1996) 45, 53–4, 91
A Hundred Camels in the Courtyard (short story collection, 1962) 135, 152
Hurston, Zora Neale (novelist; 1891–1960) 59
Hutcheon, Linda (cultural critic; 1947–) 24, 27, 46, 51, 84, 96
Huxley, Aldous (philosopher, writer; 1894–1963) 28, 100, 145

I Shot Andy Warhol (film, 1996) 98
Ibsen, Henrik (playwright; 1828–1906) 35; *Hedda Gabler* 35
India: and readings of Western literature 7; values and lifestyles 4
Indian film industry: *Dhobi Ghat* 9; *Lage Raho Munna Bhai* 63
Indiana Jones and the Temple of Doom 7
Invasion of the Body Snatchers (film) 134
Ives, David (playwright) 56

The Jajouka 146, 154
Jameson, Frederic 6
Jane, Thomas (actor; 1969–) 38–9, 41
Jdab (Moroccan trance music) 150–2
Johnson, Rob (literary critic) 128
Jones, Hettie (author, editor) 46
Jones, James T. (literary critic) 168, 207
Joyce, James (author; 1882–1941): Kerouac and 140–1; *Ulysses* (novel, 1922) 39, 207
The Junky's Christmas 20, 125–6, 149

Kay, Stephen (film director; 1963–) 36; *The Last Time I Committed Suicide* 36, 40, 41
Kerouac, Gerard (editor, writer) 64–5

Kerouac, Jan (writer, artist; 1952–1996) 44
Kerouac, John Louis (writer; 1922–1969): "The Beginning of Bop" 26; "Benzedrine Vision" 28; *Book of Haikus* (poem anthology; 1961) 84, 193; Catholicism and 26, 66; *Desolation Angels* (novel, 1965) 26, 79, 108; *Dharma Bums* (novel, 1958) 194, 206; *Dr. Sax* (novel, 1959) 174, 181, 202; drugs and 45, 47, 54, 66, 69, 75; *Mexico City Blues* (poem anthology) 202; *On the Road* (novel, 1957) 32–4, 45, 47, 55, 57, 67, 77–9, 86, 124, 188, 206; *Selected Letters, 1940–1956* 16; *The Town and the City* (novel, 1950) 24; *Tristessa* (novel, 1960) 28–9, 58, 79, 205; *The Unknown Kerouac* (Tietchen, 2016) 43; *Visions of Cody* (novel, 1972) 38, 41, 101, 205
Kesey, Ken (writer; 1935–2001): *One Flew Over the Cuckoo's Nest* (novel, 1962) 88
Kill Your Darlings 91–2
Kilmer, Val (actor; 1959–) 6
King, Dr. Martin Luther, Jr. (civil rights activist; 1929–1968) 7, 176
Kingsley, Ben (1943–) 73
Kitsch (cheap, commercialized culture arts) 16, 28, 34, 71
Knight, Shirley (film actress; 1936–) 173–7

Lage Raho Munna Bhai 3
Leary, Timothy (psychedelic theorist and therapist; 1920–1996) 19, 48–9, 105, 109, 124
Lee, Spike (film director, actor; 1957–) 35; *Do the Right Thing* (film, 1989) 35
Lennon, John (singer, The Beatles; 1940–1980) 90
Lerner, Richard (film director): *What Happened to Kerouac?* (1986) 41, 46, 48, 49
Levi-Strauss, Claude (French theorist; 1908–2009) 74–5
Leyser, Yoni (film director): *A Man Within* (film, 2010) 153, 155–6
The Life and Times of Allen Ginsberg 91
Literary Kicks (magazine) 189
Lowry, Malcolm (novelist; 1909–1957) 15
LSD (hallucinogenic drug) 49, 87, 89, 100, 107, 171–2

Mailer, Norman Kingsley (1922–2007) 15, 29, 30, 33, 34, 45, 48, 53,

105, 109, 110, 141, 175, 176; *The Naked and the Dead* (novel, 1948) 53
Malcolm X (film, 1925–1965) 63
A Man Within (film, 2010) 153, 155–6
Marcus, Alan (film critic; 1949–) 3
Martin, Steve (actor, comedian) 132
The Matrix (film, 1998) 36
McCarthy, Sen. Joseph (1908–1957) 45, 116, 124
McClure, Michael (poet, writer; 1932–) 44, 110, 117, 179, 181; Kerouac and 86
Melville, Herman (writer; 1819–1891) 13
Mexico 19, 32, 44, 71, 79, 135, 208
Mexico City Blues (poem anthology) 202
Miles, Barry (literary critic) 116, 118–9, 151
Mingus, Charlie (jazz bassist; 1922–1979) 54
Minton's (jazz club) 45
Monk, Thelonious (pianist; 1917–1982) 40, 80
Morrison, Jim (vocalist; 1943–1971) 6, 7, 87, 104
Mottram, Eric (literary critic; 1924–1995) 129, 142
Mrabet, Mohammed (storyteller and author; 1935–) 145
Muir, John (American naturalist poet; 1838–1914) 205
Murphy, Eddie (comedian; 1961–) 132

Naropa Institute 49
The Naked and the Dead (novel, 1948) 53
Naked Lunch (1993) 157–65
Naked Lunch (novel, 1959) 5, 20, 34, 114–7, 119, 123, 125, 128–9, 135, 137–140, 144, 152, 157–62, 164, 212
Naked Lunch at 50 (conference, 2009) 125
National Geographic (magazine) 183
Naylor, Gloria (writer; 1950–2016) 72, 74
New York Public Library 6
1984 14
Nixon, Richard (U.S. president; 1911–1993) 7, 63
Nolte, Nick (actor; 1941–) 31, 33, 35
Nostradamus (philosopher, mystic; 1503–1566) 143
Notes from Underground 36
NPR (radio station) 201

Oates, Joyce Carol (writer, poet; 1938–) 12
Of Mice and Men (1937) 60, 110, 117, 176
"Oil" 93

On the Road (novel, 1957) 32–4, 45, 47, 55, 57, 67, 77–9, 86, 124, 188, 206
On the Road (2012) 17, 70–2, 74–8
One Flew Over The Cuckoo's Nest (novel, 1962) 88
Orlovsky, Peter (poet; 1933–2010) 106, 108, 111
Orwell, George (writer and theorist; 1903–50) 14, 196; *1984* 14

Panther (film, 1995) 98
Parker, Charlie "Yardbird" (jazz saxophonist; 1920–1955) 27, 67–8, 74, 80, 175
Parker, Edie (novelist; 1922–93) 44, 54
A Passage to India (film, 1984) 7
Pease, Donald (literary critic; 1946–) 10
Peppard, George (actor; 1928–1994) 17
Piscopo, Joe (comedian; 1951–) 132
Pitt, Brad (actor; 1963–) 71
The Place of Dead Roads (novel) 129, 138
Poe, Edgar Allan (poet; 1809–1849) 13
Polish, Michael (film producer) 78, 84; *Big Sur* (2013) 81–83, 87, 199
Pop, Iggy (vocalist; 1947–) 153–4
postmodernism 19, 198; Burroughs and 21; stereotypes and 6
post-structuralism 4, 6–7, 23–4, 198; Burroughs and 128, 144; Ginsberg and 20; Kerouac and 41
Prince, Michael 6
"Purple Haze" (1967) 2
Pynchon, Thomas (writer; 1937–) 123, 135, 143

Queer (novel) 123

Reagan Ronald Wilson (U.S. president; 1911–2004) 127, 138, 141, 145, 170, 199
Reality Sandwiches 97
Reeves, Keanu (film actor; 1964–) 36–7, 39
rhaita (reed) 150
Riprap 192
Rollins, Henry (rock guitarist; 1961–) 169, 172

Salles, Walter (film director) 18, 76; *On the Road* (2012) 17, 70–2, 74–8
Sampas, Sebastian (writer) 12, 203
Sartre, Jean-Paul (philosopher; 1906–1980) 119
Saturday Night Live 138
Schorer, Mark (critic) 103–4
"The Secret Life of Walter Mitty" (short story, 1939) 39
Selected Letters, 1940–1956 16

Index

Shakespeare, William (playwright; 1564–1616) 200–1
Shelley, Percy Bysshe (poet; 1792–1822) 122
Shoemaker, Jack (1946–) 22, 169
Shukri, Muhammad (writer; 1935–2003) 149
Sims, Zoot (jazz saxophonist; 1925–1985) 54
Sleepy Hollow (film, 1999) 6
Slovic, Scott (cultural critic) 192–3
Smith, Patti (vocalist; 1946–) 153–4, 166
Snyder, Gary (poet, mystic, and environmentalist; 1930–): Asia and 193–4; "Oil" 193; *Riprap* 192; *Turtle Island* 192; Zen Buddhism and 193
socialist realism 32, 43, 47, 63, 95, 141
Southwest Texas Popular Association Conference 62
Spacek, Sissy (film actor; 1949–) 17, 31
Speed (film, 1994) 36
Steinbeck, John (writer; 1902–1968) 11; *Of Mice and Men* (1937) 60, 110, 117, 176
Steppenwolf 85
Sterritt, David (literary critic; 1944–) 4, 9, 156–7, 164, 182, 197
Stone, Oliver (film director; 1946–) 6
Strauss, Claude Levi (philosopher; 1908–2009) 74–5
Sufism 81

Tennyson, Alfred Lord (British poet; 1809–92) 7
Thoreau, Henry David (theorist, activist, writer; 1817–1862) 192
Thurber, James (writer): "The Secret Life of Walter Mitty" (short story, 1939) 39
Tietchen, Todd 15
The Town and the City (novel, 1950) 24
Trainspotting (film, 2000) 191
The Transcendentalists 192
Tripp, Gerard (actor) 66–9
Tristessa (novel, 1960) 28–9, 58, 79, 205
Turtle Island 192
Twain, Mark (writer, essayist; 1835–1910) 205

Ulysses (novel, 1922) 39, 207
Uncle Tom's Children 72
The Unknown Kerouac (Tietchen, 2016) 43

Visions of Cody (novel, 1972) 38, 41, 101, 205
The Visual Movement 182
Vollmer, Joan (1923–1951) 155, 163; Burroughs and 155; death 129, 141

"Wales Visitation" 50, 107
Walker, Alice (writer; 1944–) 12
The Wall (1982) 93
Waters, John (film producer) 155
Waters, Roger (bassist, Pink Floyd; 1943–) 93; *The Wall* (1982) 93
WDNA (jazz radio station, Miami) 201
Weinreich, Regina (literary critic, film producer; 1949–) 116–7, 119–21
Weir, Peter (film producer): *Dead Poets Society* 93
Weller, Peter (film actor) 157, 161
What Happened to Kerouac? (1986) 41, 46, 48, 49
"When the Music's Over" (song, 1967) 7
Whitman, Walt (American poet; 1819–1892) 45
Wilner, Hal (film producer) 131
Wilson, Peter Lamborn (ethnographer; 1948–) 148
Wolfe, Thomas (novelist; 1930–2018) 15
Woodard, David (cartographer; 1942–2004) 143–6
Words of Advice (2010) 131–2
Wright, Joe: *Anna Karenina* (2012) 76, 94
Wright, Richard (1908–1960) 72; *Uncle Tom's Children* 72

Yage (drugged drink) 210
Yeats, William Butler (Irish poet; 1865–1939): trance writing and 54, 116
Young, Lester (jazz saxophonist; 1910–1949) 27, 45

Zabriskie Point (film, 1970) 68
Zen Buddhism 195–6; Gary Snyder and 191–2; Jack Kerouac and 79, 82, 86

www.ingramcontent.com/pod-product-compliance
Lightning Source LLC
Chambersburg PA
CBHW032050300426
44116CB00007B/678